THE LITERARY PILGRIM
IN WALES

The Literary Pilgrim in Wales

A guide to the places associated with writers in Wales

Meic Stephens

GWASG CARREG GWALCH

© Text: Meic Stephens

Copyright © by Gwasg Carreg Gwalch 2000.
All rights reserved. No part of this publication may be reproduced
or transmitted,in any form or by any means, without permission.

ISBN: 0-86381-612-6

Illustrations: Dylan Williams

Published with the aid of the
Arts Council of Wales.

First published in 2000 by
Gwasg Carreg Gwalch, 12 Iard yr Orsaf, Llanrwst, Wales LL26 0EH
℡ 01492 642031   🖹 01492 641502
🖙 books@carreg-gwalch.co.uk   website: www.carreg-gwalch.co.uk

i'm gwraig
RUTH
cydymaith pob cam o'r daith

To the Reader

The literature of Wales, in both Welsh and English, is well served by a variety of histories, critical studies, anthologies and other reference works designed to help the reader over what may be unfamiliar ground. In recent years, books such as *The Companion to the Literature of Wales* have brought Welsh writing to a wider audience far beyond our borders, while providing a useful source of information for those at home who are engaged in its study. But not until now has there been an attempt to map the literary landscape of Wales in English and in a single volume intended for the visitor and general reader.

This book, which can be used with the *Companion* at the reader's elbow, presents, in alphabetical order, a list of the villages, towns and cities of Wales which have literary associations, particularly those places, mainly buildings, where writers are in some way remembered and which can be visited by members of the public. This commemoration usually takes the form of a plaque, statue or some other monument marking the spot where writers were born, lived, worked, stayed or died; in many instances, the location of their graves is given. Many of these memorials, some modest and others grandiloquent, were put up by local societies or by individuals wishing to make some permanent record of a writer's connection with the district. A valuable contribution to an awareness of the Welsh cultural heritage has thus been made and it is to be hoped that many more public bodies will choose to enrich the lives of our people in this way.

I have tried to include places associated with all the most important writers, whether they wrote in Welsh or English, although that has not proved possible in every instance. The reader who would like to draw my attention to any writer whom I have overlooked, or to any error of fact, is asked to write to me. I have also attempted to include writers from all parts of Wales, so that the literary pilgrim will be able, with this book's help, to make a short excursion to places of interest. Even so, some villages and towns do not appear here because I have not been able to discover any literary associations important enough to justify entries. Again, I hope the reader who is disappointed in this respect will contact me, so that these lacunae can be filled in any new edition which may appear.

The fact remains that Wales, a comparatively small country with a rich literary tradition, has much to offer those who are seeking some visible memorial to writers they admire. This book will help them in their quest and, at the same time, provide them with biographical, bibliographical and topographical details which will throw light on the writers' lives and work and, I hope, add to their pleasure in discovering some of the more out-of-the-way places of both rural and urban Wales. A good up-to-date road-map such as the Collins Road Atlas, on which I have depended for its clarity and accuracy, will also prove useful.

I am grateful to a number of individuals and public bodies for providing me with information for use in this book; they include: Dr R. Brinley Jones, Dr James A. Davies, Mr Sam Adams, Mr Steffan ab Owain, Mrs Kate Davies, Dr J. Gwyn Griffiths, Mr John Leeding, Mr Sam Dawson, Mr John Clifford Jones, Prof. M. Wynn Thomas, Mrs Rita Crumpton and Dr Chris Williams; the Librarians and Officers of the County Councils of Ynys Môn, Gwynedd, Conwy, Flintshire, Powys, Ceredigion, Carmarthenshire, Bridgend, Merthyr Tydfil, Monmouthshire, Newport and Cardiff; the Pontardawe and Caernarfon Civic Societies; and the Dylan Thomas Centre, Swansea. It is a matter for regret that my enquiries to the County Councils not acknowledged here failed to elicit a satisfactory response.

Meic Stephens, Whitchurch, Cardiff
March 2000

Memorial to Ann Griffiths at
Llanfihangel-yng-Ngwynfa

Y Lasynys, near Harlech, birth-place of Ellis Wynne

ABBEY CWM-HIR (W. Abaty Cwm-hir), Powys; hamlet on a minor road off the A44 or A483, about 5 m NE of Rhayader.

Here on 11 December 1282 the decapitated body of Llywelyn ap Gruffudd, the last Prince of independent Wales, was secretly buried by monks of the Cistercian Order; his head was sent to London to be exhibited at Cheapside as a sign of Edward I's conquest of Wales. The Prince's death was lamented in a powerful elegy by **Gruffudd ab yr Ynad Coch** (*fl.*1277-82) expressing the utter dismay felt by the Welsh at the end of the royal house of Gwynedd (trans.):

> Why, O my God, does the sea not cover the land?
> Why are we left to linger?

The abbey, once the largest in Wales, was demolished at the Dissolution of 1542. A marble slab marking the spot where the Prince is said to lie buried is the focus for an annual gathering of Welsh patriots. A poem by **Harri Webb** (1920-94) describing his pilgrimage to Abbey Cwm-hir ends with the line: 'Centuries later, in high summer, I feel the cold.'

ABERCUCH, Pembrokeshire; small village straddling the A484, 3 m W of Newcastle Emlyn.

It was hereabouts, in **The Mabinogion,** that the hounds of Pwyll, Prince of Dyfed, killed a stag which was also being pursued by Arawn, the king of Annwn, the Otherworld.

ABERCYNON, Rhondda Cynon Taff; former mining village at the confluence of the rivers Cynon and Taff, 3 m N of Pontypridd off the A470.

The prose-writer and oral historian **George Ewart Evans** (1909-88) was born at Bristol House, Glancynon Terrace, next to Calfaria chapel. The village and valley are lovingly portrayed in his short novel *The Voices of the Children* (1947), his collection of stories *Let Dogs Delight* (1975) and his autobiography, *The Strength of the Hills* (1983). Evans, a Welsh-speaker and Communist, spent most of his adult life in East Anglia, about the rural culture of which he wrote extensively, notably in *Ask the Fellows who Cut the Hay* (1956) and *From Mouths of Men* (1976).

ABERDARE (W. Aberdâr), Rhondda Cynon Taff; industrial town at the head of the Cynon Valley off the A465.

The best-known poet associated with the town is **Alun Lewis** (1915-44) who is commemorated by a low-relief bust in the reference department of the public library. Lewis, who died in Burma during the campaign against the Japanese, was born at 16 Llanwynno Road, Cwmaman, a village just south of the town, off the A4059, where a plaque is inscribed with a quotation from his poem 'The Mountain over Aberdare':

> I watch the clouded years
> Rune the rough foreheads of these moody hills,
> This wet evening, in a lost age.

His *Collected Stories* appeared in 1990 and his *Collected Poems* in 1994.

The novelist **T. Rowland Hughes** (1903–49) lodged at 34 Gospel Hall Terrace from 1926 to 1928 when he was a teacher of Welsh and English at the Boys' County School.

The poet and novelist **Rhydwen Williams** (1916–97) lived the last years of his life at 30 Llewelyn Street, Trecynon, on the N side of the town. His collected poems appeared in 1991; his most important prose-work was the trilogy of novels *Cwm Hiraeth*: *Y Briodas* (1969), *Y Siôl Wen* (1970) and *Dyddiau Dyn* (1973).

The poet **Gwilym R. Tilsley** (1911–97), who won the Chair at the National Eisteddfod in 1950 with his *'Moliant i'r Glöwr'*, a poem in praise of the collier, was living at the time in the manse of Seion, the Wesleyan chapel in Wynn Street, near the town centre.

ABERDARON, Gwynedd; village at the end of the B4413 almost at the extreme tip of the Llŷn peninsula.

In medieval times this was the place from which pilgrims crossed to the island of Bardsey (Ynys Enlli) and it is still used as an embarkation point.

The house known as Bodwrda, about I m to the

E, was for generations the home of the Gwyn family, who were generous patrons of poets. The poet **Gruffydd Bodwrda** (*c*.1578-1649), who was a member of this family, was buried at Llangwnnadl.

Perhaps the most colourful character associated with the village was Richard Robert Jones (Dic Aberdaron; 1780-1843), eccentric and self-taught speaker of 14 languages, who roamed the countryside with his books and cats; in a poem about him, **T.H. Parry-Williams** (1887-1975) wrote (trans.), 'Not everyone goes dotty in quite the same way.' Dic Aberdaron's home was Cae'r Eos, where there is a commemorative plaque; he died and was buried in St Asaph.

The most famous poem associated with the village is the one by **Albert Evans-Jones (Cynan**; 1895-1970), of which the first verse is (trans.):

> When I am old and respectable,
> With silver in my purse,
> Criticised no longer
> And all men singing my praise,
> I shall buy a lonely cottage
> With nothing beyond its door
> But the rocks of Aberdaron
> And the wild waves of the shore.

ABERDOVEY (W. Aberdyfi), Gwynedd; village on the Dyfi estuary and the A493.

The song *'Clychau Aberdyfi'* ('The Bells of Aberdovey') refers to the traditional belief that the bells of *Cantre'r Gwaelod* (The Lower Hundred), the drowned kingdom of Gwyddno Garanhir under the waters of what is today Cardigan Bay, can still be heard on calm evenings in summer. The tune dates from before 1840 but the name of its composer is not known for certain; the Welsh words were written by **John Ceiriog Hughes** (1832-87).

The tale inspired the historical romance by the English novelist **Thomas Love Peacock** (1785-1866), *The Misfortunes of Elphin* (1829), in which Seithenyn, the man held responsible for the drowning of *Cantre'r Gwaelod,* is portrayed as a drunkard of Gargantuan proportions. The novel includes the well-known 'War Song of Dinas Vawr', the first verse of which is:

> The mountain sheep are sweeter
> But the valley sheep are fatter;
> We therefore deemed it meeter
> To carry off the latter.

The English novelist **Oliver Onions** (1873-1961) and his wife **Berta Ruck** (1878-1978), also a writer, lived in Aberdovey from 1939; his best historical novels are *Poor Man's Tapestry* (1946) and *A Penny for the Harp* (1951), both of which are set in mid-Wales.

Berta Ruck was the sister of **Richard Ruck** (1887-1973), who is remembered as the translator of the five novels of **T. Rowland Hughes** (1903-49).

ABEREDW, Powys; small village on the B4567, 3 m S of Builth in the valley of the Wye.

The rocky, wooded hillside inspired **Francis Kilvert** (1840-79), the curate of Clyro, in an entry in his diary for 13 April 1875, to rhapsodize thus:

> Oh, Aberedw, Aberedw. Would God I might dwell and die by thee. Oh, Aberedw, Aberedw. I never pass thy enchanted gorge and look up through the magic gateway of thy Rocks without seeming for a moment to be looking in at the gates of Paradise just left ajar . . . Oh, Aberedw, Aberedw.

It is not known what special significance the rocks of Aberedw held for the diarist, although it is thought he may have had an amorous experience in the vicinity while walking in the district some years before.

ABER-ERCH, Gwynedd; hamlet off the A497 and A499 between Cricieth and Pwllheli.

The poet and hymn-writer **Robert Williams (Robert ap Gwilym Ddu**; 1766-1850) is buried in the churchyard. The elegy which he wrote for his daughter, who died in 1834 at the age of 18, is one of the most moving in the Welsh language. His best-known hymn is the one beginning *'Mae'r gwaed a redodd ar y Groes'* and his finest verse, which is quite different from the eisteddfodic verse of his day, is to be found in the volume *Gardd Eifion* (1841).

ABER-FAN, Merthyr Tydfil; former mining village off the A470 in the valley of the Taff.

On 21 October 1966 part of a coal-tip slid into the valley, crushing houses and burying the Pant-glas Junior School; in all, 116 children and 28 adults lost their lives. A good deal of verse was written in response to the disaster, but most of it was of inferior quality. The graves of the victims of the disaster are in the cemetery above the village.

ABERFFRAW, Anglesey; small coastal village on the A4080 in the SW of the island.

In **The Mabinogion** the wedding-feast of Matholwch and Branwen is held here. The Princes of Gwynedd had their court at Aberffraw in medieval times. The heritage centre in the village, known as Llys Llywelyn, is devoted to the history of the isle of Anglesey.

A little to the N of the village is Henllys Fawr,

the former home of **W.J. Griffith** (1875-1931), author of a celebrated collection of humorous short stories, *Storïau'r Henllys Fawr* (1938).

ABERGAVENNY (W. Y Fenni), Monmouthshire; market town on the junction of the A40, A465 and A4042 at the confluence of the rivers Gavenny and Usk.

The Marcher lord William de Braose (*c.*1150-1211) was known in Welsh tradition as 'The Ogre of Abergavenny' on account of his treachery in inviting his neighbour Seisyll ap Dyfnwal and other Welsh leaders to a banquet at which he ordered them to be slaughtered. The man of the same name who was hanged as punishment for his liaison with Joan, the wife of Llywelyn Fawr, was one of his grandsons; see under Abergwyngregyn.

The massacre was the subject of an English poem by **William Williams (The Poet of Mount Pleasant;** 1850-1917) with which he won a prize at the National Eisteddfod held at Abergavenny in 1913; the poem is to be found in the author's only book, *Songs of Siluria* (1916).

The scholar and Catholic mystic **Augustine Baker** (1575-1641) was a native of Abergavenny. His book *Sancta Sophia* (1657), translated as *Holy Wisdom*, remained part of Benedictine life for nearly three centuries.

The Reverend **William Jones** (1755-1821), diarist, was also born in the town and attended the Grammar School; his diary was edited by O.F. Christie and published in 1929.

In the 19th century Abergavenny was an important centre in the movement to revive the literary culture of Wales. At the Sun Inn (now the Coach and Horses) in Cross Street, the patriotic society known as *Cymreigyddion y Fenni* was inaugurated in 1833. For some thirty years the town's annual eisteddfod, under the patronage of Lady Llanover (Augusta Waddington Hall; 1802-96), attracted many visitors from Wales and abroad, among them the French poet Alphonse de Lamartine (1790-1869) in 1839. The previous year a deputation of Bretons led by Hersart de la Villemarqué (1815-95), author of *Barzaz Breiz; Chants Populaires de la Bretagne*, took part in a ceremony symbolic of the ancient links between Wales and Brittany.

It was at the Abergavenny Eisteddfod that the great literary critic **Thomas Stephens** (1821-75) won a prize for an essay which was subsequently published as *The Literature of the Kymry* (1849), for long thereafter regarded as the authoritative work on Welsh literature.

The English novelist **Alexander Cordell (George Alexander Graber**; 1914-97) came to live in Abergavenny in 1950, making his home first at nearby Llanelen and then at 7 Holywell Crescent before moving to Pembrokeshire in 1963. During his time here he wrote *Rape of the Fair Country* (1959) and *The Hosts of Rebecca* (1960), the first of a number of novels dealing with the Industrial Revolution in SE Wales.

ABERGELE, Conwy; small coastal resort off the A55, 11 m E of Llandudno.

Felicia Hemans (1793-1835), whose most famous poem 'Casabianca' begins, 'The boy stood on the burning deck', lived at Hen Gwrych, a house in the grounds of Gwrych castle, from about 1800, and several of her poems describe local scenes.

The writer **Robert Ambrose Jones (Emrys ap Iwan**; 1848-1906), sometimes called 'the father of Welsh nationalism' on account of his staunchly patriotic writings, was born at Bryn Aber, a large house where his father was gardener. His mother had been invited to have the child there by the housekeeper while the owner was away; his parents lived in a smaller house near by. The commemorative plaque on the wall of the house bears the inscription: *'Gŵr a garodd ei Dduw a'i iaith a'i genedl'* (A man who loved his God and his language and his nation). Trained for the ministry at the Calvinistic Methodists' Theological College in Bala, Emrys ap Iwan was particularly critical of his denomination's readiness to promote 'English causes' (that is to say, to allow chapels to use the English language), and more generally, was opposed to all forms of anglicization, expressing his disapproval with great eloquence and withering scorn for those of his compatriots who were prepared to abandon the Welsh language. In his *Homiliau* (1906) he wrote (trans.): 'To destroy a nation is a disaster next to destroying the human race, and to destroy a nation's language is a disaster next to destroying the nation, because a nation ceases to exist, sooner or later, after losing its language.'The secondary school in Abergele is named after Emrys ap Iwan. The standard edition of his writings is the one compiled by D. Myrddin Lloyd (3 vols., 1937, 1939, 1940).

ABERGLASLYN, Gwynedd; a pass 2 m S of Beddgelert on the A4085.

This well-known beauty-spot attracted the attention of many tourists during the 18th century, including **John Cradock** who declared that it was 'the noblest specimen of the Finely Horrid the eye can possibly behold . . . 'tis the last approach to the mansion of Pluto through the regions of Despair.' The landscape immediately to the S of the pass is indeed among the wildest in Wales, but many English tourists were given to hyperbole when describing the landscape of Wales.

ABERGLASNEY, see under **LLANGATHEN**

ABERGWILI, Carmarthenshire; small village on the A40, 2 m NE of Carmarthen town.

A minor road leading steeply to the N leads to Merlin Hill, where the enchantress Nimue ('The Lady of the Lake') is said to have lured the aged Merlin and then buried him deep under a rock; a finger-post shows the way to Merlin's Grove.

The Bishops of St David's had their residence at Abergwili and their palace was for long a centre of learning and a source of generous patronage for Welsh poets. It was here that the work of translating the New Testament into Welsh was begun during the episcopacy of Richard Davies (1501?-81).

Among other literary men associated with Abergwili were **John Howell (Ioan ap Hywel;** 1774-1830), editor of the anthology *Blodau Dyfed* (1824), and Thomas Burgess (1756-1837), an Englishman who as Bishop of St David's (1803-25) played a leading role in organizing the eisteddfod held at Carmarthen in 1819.

ABERGWYNGREGYN, Gwynedd; small village 5 m E of Bangor on the A55.

Llywelyn Fawr, Prince of Gwynedd, had his court here in the early 13th century. His wife Joan, known in Welsh as Siwan, daughter of the English King John, was alleged to have had a brief liaison with the young Marcher Lord William de Braose, who was hanged for treason in 1230. One of the finest verse-plays in Welsh, *Siwan* (1956) by **Saunders Lewis** (1893-1985), is set at Llywelyn's court, said by its owners to have been on the site where the late-medieval house known as Pen-y-bryn now stands a little outside the village; it may also have been where Ty'n-y-mwd is now situated near by – both sites are currently under archaeological investigation.

ABERMAD, see under **LLANGATHEN**

ABERMULE (W. Abermiwl), Powys; small village on the junction of the A483 and B4386, 4 m NE of Newtown.

Across the river Severn is the site of Castell Dolforwyn, built by Llywelyn ap Gruffudd, the last Prince of independent Wales, in the 13th century. The meadow below is known as Dolforwyn (Maiden's meadow). Local tradition places here the scene of the drowning of the unfortunate nymph Sabrina, the daughter of Locrine. This tale sprang from the fertile imagination of **Geoffrey of Monmouth** (*c.*1090-1155) who, in his *Historia Regum Britanniae* (*c.*1136), related how Locrine, King of Britain, fell in love with Estrildis and had a daughter by her; his wife, Gwendolen, overcome by envy and wrath, hurled the child Sabrina into the river. Thereafter, according to Geoffrey, the river was known as Sabrina in Latin and in Welsh,

Habren (the modern name is Hafren). The story was used by the English poet **John Milton** (1608-74) in his masque *Comus* (1637), where Sabrina is invoked as the goddess of chastity.

ABER-NANT, Carmarthenshire; hamlet on a minor road about 4 m NW of Carmarthen and 3 m SW of Cynwyl Elfed, reached from the A484 or A40.

The writer **James Howell** (1593-1666) was born here, the son of the rector. An able linguist, he had a distinguished career in the king's service but during the Civil War was clapped into the Fleet prison by the Parliamentarians and there remained until the amnesty of 1650. The eight years of his incarceration made a writer of him. Among his forty books the most notable is *Epistolae Ho-Elianae* (1645; trans. *Familiar Letters*), the first collection of letters in the history of writing in English addressed to named individuals but intended for publication.

ABERPERGWM, Neath-Port Talbot; a mansion on S side of Glyn Neath off the A465.

The house was once renowned for its bardic patronage and its library of manuscripts. The poet most frequently associated with it is **Iorwerth Fynglwyd** (*fl.*1485-1527).

In the 18th century Aberpergwm was the home of Rees Williams (d.1820), believed to have been the last to employ a household poet in the person of **Dafydd Nicolas** (1705?-74). A daughter of his, **Maria Jane Williams (Llinos**; 1795-1873), was a famous singer and collector of manuscripts.

ABERYSTWYTH, Cardiganshire; seaside resort, university town and cultural centre facing Cardigan

Bay and at the end of the A44 at its junction with the A487.

The University (formerly known as the University College of Wales and housed on the promenade) was founded in 1872; its main campus is now on Penglais Hill, on the A487 which climbs E out of the town.

The National Library of Wales, founded in 1907 and also on Penglais, houses a unique collection of books, manuscripts and other artefacts relating to the language and literature of Wales. Among its treasures are the medieval manuscripts known in English as *The Black Book of Carmarthen*, *The White Book of Rhydderch* and *The Book of Taliesin*. The Library houses many portraits of Welsh writers but they are not all on public display; a bust of **Saunders Lewis** (1893-1985) by Ivor Roberts-Jones and one of **Alun Lewis** (1915-44) by R.L. Gapper are sometimes exhibited.

The Welsh Books Council, founded in 1961, is based at Castell Brychan, a former Roman Catholic seminary, on Constitution Hill at the N end of the town; the Council's Books Centre, a warehouse which distributes books to all parts of Wales, is situated on the Glanyrafon Estate at Llanbadarn, a little to the S.

Among other bodies which have their headquarters in Aberystwyth are *Urdd Gobaith Cymru* (The Welsh League of Youth) and *Cymdeithas yr Iaith Gymraeg* (The Welsh Language Society); the former has offices in Llanbadarn Road and the latter at Penroc, at the junction of Pier Street and the promenade. There is a good Welsh bookshop, *Siop y Pethau*, on the corner of Great Darkgate Street and Terrace Road.

Among the many Welsh writers who were

educated at the University College are **Owen Morgan Edwards** (1858-1920), **Robert Willliams Parry** (1884-1950), **T.H. Parry-Williams** (1887-1975), **D.J. Williams** (1885-1970), **Waldo Williams** (1904-71), and **D. Gwenallt Jones** (1899-1968).

Thomas Gwynn Jones (1871-1949), after four years on the staff of the National Library, was appointed Lecturer in Welsh at the College in 1913 and became Professor of Welsh Literature six years later. He lived first at Eirlys (now the Vicarage) on the Buarth, moving later to Hafan in the village of Bow Street, just N of the town, and died at Willow Lawn in Caradog Road; he was buried in the cemetery off Llanbadarn Road.

T.H. Parry-Willliams joined the staff of the Welsh Department in 1914 and was appointed Professor in 1920. he lived for many years in lodgings at Lynhurst in North Road and, after marrying in 1942, at Y Wern in the same road, where he died.

D. Gwenallt Jones was appointed to a lectureship in Welsh in 1927 and ended his career as Reader in 1967; he lived at Rhyd-y-môr, a house with a commemorative plaque, in Ffordd Rheidol, Penparcau, on the southern outskirts of the town, and was buried in the cemetery off Llanbadarn Road, about ten yards from the grave of his old professor, T. Gwynn Jones.

Thomas Levi (1825-1916) and **Richard Hughes Williams (Dic Tryfan**; 1878?-1919) are also buried in the cemetery; the latter lived at Dairy Cottage in Llanbadarn Road.

Among other writers domiciled in Aberystwyth, **Caradoc Evans** (1878-1945) was certainly the most notorious. Returning from London to his native county in 1939, he spent the rest of his life in or near the town, first at New Cross, a village 6 m SE on the B4340, and later at Queens House and 36a North Parade in the centre of town. While living in Aberystwyth he and his wife, Marguerite, the Baroness Barcynska (1886-1964), who wrote under the pseudonym **Oliver Sandys**, founded a theatre company but it was short-lived. Evans courted unpopularity by expressing such sentiments as: 'Wales would be brighter and more Christian-like if every chapel were burnt to the ground and a public house raised on the ashes thereof.' He revelled in his reputation as 'the most hated man in Wales'. It is only recently that his achievements as a writer of short stories have been acknowledged.

The Marxist poet **T.E. Nicholas** (1878-1971) settled in the town in 1921, practising as a dentist; he died at his home, Glascoed, in Elm Tree Avenue. He wrote mainly in Welsh, but a volume of his verse in English translation appeared under the title *Prison Sonnets* in 1948 and a bilingual selection of his political poems in 1981. It was while living in Aberystwyth that he and his son were imprisoned for alleged sedition and their opposition to the second world war.

Goronwy Rees (1909-70), who was born and brought up in Aberystwyth, the son of a minister of the Presbyterian Church, returned in 1953 as Principal of the University College, but stayed only four years; he was born and brought up at Pen-y-geulan in North Road, a house now named Rhos. His idyllic childhood and the stormy course of his principalship are described (not altogether accurately and with great animus) in his two volumes of autobiography, *A Bundle of Sensations* (1960) and *A Chapter of Accidents* (1972).

After his release from prison in 1937 and

dismissal from his post as a Lecturer in Welsh at University College, Swansea, the playwright **Saunders Lewis** (1893-1985) supported himself by journalism and teaching. He lived first at Yr Hen Dŷ in Abermad, a village on the B4575 about 4 m SE of Aberystwyth, and then at nearby Llygad-y-glyn in Llanfarian on the A4870.

E. Prosser Rhys (1901-45), the editor of the weekly newspaper *Baner ac Amserau Cymru*, had an office at 33 North Parade from 1923 until his death; his press, known as Gwasg Aberystwyth, was later bought by Gomer Press of Llandysul. He won the Crown at the National Eisteddfod in 1924 with his poem *'Atgof'*, which caused some controversy on account of the homosexual feelings it expressed. His collected poems were published in 1950. He was buried in the cemetery off Llanbadarn Road.

The author **T.I. Ellis** (1899-1970), the posthumous son of T.E. Ellis (1859-99), the Liberal MP for Merioneth, lived at 4 Laura Place, near the Old College. He wrote six volumes in the *Crwydro Cymru* series (1953-59), numerous pamphlets on cultural and political topics, a biography of his father and a volume of essays, *Ym Mêr fy Esgyrn* (1955).

At 8 Laura Place lived **Alwyn D. Rees** (1911-74). As editor of the monthly magazine *Barn* from 1966 until his death, he gave unstinting support to those who were campaigning for enhanced status for the Welsh language, including *Cymdeithas yr Iaith Gymraeg* (The Welsh Language Society) during its most militant phase. He was the author of *Life in a Welsh Countryside* (1950) and, with his brother Brinley Rees, wrote *Celtic Heritage* (1961). A selection of his articles was published as *Ym Marn Alwyn D. Rees* in 1976.

The prose-writer and Viking scholar **Gwyn Jones** (1907-99) was Professor of English at the University College from 1940 to 1964. He published several novels and volumes of short stories while living in the town, notably *The Buttercup Field* (1945), *The Flowers beneath the Scythe* (1952), *Shepherd's Hey* (1953) and *The Walk Home* (1962). But his major achievement was his collaboration with Thomas Jones, the College's Professor of Welsh, in the translation of *The Mabinogion*. This work, first published in a fine edition by the Golden Cockerel Press in 1948, not only satisfied Welsh scholars but also delighted a wider readership with its subtle rendering of the original and the unfailing elegance of its prose-style. It was this translation, still regarded as definitive, which was largely responsible for re-awakening world-wide interest in these tales. After retiring from the Chair of English at Cardiff in 1975, Gwyn Jones returned to Aberystwyth and lived at Castle Cottage in Sea View Place. During his retirement he edited *The Oxford Book of Welsh Verse in English* (1977); his *Collected Stories* appeared in 1997.

The poet and translator of Welsh poetry **Gwyn Williams** (1904-90) spent the last seven years of his life at 40 Queen Street; he had previously lived at Trefenter, a few miles to the S of Aberystwyth beyond Llangwyryfon. Born in Port Talbot, he spent many years as Professor of English Literature at the Universities of Cairo, Alexandria, Libya and Istanbul. His translations of Welsh poetry were published as *To Look for a Word* in 1976 and his *Collected Poems* appeared in 1987.

The poet, critic and prose-writer **R. Gerallt Jones** (1934-99) lived at Leri, Dol-y-bont, off the A487 and on the B4353, about 8 m to the N of Aberystwyth.

He was the author of five novels, all of which deal with contemporary issues, and his collected poems appeared in 1989.

The renowned Celtic scholar **J.E. Caerwyn Williams** (1912-99), Professor of Irish at the University College from 1965 to 1979, lived at Iwerydd, 6 Pant-y-rhos, Waunfawr, on the outskirts of Aberystwyth.

Llanbadarn Fawr, about 1 m SE of Aberystwyth and originally its parent village, has a parish church dating from the 13th century which is the setting of *'Merched Llanbadarn'* (The Girls of Llanbadarn) by **Dafydd ap Gwilym** (*fl.*1315/20-1350/70), one of the funniest poems about sexual frustration in the Welsh language.

Statue of Dafydd ap Gwilym, Cardiff City Hall

Within the chancel of the church at Llanbadarn are buried members of the Gogerddan and Nanteos families, together with their opponent, **Lewis Morris** (1701-65), the antiquary. Morris lived at Galltfadog, near Capel Dewi, and died at Pen-bryn, Goginan.

The writer **William Ambrose Bebb** (1894-1955) was born at a farm known as Blaendyffryn, now a ruin, at Goginan, about 7 m to the E of Aberystwyth on the A44, and brought up at Gamer Fawr, where there is a plaque. He wrote mainly about the history of Wales and was an early member of Plaid Cymru.

In the parish of Llangynfelyn, off the B4572 about 3 m N of Aberystwyth, the poet **Deio ab Ieuan Du** (*fl.*1450-80) was born. His most famous poem is one thanking Siôn ap Rhys of Glyn-nedd for the gift of a bull. It contains the line '*Y ddraig goch a ddyry cychwyn*' (The red dragon will show the way), which is used on the royal badge of Wales; the 'dragon' is, of course, a reference to the bull's penis.

In the same parish, at a house called Cwmcynfelyn, the poet **Isaac Williams** (1802-65) was born. He spent most of his life as a curate in England but was a frequent visitor to Llangorwen, where his brother owned land. Most of his verse is devotional; his books include *The Cathedral* (1838), *The Baptistery* (1842) and *The Altar* (1842).

AFON-WEN, Gwynedd; hamlet on the A497 between Cricieth and Pwllheli.

From here access can be gained to Y Lôn Goed, a treelined track which runs for nearly 5 m to the N as far as Mynydd y Cennin. It was designed by an Englishman named John Maugham, shortly after he had become agent to the Plas-hen estate, to serve the farms of the district; it is also sometimes called Ffordd Môn, a corruption of its builder's name. Its quiet beauty was celebrated by **R. Williams Parry** (1884-1956) in a famous poem, *'Eifionydd'*, which has been translated by **Harri Webb** (1920-94):

> Far from the scowl of progress,
> From drab industry afar,
> There's a land of sea and wildness
> That bears no stain or scar
> Save where the hillside plough lays bare
> The sweet spring earth in the mountain air . . .
>
> And Lôn Goed's a green heaven
> Where quiet is complete
> From its roof of branches woven
> To the soft grass at my feet;
> It leads to nowhere, the leafy lane,
> But none who linger there complain . . .

ALLT-WEN, see under PONTARDAWE

AMMANFORD (W. Rhydaman), Carmarthenshire; industrial town in the Llwchwr (Loughor) Valley on the junction of the A483 and the A474.

The poet and teacher **Watcyn Wyn (Watkin Hezekiah Williams;** 1844-1905) came here in 1880 to open a school, later called the Gwynfryn Academy, which still stands in College Street nearly opposite Gwynfryn Chapel, where young men were prepared for the Congregationalist ministry. Under his influence many discovered an interest in the writing of poetry, so that the town became the cultural centre of the anthracite coalfield of west Wales. The most famous of Watcyn Wyn's hymns is *'Rwy'n gweld o bell y dydd yn dod'* (I see, far off, the day a 'coming'). Several of his poems, in English translation, were introduced by **Edward Thomas** (1878-1917) into *Beautiful Wales* (1905). There is a plaque commemorating the Welsh writer in Gwynfryn Chapel and he is buried in the graveyard of Gellimanwydd (The Christian Temple).

The poet **William Nantlais Williams** (1874-1959) was minister at Bethany Chapel, where he is buried. His memoirs were published as *O Gopa Bryn Nebo* in 1967.

The poet **Amanwy (David Rees Griffiths**; 1882-1953) was born in Betws, near Ammanford, one of the eight children of the village blacksmith; his brother, James Griffiths (1890-1975), became the first Secretary of State for Wales in 1964. The poet's work was published posthumously as *Caneuon Amanwy* in 1956. He too was buried in the Gellimanwydd cemetery and is commemorated by a plaque in the village hall.

There is a Welsh bookshop in Ammanford known as *Siop y Cennen* in Shopper's World.

ARTHOG, Gwynedd; small village on the S shore of the Mawddach estuary and the A493, about 6 m SW of Dolgellau.

Here, at 7 Mawddach Crescent, lived the novelist and topographical writer **Cledwyn Hughes** (1920-78), whose many books include *A Wanderer in North Wales* (1949), *West with the Tinkers* (1954) and *Portrait of Snowdonia* (1967).

ATPAR, see under **NEWCASTLE EMLYN**

BALA, Gwynedd; market town on the junction of the A494 and A4212, at the N head of Llyn Tegid (Bala Lake).

It became an early centre of Welsh Methodism

after **Thomas Charles** (1755-1814), one of the founders of the British and Foreign Bible Society, married a local woman and settled in the town. His house in the High Street is now a branch of Barclays Bank; his statue stands in front of Capel Tegid. He is buried in the graveyard of the church at Llanycil, about 1 m to the S on the A494 on the N side of Bala Lake.

Here, in 1837, **Lewis Edwards** (1809-87), considered in his day to be the foremost literary critic and theologian in Wales, founded the Presbyterian College and became its first Principal; his statue stands in front of the building, which is no longer a college. Edwards, too, is buried at Llanycil.

Many prominent men in the religious life of Wales were born in Bala, including **John Jones (Ioan Tegid;** 1792-1852), **Roger Edwards** (1811-86), and **John Puleston Jones** (1862-1925).

The town also has a tradition of sturdy independence in politics. The Liberal politician Thomas Edward Ellis (1859-99), a native of Cefnddwysarn and MP for Merioneth until his early death, is commemorated by a statue in the High Street, on which there is a quotation from **Morgan Llwyd** (1619-59) which reads (trans.): 'A man's time is his inheritance and woe to him who wastes it.' Ellis is buried in the graveyard of the Methodist chapel at Cefnddwysarn.

Near the Theological College, to the NW of the town centre, stands Bodiwan, the former home of Michael D. Jones (1822-98), Principal of the College, proto-nationalist and the man who promoted the idea of a Welsh settlement in Patagonia; there is a commemorative plaque at the entrance.

The historian **R.T. Jenkins** (1881-1969) was brought up by his grandparents at Arran House. He joined the staff of the History Department of the University College of North Wales, Bangor, and was later appointed Professor. He wrote, besides two histories of Wales in the 18th and 19th centuries, a short novel, *Orinda* (1943), and a volume of entertaining essays, *Cwpanaid o De a Diferion Eraill*, which was published posthumously in 1997.

There is a Welsh bookshop, *Awen Meirion*, near the statue of T.E. Ellis.

BANGOR, Gwynedd; cathedral and university town off the A5, overlooking the E end of the Menai Straits and Anglesey.

The diocese of Bangor is the oldest in the countries of Britain. The cathedral was founded by St Deiniol in 456 AD; the present building was built during the reign of Gruffudd ap Cynan (*c.*1055-1137), King of Gwynedd; his son Owain Gwynedd and grandson **Hywel ab Owain Gwynedd** (*fl.*1140-70), who was a distinguished poet, are buried near the main altar.

Many medieval poets composed verse in honour of the cathedral and its bishops, notably **Dafydd ap Gwilym** (*fl.*1315/20-1350/70). There are memorials to **Edmwnd Prys** (1543/4-1623), **Goronwy Owen** (1723-69) and **Morris Williams** (**Nicander**; 1809-74) in the cathedral.

The Archdeacon's House near the cathedral is where in Shakespeare's play *Henry IV, Part I* (*c.*1597) Owen Glendower, Hotspur and Mortimer plan to divide the kingdom between them.

The city is sometimes called 'the Athens of north Wales', mainly on account of its rich intellectual life. The Normal College, situated on the Menai Straits, was opened in 1858 for the training of teachers, the Independents' Theological College in 1886, the Baptist College in 1892, and the University College of North Wales (now the University of Bangor) in 1901.

Theatr Gwynedd is situated in Deiniol Road and the studios of BBC Cymru are housed at Bryn Meirion near the University. There is a Welsh bookshop known as *Siop Pendref* in the Wellfield Shopping Centre.

Many Welsh writers were educated at the University College and a number taught there. **John Morris-Jones** (1864-1929), scholar, critic and poet, attended Friars School (1876-79) and, after graduating in Mathematics at Oxford, returned to Bangor in 1889 as lecturer in Welsh at the University College; he was appointed Professor of Welsh six years later. His major works of scholarship were *A Welsh Grammar Historical and Comparative* (1913) and *Cerdd Dafod* (1925), a study of traditional Welsh prosody. There is a bust of him by R.L. Gapper near the entrance to the Library and Neuadd John Morris-Jones is a hostel for Welsh-speaking students.

Among his students was the prose-writer **Kate Roberts** (1891-1985).

The poet **Robert Williams Parry** (1884-1950) was assistant lecturer in the Welsh Department and taught extra-mural classes from 1921 to 1944.

Albert Evans-Jones (Cynan; 1895-1970) entered the University College in 1913 and later became a lecturer in Welsh literature for the Extra-Mural

Department (1931-60); a collection of his poems, *Cerddi Cynan,* was published in 1959 (enlarged edn., 1967).

The novelist **T. Rowland Hughes** (1903-49) graduated in English in 1925.

The literary historian **Thomas Parry** (1904-85), a former student of the College, was Professor of Welsh from 1947 to 1953; he lived first at Peniarth (now Penmaen) in Lôn Meirion and, after his return to Bangor from Aberystwyth, at Gwyndy in Victoria Terrace, a house named after his old home at Carmel.

The playwright **John Gwilym Jones** (1904-88) was a student at the College and returned in 1953 as a lecturer in Welsh.

The last home of **W.J. Gruffydd** (1881-1954) was at Y Rhiw, near Griffith's Crossing between Bangor and Caernarfon.

The poet and critic **Alun Llywelyn-Williams** (1913-88) was Director of Extra-Mural Studies from 1948 until his retirement; he lived at Penylan in Richmond Road and then at Cwm Bychan in Ffriddoedd Road; he is buried in Bangor Cemetery and on his tombstone there is a quotation from his poem *'Pan Oeddwn Fachgen'*.

From 1974 until his death, the critic **Bedwyr Lewis Jones** (1933-92), who lived at Bodafon in Siliwen Road, was Professor of Welsh at the College; with **R. Gerallt Jones** (1934-99), who read English at Bangor, he edited the magazine *Yr Arloeswr* from 1957 to 1960. The Bedwyr Centre, named after the former Professor of Welsh, is in College Road near the entrance to the University.

The writer **Dyfnallt Morgan** (1917-94), who was a lecturer in the Department of Extra-Mural Studies at the University College, lived at 56 Upper Garth Road.

Among writers born in Bangor were **J.E. Daniel** (1902-62), **A.O.H. Jarman** (1911-99) and **Brenda Chamberlain** (1912-71). The last-named lived the last years of her life at 10 Menai View Terrace and was buried in Glanadda Cemetery off Ffordd Caernarfon.

The prose-writer and historian **William Ambrose Bebb** (1894-1955) was on the staff of the History Department at Bangor Normal College from 1925 until his death. He lived at Llwydiarth in Ffriddoedd Road. He died suddenly outside Hillgrove School in Upper Bangor; he too was buried at Glanadda Cemetery.

Above the door of the offices of the Workers' Educational Association in College Road there is a slate plaque in memory of **Robert Silyn Roberts** (1871-1930), the founder of the movement's North Wales branch.

The English novelist **Alexander Cordell (George Alexander Graber**; 1914-97) lived for a few years at Afallon, Waun Wen, at Glasinfryn, a village off the B4409 about 2 m to the S.

The city and University College are partly the setting for Islwyn Ffowc Elis's novel *Cysgod y Cryman* (1953; trans. Meic Stephens, *Shadow of the Sickle*, 1998).

BARDSEY (W. Ynys Enlli), Gwynedd; small island 2 m off the extreme SW tip of the Llŷn peninsula, reached by boat from Aberdaron or Aber-soch.

A monastic community was established on the island in the 6th century and, according to a spurious local tradition, some 20,000 saints −

including Beuno, Dyfrig and Padarn – are buried here; they were eulogized in poems by **Lewis Glyn Cothi** (*c*.1420-89) and **Hywel ap Rheinallt** (*fl*.1461-1506), among others. In the Middle Ages the island was a place of pilgrimage; it was believed that three pilgrimages to Bardsey were the equivalent of one to Rome. The religious house, a community of Augustinian Canons, was dissolved about 1537 and it subsequently became a place of refuge for pirates.

Two notable women writers lived on Bardsey: **Dilys Cadwaladr** (1902-79), a teacher at the school until it closed in 1945 and the first woman to win the Crown at the National Eisteddfod, a feat she accomplished in 1953, and **Brenda Chamberlain** (1912-71), whose book *Tide Race* (1962) reflects the rigours of life on the island; the latter lived at Carreg-fawr, where one of her paintings can still be seen on the wall of the landing.

Among other writers attracted to Bardsey was **R. Gerallt Jones** (1934-99), who wrote a journal entitled *Bardsey* (1976).

The island, which has only a handful of permanent residents, was bought by the Bardsey Island Trust in 1979 and is now run as a sanctuary for wild life.

BARMOUTH (W. Abermo or Y Bermo), Gwynedd; seaside resort on the A496 on the N shore of the Mawddach estuary.

Hereabouts 'the Mawddach Monster' is said to live, a folk-belief celebrated in the amusing poem 'Welsh Incident' by the English poet **Robert Graves** (1895-1985):

> Criccieth's mayor addressed them
> First in good Welsh and then in fluent English,

> Twisting his fingers in his chain of office,
> Welcoming the things . . .

About 3 m N of the town stands Egryn Abbey, which was once the home of **William Owen Pughe** (1759-1835), lexicographer, whose theories about the origins of Welsh had a baneful effect on the orthography of the language, which he believed was the primeval language of Mankind; it was he, too, who first claimed that Welsh is 'the language of heaven'.

In the Dragon Theatre there is a memorial to the poet **W.D. Williams** (1900-85), who was headmaster of the primary school from 1942 to 1961; he lived at Twyni, 1 North Avenue. He is remembered as the author of the *englyn* which is often said as grace before meals:

> O Dad, yn deulu dedwydd, y deuwn
> Â'n diolch o'r newydd,
> Cans o'th law y daw bob dydd
> Ein lluniaeth a'n llawenydd.

(Trans. O Father, as a happy family, we thank thee once again, for from thy hand each day comes our sustenance and joy.)

BASSALEG, see under NEWPORT

BEAUMARIS (W. Biwmares), Anglesey; town at the E end of the Menai Straits on the A545.

Here the poet and genealogist **Richard Llwyd (The Bard of Snowdon**; 1752-1835) was born. His long poem 'Beaumaris Bay' has notes twice as copious as the text, but many others are witty, allusive and technically accomplished; his *Poetical Works* were published in 1837.

BEDDGELERT, Gwynedd; village on the junction of the A4085 and A498 about 1 m N of Aberglaslyn.

It is said to be the burial-place of Gelert, the favourite hound of Llywelyn Fawr (1173 -1240) who, returning from the hunt, found the dog covered with gore and, assuming that it had killed his infant son, slew it -- only to discover that it had killed a marauding wolf and that the child was safe. Although this folk-tale is found in early Welsh prose, it was unknown in the village before the end of the 18th century for it was the fabrication of one David Prichard, landlord of the Royal Goat. The cromlech said to be Gelert's grave, and the well-known poem by **W.R. Spencer** (1769-1834) which Haydn set to music, were based on details supplied by Prichard, who was anxious to promote tourism in the district. A more likely explanation of the village's name is that, in the 6th century, it was the site of a priory dedicated to Celert. Prichard's hoax was neatly summed up in the couplet by **Israel Zangwill** (1864-1926):

Pass on, O tender-hearted, dry your eyes;
Not here a greyhound, but a landlord lies.

The poet **Rhys Goch Eryri** (*fl.*1385-1448) is reputed to have been born in the district and the remains of **T.H. Parry-Williams** (1887-1975) are buried in the cemetery.

BENLLECH, Anglesey; seaside village on the A5025.

At Brynteg, on the B5110 in the direction of Llangefni and in the parish of Llanfair-mathafarn-eithaf, the poet **Goronwy Owen** (1723-69) was born in the cottage Tafarn-goch, the home of his father's family, who were tinkers; the initials G.O. are cut on a stone in the wall but 'the Red Tavern' is now painted white. Ordained deacon by the Anglican Church in 1746, but unable to find a living in Wales, he took a teaching post at William and Mary College in Williamsburg, Virginia, in 1757. On the voyage to America both his wife and youngest child died. He married again but his second wife died soon afterwards. He then turned to alcohol and prodigal living, spending the last nine years of his life as vicar of a parish in Brunswick County, where he became a tobacco planter, and married for a third time; he was buried on his plantation near Dolphin, to the N of Lawrenceville. Owen was the greatest Welsh poet of his time and his verse was widely imitated. His most famous poem is *'Cywydd y Farn Fawr'*; others speak of his longing for the scenes of his youth. One of his many descendants was the founder of Interflora.

At Red Wharf Bay there is a plaque commemorating **Hywel ab Owain Gwynedd** (*fl.*1140-70), prince and poet. The illegitimate son of Owain Gwynedd, he was killed in battle against two of his half-brothers near the village. Only nine of his poems have survived, most of which are love-poems and poems in praise of his beloved Meirionnydd and its beautiful women.

BETHEL, Gwynedd; village on the B4366, about 3 m NE of Caernarfon.

The poet and critic **W.J. Gruffydd** (1881-1954) was born at Gorffwysfa in Erw Terrace, where a memorial stone marks his childhood home; he is buried at Llanddeiniolen, NE of the village, under the yew-tree of his most celebrated poem, which includes the chilling line (trans.), 'The yew-tree is patient; its time will come'. Gruffydd, who was Professor of Welsh at the University College,

Cardiff, from 1918 until his retirement in 1946, was editor of several influential anthologies, including *Y Flodeugerdd Gymraeg* (1931), and from 1922 to 1954 of the literary magazine *Y Llenor*. His memoirs were published as *Hen Atgofion* in 1936 (trans. D. Myrddin Lloyd, *The Years of the Locust*, 1976). A man of independent and often rebellious mind, he represented the University of Wales at Westminster from 1943 until the seat was abolished in 1950. Although he spent most of his life in Cardiff, he wrote in his memoirs that he resided, rather than lived there, and looked back on his boyhood in Bethel as the main influence upon him. A volume of his literary criticism, *Yr Hen Ganrif*, was published in 1991.

BETHESDA, Gwynedd; former slate-quarrying town on the E side of the A5, some 5 m SSE of Bangor; its satellite villages are Llanllechid, Rachub, Carneddi, Gerlan, Llandygái, and Tregarth.

The town grew around the Independent chapel, built in 1820, from which it took its name. The Penrhyn quarries which are such a prominent feature of the landscape hereabouts were first developed by Richard Pennant about 1765 and by 1875 they were the largest in the world, employing more than 2,000 workers. The Penrhyn Lockouts of 1896-97 and 1900-03 were one of the most serious disputes in the history of Welsh industry. At the heart of the confrontation between the men and the owner was the right to belong to a union and the way in which wages were fixed by management. The community suffered grievous damage as a result of the owners' intransigence, with many people leaving the district in search of work elsewhere. The strikes are the background to the novel *Chwalfa* (1946) by **T. Rowland Hughes** (1903-49), which was translated by Richard Ruck as *Out of their Night* (1954).

From 1898 to 1917 **J.T. Jôb** (1867-1938) was a minister with the Calvinistic Methodists in Bethesda. He won the Crown at the National Eisteddfod on three occasions (1897, 1903 and 1918), the Crown in 1900 and the Chair at the eisteddfod held in San Francisco in 1915. A selection of his poems was published under the title *Caniadau Jôb* in 1929.

The poet **Robert Williams Parry** (1884-1950) lived in Bethesda after his marriage in 1923, first at 18 Ffrydlas Road, then at Heulfryn (Tŷ'r Ysgol) in Carneddi, then at 10 Coetmor Estate (now 20 Ystâd Coetmor), and finally at 3 Coetmor Estate; he was employed on the staff of the University College of North Wales, Bangor. He and his wife Myfanwy (1898-1971) are buried in Coetmor Cemetery, just up the hill from the A5 and on Ffordd Coetmor, where their tombstone bears a low-relief carving of Y Lôn Goed, a grassy, tree-lined track in Eifionydd which is celebrated in one of his best-known poems. The grave is on the right of the path a few yards from the main gate and the inscription reads: *'O'r addfwyn yr addfwynaf'* (Of the mild, the mildest).

Also buried here are **Robert Lloyd Jones** (1878-1962), author of the children's novels *Capten* (1928) and *Mêt y Mona* (1929), and **J.O. Williams** (1892-1973) who, in collaboration with **Jennie Thomas** (1898-1979), wrote the popular series, *Llyfr Mawr y Plant* (4 vols.,1931-75).

The poet and novelist **Caradog Prichard** (1904-80) was born at a house known as Llwyn Onn, near Pen-y-bryn School and across the road from Wenallt, where J.O. Williams was born and brought up. The district forms the background of his important novel *Un Nos Ola Leuad* (1961; trans. Philip Mitchell, *One Moonlit Night*, 1999). The writer spent many years in London as a journalist with *The News Chronicle* and *The Daily Telegraph*. He too is buried in Coetmor Cemetery but in the Church section, as is the Celtic scholar **Idris Ll. Foster** (1911-84), another native of Bethesda. The latter's grave is immediately in front of the chapel's main door and Prichard's, three rows off, to the right and near the hedge.

A plaque commemorates the scholar **Ifor Williams** (1881-1965), his father and grandfather, on the wall of their home, Pendinas, at Tregarth, a village on the W side of the A5 and on the B4366; a council estate in the village is also named after Sir Ifor. He was Professor of Welsh at Bangor from 1920 until his retirement in 1947 and his life's work was the editing of early Welsh poetry and prose. Among the many texts he edited were the Llywarch Hen cycle, **Aneirin**'s *Gododdin*, the poems attributed to **Taliesin** and the Four Branches of the **Mabinogi**.

The writer **E. Tegla Davies** (1880-1967), who was a Wesleyan minister in the village, is buried in the churchyard at Tregarth.

Before the second world war the writer and painter **Brenda Chamberlain** (1912-71) lived with the artist John Petts at Ty'n-y-mynydd on the hillside above Rachub. It was here they began printing broadsheets on the Caseg Press, named after a nearby river, which included work by **Dylan Thomas** (1914-53) and **Alun Lewis** (1915-44). There is a fine inscription by Petts on the chimney-breast of the house which reads: '*Bydded tangnefedd yn y tŷ hwn*' (Let peace be in this house).

The writer **Ioan Bowen Rees** (1929-99), who was

Chief Executive of Gwynedd County Council from 1980 to 1991, lived at Talsarn, a house on a lane between and to the S of Rachub and Llanllechid. He wrote essays, many about climbing, and edited the anthology *The Mountains of Wales* (1992). He is buried in the graveyard at Brithdir, near Dolgellau, the town where he was born.

BETHLEHEM, Carmarthenshire; village on a minor road off the A4069 about 4 m SW of Llangadog and 4 m NE of Llandeilo.

The poet and local historian **Gwilym Teilo (William Davies**; 1831-92) was born at Pontbrenaraeth near the village. His collected poems were published as *Gweithiau Gwilym Teilo* in 1927.

The writer and editor **Keidrych Rhys (William Ronald Rees Jones**; 1915-87) was born here at a farm called Blaen Sawdde in Dyffryn Ceidrych on Boxing Day; an ebullient man with a keen taste for controversy, he described himself in a poem as 'almost a second Christ!'. He founded the influential magazine *Wales* in 1937 and edited the anthology *Modern Welsh Poetry* (1944). Many of his own poems, to be found in the rare booklet *The Van Pool* (1942), are set locally.

His wife, **Lynette Roberts** (1909-95), was also a poet. They lived after their marriage at Tŷ Gwyn in Llanybri, a village on a minor road about 2 m NW of Llanstephan. Born in Buenos Aires, she published two volumes of poetry, *Poems* (1944) and *Gods with Stainless Ears* (1951), but gave up writing in 1956 on becoming a Jehovah's Witness.

BETWS, see under **AMMANFORD**

BETWS BLEDRWS, Cardiganshire; small village on the A485 about 3 m NE of Lampeter.

Here are the ruins of the mansion known as Derry Ormond, where **Elizabeth Inglis-Jones** (1900-94) was brought up. The district is the setting of her first romantic novel, *Starved Fields* (1929), but she is now remembered as the author of *Peacocks in Paradise* (1950), the story of Thomas Johnes (1748-1816) and his estate at Hafod.

BETWS CEDEWAIN, Powys; small village on the B4389 about 4 m N of Newtown.

The poet and genealogist **Lewys Dwnn** (*fl*.1568-1616) was born here. His verse is uninspired but rich in genealogical detail about eminent families of the district.

His son, **James Dwnn** (*c*.1570-*c*.1660), was also a poet.

BETWS-YN-RHOS, Conwy; village on the B5381 about 10 m W of St Asaph.

The great poet **Thomas Gwynn Jones** (1871-1949) was born at Gwyndy Uchaf, a farm in the vicinity a little to the W, and was educated locally; a plaque marks his birthplace. After beginning his career as a journalist at Denbigh, he worked in Liverpool, Caernarfon and Mold before settling in Aberystwyth, where he was appointed to the Gregynog Chair of Welsh Literature at the University College of Wales in 1919. He was a prolific poet in the traditional metres who addressed some of the great issues of his time, especially the threat to western civilization by the forces of barbarism and totalitarianism, although he once described himself as 'a pacifist with the accent on the fist'. The most famous of his poems are to be found in the volumes *Caniadau* (1934) and *Y Dwymyn* (1944).

Y Gwyndy Uchaf, Betws-yn-Rhos,
birth place of T. Gwynn Jones

BLAENAU FFESTINIOG, Gwynedd; slate-quarrying town on the A470, 13 m NW of Porthmadog.

Tyddyn-du, the home of the poet **Edmwnd Prys** (1543/44-1623), is the last house on the right on the A470 from Llan Ffestiniog before it joins the road from Maentwrog to Trawsfynydd.

The Puritan author **Morgan Llwyd** (1619-59) was born at Cynfal Fawr, a farmhouse 1 m S of Ffestiniog off the A470. Part of the original house can still be seen and his birth here is recorded by a plaque. He was the author of books in Welsh and English, notably *Llyfr y Tri Aderyn* (1653), a clarion-call to the Welsh to prepare themselves for the imminent coming of Christ to reign as King on earth.

Cynfal Fawr, near Blaenau Ffestiniog,
birth-place of Morgan Llwyd

Less than 1 m from Cynwal Fawr, on the land of Bryn Saeth, there is a large standing stone with a hole in it which, according to tradition, was made by the arrow of Gronw Pebr, as related in **The Mabinogion**.

It is thought that Cynwal Fawr was built by **Huw Llwyd** (1568?-1630?), who may have been the father of Morgan Llwyd.The large boulder known as Huw Llwyd's Pulpit, where he used to meditate, and perhaps practise as a wizard, is situated on a public footpath in a gorge about ten minutes' walk from Cynwal Fawr.

The novelist **John Cowper Powys** (1872-1963) moved into 1 Waterloo in 1955 and spent his last years at nearby Manod. Among his works published while he was here were the novels *Atlantis* (1956) and *All or Nothing* (1960), and *Poems* (1964) was published in the year after his death in Blaenau Ffestiniog.

The poets **William Morris** (1889-1979) and **R. Bryn Williams** (1902-81) were born in Blaenau

Ffestiniog; both served as Archdruids.

The bookshop known as *Siop yr Hen Bost* is at 45 High Street.

BLAENCLYDACH, Rhondda Cynon Taff; former mining village with Clydach Vale near Tonypandy off the A4119 in a side-valley of the Rhondda Fawr.

The novelist **Lewis Jones** (1897-1939) was born at 4 Sunny Bank. At the age of 12 he went to work in the Cambrian Colliery, where the Tonypandy Riots of 1910 had their origin; married at 20, he spent the rest of his life in the village, latterly at 61 Brynhyfryd Street, Clydach Vale, and worked as a check-weigher. His two novels, *Cwmardy* (1937) and *We Live* (1939), are authentic and passionate accounts of working-class life in the Rhondda during the inter-war years. A Communist, Lewis Jones organized and led hunger-marches from south Wales to London and, during the last three years of his life, served as a member of Glamorgan County Council. He also played a prominent part in the campaign for the defence of the Spanish Republic. His secular funeral, which took place at the Judges' Hall, Trealaw, the coffin draped with a Communist flag, seemed to many observers to be the end of 'Red Rhondda'; he was buried in Trealaw cemetery.

Rhys Davies (1901-78), one of the most prolific and accomplished of Welsh writers in English, was born at 6 Clydach Road, where his parents kept a grocer's shop known rather grandly as Royal Stores; it is now a private house distinguished only by a plaque put up by the Rhys Davies Trust. Opposite stands the Central Hotel, on which he based the Jubilee Arms which appears in many of his stories.

In his early twenties and aware of his homosexuality, Davies left for London, there to live as a professional writer for the rest of his life. The Rhondda left an indelible mark on him and features in almost all his work; the trilogy of novels *Honey and Bread* (1935), *A Time to Laugh* (1937) and *Jubilee Blues* (1938) are set in Blaenclydach and his autobiography, *Print of a Hare's Foot* (1969), refers to his boyhood in the village; his *Collected Stories*, edited and with an introduction by Meic Stephens, appeared in three volumes in 1996 and 1998.

BLAEN-CWM, Rhondda Cynon Taff; village at the top end of the Rhondda Fawr off the A4061 about 1 m NW of Treherbert.

The novelist **Ron Berry** (1920-97) was born here; he left school at the age of 14 and worked as a miner in local pits. He wrote six novels, including *Hunters and Hunted* (1960) and *This Bygone* (1996), and an autobiography, *History is What you Live* (1998).

BODEDERN, Anglesey; village off the A5025 and on the B5109 about 3 m SE of Llanfachraeth.

The novelist **William David Owen** (1874-1925) was born at Ty'n-franan, a smallholding near a marshy area in which his novel, *Madam Wen* (1925), is set. A barrister until obliged to retire by ill health, he worked towards the end of his life as a solicitor at Rhosneigr, a coastal village to the S off the A4080. His novel is a popular romance about a female Robin Hood and its heroine, Einir Wyn, may have been based on Margaret Wynne, the wife of Robert Williams, squire of Chwaen Wen in the mid-18th century. There is a commemorative plaque on the wall of the school at Bryngwran, a village a little to the S on the A5.

Near Rhosneigr is Llyn Traffwll, a lake mentioned in the poem *'Anfon y Nico'* by **Cynan (Albert Evans-Jones**; 1895-1970) in which he yearns for Anglesey from the battlefield of Macedonia during the first world war.

Above the lake is Tregwehelyth, the birth-place of **Gruffudd Gryg** (*fl.*1357-70), a contemporary of **Dafydd ap Gwilym** (*fl.*1315/20-1350/70) with whom he engaged in bardic contention.

BODORGAN, Anglesey; village on a minor road off the A4080 about 2 m SE of Aberffraw.

The poet and short-story writer **Tom Parri Jones** (1905-95) is commemorated at Malltraeth, his home for many years. His most lively writing is found in his racy tales of village life in Anglesey: *Teisennau Berffro* (1958), *Yn Eisiau, Gwraig* (1958), *Traed Moch* (1971) and *Y Felltith* (1977).

BRECON (W. Aberhonddu), Powys; cathedral, market and former county town on the junction of the A40 and A470.

John Price (1502-55), royal administrator and early Protestant scholar, was born here; among the public offices he held were those of Chief Registrar of the Crown and Secretary of the Council of the Marches. He took a keen interest in the history and literature of Wales and was the first to publish a book in Welsh, namely *Yn y lhyvyr hwnn* (1546); his *Historiae Britannicae Defensio*, in which he defended **Geoffrey of Monmouth** (*c.*1090-1155) against Polydore Vergil, was published posthumously in 1573.

William Aubrey (*c*.1529-95), known as the Great Civilian, was born at Cantref, near Llanfrynach, on the S side of the Wye; his grandson, **John Aubrey** (1626-97), was the author of *Brief Lives* (1813).

The scholar **Siôn Dafydd Rhys** (1534-*c*.1619) practised medicine from his home (unidentified) in Cwm Llwch in the Brecon Beacons.

The poet **John Lloyd** (1797-1875) was born in the town and educated at Christ College; he lived at Dinas, a house demolished in 1980 to make way for a by-pass. Unusually for a member of the squirearchy of his time, he thought of himself as a Welsh patriot, writing of the glory of Welsh arms in the royal service. His verse was published in two volumes: the first was plainly entitled *Poems* (1847) and the second, somewhat surprisingly, *The English Country Gentleman* (1849).

The poet's son, also called **John Lloyd** (1833-1915), had antiquarian interests and supported commoners' rights in the Great Forest of Brecknock.

Two other poets born in Brecon were **Walter Churchey** (1747-1805), one of the earliest pillars of Methodism in the town, and **Jane Cave** (*c*.1754-1813), the daughter of an English exciseman who, while stationed at Talgarth, was converted by the preaching of Howel Harris (1714-73).

Like her brother Charles Kemble (1775-1854), the actress Sarah Siddons (1755-1831) was born at the inn known as The Shoulder of Mutton, which still stands in the centre of the town. Both her first stage appearance and the crisis caused by her love for fellow-actor William Siddons took place in Brecon.

The novelist **Alice Mallt Williams** (1867-1950) grew up at Aberclydach House in Talybont-on-Usk, a village some 7 m SE of Brecon on the opposite side of the valley from Llansantffraid; she lived later at Llanarthne in Carmarthenshire and St Dogmael's in Pembrokeshire. With her sister Gwenffreda she wrote, under the pseudonym *Y Ddau Wynne*, two novels, *One of the Royal Celts* (1889) and *A Maid of Cymru* (1901). Of considerable private means, she was a pioneer feminist and early member of Plaid Cymru, to which she made generous financial contributions.

BRIDGEND (W. Pen-y-bont ar Ogwr), Bridgend; large industrial town off the M4 and at the junction of the A48, A4063 and A473

The public library in Wyndham Street has plaques commemorating the philosopher **Richard Price** (1723-91), a native of Llangeinor, and the harpist John Thomas (Pencerdd Gwalia; 1826-1913), who was born in Bridgend; the latter is buried in Nolton churchyard in the town.

The poet **Wil Ifan (William Evans**; 1888-1968) was a minister here from 1909 to 1917 and from 1925 to 1949 and lived at Yetygarn in Park Street; there is a bust of him in the Reference Library at Coed Parc.

The offices of Seren Books, publishers of *Poetry Wales* and many English-language books by Welsh writers, are at 2 Wyndham Street.

The bookshop *Siop yr Hen Bont* is in Old Bridge Street.

BRO GYNIN, Cardiganshire; a ruined farmhouse about 6 m NE of Aberystwyth in the parish of Llanbadarn Fawr; it can be reached by following a right-hand turn off the A487 to Penrhyncoch and then left to Salem and left again.

Widely accepted as the birthplace of the poet **Dafydd ap Gwilym** (*fl.*1315/20-1350/70), the spot is marked by a plaque which was unveiled by **Thomas Parry** (1904-85) in 1977; but see also the entry for Talley. Dafydd ap Gwilym was the most accomplished Welsh poet of the medieval period and is generally regarded as one of the greatest of all time. The standard edition of his work was edited by Thomas Parry, *Gwaith Dafydd ap Gwilym* (1952); his poems can be read in English translation by Joseph P. Clancy, *Medieval Welsh Lyrics* (1965) and Rachel Bromwich, *Dafydd ap Gwilym: a Selection of Poems* (1982).

BRYNREFAIL, Gwynedd; village off the A4086 about 5 m E of Caernarfon.

The novelist **T. Rowland Hughes** (1903-49) entered the County School in 1915, a fact recorded by a plaque on the school wall.

BUILTH (W. Llanfair-ym-Muallt), Powys; market town on the river Wye at the junction of the A470 and the A483.

Here was born, at a place as yet unidentified, **Thomas Jeffery Llewelyn Prichard** (1790-1862), actor and author of *The Adventures and Vagaries of Twm Shon Catti* (1824), sometimes said to be the first novel by a Welsh writer in English. The exact place of his birth has so far eluded scholars, but it is thought that his boyhood was spent at Bryn Du, an isolated farmhouse on the mountainside a little to the N of Sennybridge. He settled in Builth with his wife Naomi in about 1826 and earned a living as a bookseller. The 1841 Census shows the family living in the town's High Street and that for 1851 shows them in Broad Street. He is commemorated by a stone memorial, the work of the Japanese artist Hideo Furuta, in the yard of Builth High School. After 1839 Prichard led the life of a strolling player, but spent his last years in penury; having lost his nose in an accident with a sword, he died in a poor quarter of Swansea known as World's End after falling into his own fire, and was buried in an unmarked grave in Dan-y-graig Cemetery.

The novelist **Hilda Vaughan** (1892-1985), who later became the wife of the English novelist Charles Morgan (1894-1958), was born at a house known as The Castle, a small Victorian mansion. The house is no longer there; only a row of Wellingtonians, which once lined the drive, are still to be seen, near the police station. Some of her novels are set in Radnorshire; they include *The Battle to the Weak* (1925), *Her Father's House* (1930) and *The Invader* (1928), while *The Soldier and the Gentlewoman* (1932) is set in Carmarthenshire. Perhaps her most exquisite writing is to be found in the novella, *A Thing of Nought* (1934), a tale of star-crossed love again set in the hills of Radnorshire.

The poet **T. Harri Jones** (1921-65) was born at Cwm Crogau, a farmhouse in the Hirnant valley off the B4358 between Newbridge and Llanafan, and educated at Builth High School. He emigrated to Australia in 1959 and there made his name as the author of *The Enemy in the Heart* (1957), *Songs of a Mad Prince* (1960) and *The Beast at the Door* (1963); his *Collected Poems* appeared in 1977. After his death by drowning, his ashes were buried in the churchyard of St Michael's at Llanfihangel Brynpabuan, near the entrance to Cwm Crogau. In 'Land of my Fathers' he wrote:

Always I feel the cold and cutting blast
Of winds that blow about my native hills,
And know that I can never be content
In this or any other continent
Until with my fathers I am at last
Back in the old country that sings and kills.

The hill Allt-y-clych, which is mentioned in several of his poems, overlooks the church. A bust of T.H. Jones is kept at Builth High School; a commemorative plaque erected on the school wall by the Rhys Davies Trust in 1999 can be seen from North Road.

At Cilmeri, about 6 m to the W of Builth on the A483, there is a magnificent monument to Llywelyn ap Gruffudd, the last Prince of independent Wales, who was killed on the nearby bank of the Irfon on 11 December 1282.

At a farmhouse known as Hendre Einion in the parish of Llanfaredd, off the A481 about 3 m NE of Builth, was born the antiquary **Edward Davies (Celtic Davies;** 1756-1831). He earned his sobriquet on account of his books *Celtic Researches* (1804) and *The Mythology and Rites of the British Druids* (1809). A keen collector of manuscripts, he nevertheless lacked a sufficient grasp of Welsh to interpret accurately the ancient poetry in which he delighted.

The antiquary **Thomas Price (Carnhuanawc;** 1787-1848) was born at Pencaerelin, a smallholding in the parish of Llanfihangel Brynpabuan. Educated at Christ College, Brecon, he was ordained priest in the Church of England in 1812 and preferred to the living of Llanfihangel Cwm Du in his native county in 1825. A patriot, he was an ardent advocate of education through the medium of the Welsh language and criticized the Anglican Church for condoning the use of English in its services. He wrote mostly on the history and antiquities of Wales and did much to foster relations between Wales and Brittany.

CADAIR IDRIS, Gwynedd; mountain situated between the rivers Mawddach and Dysynni, to the S of Dolgellau.

It is said that whoever spends a night alone on its summit (alt. 893 metres) will come down next morning mad, blind or endowed with poetical powers. This local tradition was given wider currency by **Felicia Hemans** (1793-1835) in a poem, 'The Rocks of Cader Idris', which appeared in her book *Welsh Melodies* in 1832.

In a letter to E.J. Hookham, the English novelist **Thomas Love Peacock** (1785-1866) wrote: 'On the top of Cadair Idris, I felt how happy a man may be with a little money and a sane intellect, and reflected with astonishment and pity on the madness of the multitude.'

CAEATHRO, Gwynedd; village on the A4085 about 2 m SE of Caernarfon.

The poet **T. Arfon Williams** (1935-98) lived the last ten years of his life at Y Wern, where some of his ashes were buried under a tree in the garden.

CAEO, Carmarthenshire; small village on a minor road off the A482 about 5 m NE of Llansawel.

It is famous as the birth-place of the hymn-writer **Dafydd Jones** (1711-77), whose home was in Cwm Gogerddan. By trade a drover, he was converted at Troedrhiwdalar while on his way home from a cattle-drive into England. He joined the Independent chapel at Crug-y-bar, about 2 m distant, and was a member there for the rest of his life. Dafydd Jones o Gaeo, as he is known, translated the hymns of **Isaac Watts** (1674-1748) into dignified, powerful, singable Welsh and many of his own hymns are still sung by Welsh congregations.

CAERLEON (W. Caerllion), Newport; town on the river Usk, off the M4 and A449, about 3 m NE of Newport. The town's name is derived from 'Camp of the Legion' and the extensive remains of the amphitheatre and barracks of the stronghold dating from AD 80 can still be seen, as well as a Roman museum.

The most impressive description of Roman Caerleon is in **Geoffrey of Monmouth**'s *Historia Regum Britanniae (History of the Kings of Britain, c.1136)*, on which the English novelist **Thomas Love Peacock** (1785-1866) drew for his novel, *The Misfortunes of Elphin* (1829).

The town is also probably the Carlion of **Malory**'s *Le Morte d'Arthur* (1485), where Arthur was crowned and held court.

The English poet **Alfred, Lord Tennyson** (1809-92), stayed at the Hanbury Arms in 1856 while gathering material about the Arthurian legends which he used in *The Idylls of the King* (1859), a fact noted by a plaque inside the hotel.

Arthur Machen (1863-1947) was born Arthur Llewellyn Jones at 33 High Street, although soon after his birth he was taken to Llanddewi, where his father was rector. Machen, in his autobiography *Far Off Things* (1922) wrote: 'I shall always esteem it as the greatest piece of fortune that has fallen to me that I was born in that noble, fallen Caerleon-on-Usk in the heart of Gwent. The older I grow, the more firmly am I convinced that anything I may have accomplished in literature is due to the fact that when my eyes first opened in early childhood, they had before me the vision of an enchanted land.' Machen won fame during the first world war as the author of a story, later published in *The Bowmen and Other Legends* (1915), in which he described how the ghosts of Welsh archers had intervened in the battle of Mons by discharging their arrows at the German positions. They were described as 'a long line of shapes, with a shining about them', and their arrows were said to kill without leaving visible wounds. Within a week Machen's archers had been transformed into 'the Angels of Mons' and, much to his distress, what he had written as fiction was being taken as fact, especially by jingoists who claimed that it was unpatriotic to doubt it.

The poet **Clifford Dyment** (1914-70) spent part of his childhood at 1 Ashwell Terrace (gone). In his autobiography, *The Railway Game* (1962), he wrote: 'The town you call your native town should be your *family home* . . . The place I was taken to [from Alfreton, Derbyshire], at one month old, was the place I should like to have been born: my private and adopted town, Caerleon-upon-Usk.' His *Collected Poems* were published in 1970.

CAERNARFON, Gwynedd; county town on the A487 near the SW end of the Menai Straits.

It stands on the site of the Roman fort Segontium and is featured in many early Welsh tales, notably that of Macsen Wledig (Maxen Maximus) and Helen of the Hosts.

The castle was the scene of the investitures of the prince of Wales in 1911 and 1969. The memorial to

Llywelyn ap Gruffudd, the last Prince of independent Wales, was erected by Gwynedd County Council in 1982, the seventh centenary of his death.

There are two statues on the square: one to David Lloyd George (1863-1945), who was elected Liberal MP for Caernarfon Boroughs in 1890, and the other to Hugh Owen (1804-81), pioneer of the movement to establish a university for Wales.

The offices of *Yr Herald Cymraeg,* established in 1855, are situated in the town and many prominent Welsh literary figures have worked on the paper, notably **T. Gwynn Jones** (1871-1949).

The journalist and poet **R.D. Rowland (Anthropos**; 1853?-1944) was a prominent member of a cultural society known as *Clwb Awen a Chân* in Caernarfon and was its President from 1908 to 1932.

The poet **Huw Owen Williams (Huw Menai**; 1888-1961) was born in the town but left school at the age of 12 to seek work in the coal industry in Merthyr Tydfil; he lived the rest of his life in the industrial valleys of Glamorgan. He published four volumes of verse: *Through the Upcast Shaft* (1920), *The Passing of Guto* (1929), *Back in the Return* (1933) and *The Simple Vision* (1945). He was cremated at Glyntaf Crematorium, near Pontypridd.

There are two Welsh bookshops in Caernarfon, one in Twll-yn-y-wal Street and the other in Stryd y Porth Mawr.

CAERPHILLY (W. Caerffili), Caerphilly; industrial town 6 m N of Cardiff on the A468.

The philosopher **David Williams** (1738-1816) was born at Waun Waelod, a house now in ruins behind the Old Carpenters' Arms, in the parish of Eglwys Ilan to the W of the town. There is a memorial in a small park named after him on the S side of the castle. Williams attracted the attention of Benjamin Franklin (1706-90) with his *Treatise on Education* (1774) and his *Liturgy on the Universal Principles of Religion and Morality* (1776) was praised by Voltaire and Rousseau. His reputation in France was established by a translation of his *Letters on Political Liberty* (1782), a defence of the American colonists. Ten years later he was awarded the honorary citizenship of France and invited to Paris to help draw up a constitution for the Girondists. His chief claim to literary fame lies in his establishment in 1790 of the Royal Literary Fund, which helps authors in need.

At Groes-wen, on a hill about 2 m W of the town, the literary critic **William Williams (Caledfryn;** 1801-69), who was Independent minister here, is buried at the top end of the graveyard, not far from his friend **Evan Jones (Ieuan Gwynedd;** 1820-52). Caledfryn's tombstone, in red marble, has a low-relief portrait of him and is inscribed simply with his bardic name and dates.

The dramatist **Eynon Evans** (1904-89) lived at 4 Celyn Grove and later at Bryngolau, Court Road in Energlyn. He worked for many years as a bus-driver in Caerphilly, where he helped to found the Tonyfelin Dramatic Society, for which he wrote an annual three-act play; his ashes are buried in the cemetery at Tonyfelin. His work was extremely popular with amateur dramatic societies in south Wales and some of his plays achieved success on the London stage. His best-known work and the play which established him as a full-time writer was *Wishing Well* (1946), which was filmed as *The Happiness of Three Women*, with the author playing one of the leading roles. He also published a collection of short stories, *Prize Onions* (1951). One of the characters he created in a series of radio sketches, namely Tommy Trouble, delighted listeners to the BBC Welsh Home Service from 1943 to 1953. Ffordd Eynon Evans in Pen-yr-heol is named after the playwright.

CAERWYS, Flintshire; village just off the A541 about 7 m SW of Holywell.

Two important bardic sessions were held here in the 16th century at which poets met to discuss the rules governing their craft, with a view to protecting their professional status against encroachment by inferior practitioners. The first 'eisteddfod' took place in 1523 and the second in 1567, both probably under the patronage of the Mostyn family.

The antiquary **Angharad Llwyd** (1780-1866), one of the most able Welsh women of her day, was a native of the place and lived at a house known as Siambar Wen, which once stood at the rear of the modern house of the same name. A member of the Honourable Society of Cymmrodorion, she won prizes for her essays on genealogical and historical subjects. She also edited a new edition of **Sir John Wynn's** *History of the Gwydir Family* (1827) and wrote *The History of the Island of Mona* (1832), which won the premier prize at the Beaumaris Eisteddfod of 1833. Her father, John Lloyd (1733-93), vicar of Caerwys, accompanied **Thomas Pennant** (1726-98) on his tours of Wales.

CAPEL BANGOR, Cardiganshire; village 6 m E of Aberystwyth on the A44.

At the farm known as Pwllcenawon near the river Rheidol, the essayist **Lewis Edwards** (1809-87)

59

was born. He was the founder in 1843 of the influential magazine *Y Traethodydd*, which is still published by the Presbyterian Church of Wales. His literary essays appeared in the volume *Traethodau Llenyddol* (1865). There is a bust of the author against the wall of Pen-llwyn chapel in the village, which is visible from the road.

CAPEL-Y-FFIN, Powys; hamlet in the valley of the Honddu on a minor road about 7 m S of the Hay.

Here Father Ignatius (J.L. Lyne; 1837-1908) tried to revive Benedictine monasticism by founding a monastery in 1870. **Francis Kilvert** (1840-79) sought him out, recording their meeting in an entry in his diary for 2 September 1870: 'He struck me as being a man of gentle simple kind manners, excitable, and entirely possessed by the one idea.'

The English sculptor Eric Gill (1882-1940) lived here during the 1920s in a community of artist-craftmen which included the writer and painter **David Jones** (1895-1974). Jones's two great works are *In Parenthesis* (1937) and *The Anathémata* (1952).

CARDIFF (W. Caerdydd), Cardiff; capital city of Wales, situated to the S of the M4 and on the river Taff.

In 1830 the city was no more than a small market-town, but grew rapidly after the discovery of coal in the valleys to the N during the latter part of the 19th century until, in the Edwardian period, it outstripped Merthyr Tydfil and became the largest town in Wales and the greatest coal-exporting port in the world. It was declared a city in 1905 and the capital of Wales in 1955.

In Cathays Park, the gift of the Bute family whose wealth created Cardiff, are: the National

Museum of Wales; the University of Wales, Cardiff; the Temple of Peace; the Law Courts; and the administrative offices, formerly the Welsh Office, which are now part of the National Assembly, which is situated in temporary premises on Cardiff Bay.

At the old City Hall can be seen a number of statues, in Serravesa marble and unveiled by David Lloyd George in 1916, which commemorate Welsh national heroes such as St David, Llywelyn ap Gruffudd and Owain Glyndŵr; the writers **Giraldus Cambrensis** (*c*.1146-1223), **Dafydd ap Gwilym** (*fl*.1315/20-1350/70), **William Morgan** (1545-1604) and **William Williams (Pantycelyn**; 1717-91) are also honoured here.

Among cultural bodies which have their headquarters in the city are the Arts Council of Wales in Museum Place, the Registry of the University of Wales in King Edward VII Avenue, the Welsh Language Board in St Mary Street, the Welsh Academy in Mount Stuart Square and the University of Wales Press in Gwennyth Street in Cathays, a district to the N of the city centre. The National Rugby Stadium (formerly Cardiff Arms Park) opened off Westgate Street in 1999 and an Arts Centre is planned for the Bay. The headquarters of BBC Wales are in Llandaf and HTV Wales is located at Culverhouse Cross, near the A4050, on the W side of the city.

The city has several good bookshops, including The Stationery Office (Oriel) in the High Street, which specializes in the books of Wales, Waterstones in The Hayes and St David's Link, Blackwells in the Royal Arcade and Siop y Felin in the main street of the northern suburb of

Statue of Giraldus Cambrensis, Cardiff City Hall

Whitchurch.

The City Library just off The Hayes houses a number of old Welsh manuscripts, including *Llyfr Aneirin* (*The Book of Aneirin*, *c*.1265), which contains the long heroic poem 'Y Gododdin' by the 6th-century poet **Aneirin**. The poem describes the defeat of a British war-band by Mercian forces at Catraeth – perhaps Catterick in modern Yorkshire.

The prose-writer **Dorothy Edwards** (1903-34) lived during her teens in Penydre in the Garden Village in Rhiwbina, a northern suburb of the city, and was educated at Howell's Girls' School in Llandaf and at the University College. She published only two books, namely *Rhapsody* (1927), a collection of short stories, and a novel, *Winter Sonata* (1928), which was hailed by English critics as one of the best books of its year. She put an end to her life by throwing herself under a train near Caerphilly station. The reason remains a mystery, but a note found on her body read: 'I am killing myself because I have never sincerely loved any human being all my life. I have accepted friendship, and even love, without gratitude and given nothing in return.'

The poet and critic **W.J. Gruffydd** (1881-1954), a native of Bethel, was appointed to the Chair of Welsh at the University College in 1918. From 1922 to 1951 he was editor of the influential literary magazine *Y Llenor*. His home in Cardiff was at 22 Lôn y Dail in the Garden Village of Rhiwbina, although in his autobiography, *Hen Atgofion* (1936; trans. D. Myrddin Lloyd, *The Years of the Locust*, 1936) he wrote (trans.): 'The truth is I have never lived in a community since I left Llanddeiniolen for Cardiff a quarter of a century ago. Here I simply reside – sleeping, working and eating; I do not *live* here . . . How sad it is that a Welshman should be an exile in Wales, for every Welshman living in Cardiff or its suburbs is an exile.' The Welsh character of Cardiff has developed since Gruffydd's day and the city now has many thousands of

Welsh-speakers and a thriving cultural life.

The playwright **Saunders Lewis** (1893-1985) lived during the early 1920s at 10 Hamilton Street while employed in the County Library at Bridgend. Here he wrote *Gwaed yr Uchelwyr* (1923). There is a bust of him by Ivor Roberts-Jones in the National Museum of Wales.

The poet and essayist **Iorwerth C. Peate** (1901-82), the first Curator of the Folk Museum at St Fagans, lived from 1929 at 29 Lôn y Dail, Rhiwbina.

The novelist **Howard Spring** (1889-1965) was born at 32 Edward Street, Canton, now an inner suburb. The street was renamed Albert Street in 1892 and the house is now the Canton Branch of Barclays Bank, which sponsored the commemorative plaque. After his father's death Spring left school and worked in a butcher's shop. Later he became an office boy at *The South Wales News* and attended evening classes at the University College, for which his editor paid. Most of his adult life was spent in England, but his childhood in Cardiff is charmingly evoked in his memoir *Heaven Lies about Us* (1939).

Ivor Novello (1893-1951), man of the theatre, was born **David Ivor Davies** at 95 Cowbridge Road, now marked by a blue plaque. A few months later his family moved to 11 Cathedral Road, now the offices of Lloyds Bank and known as Novello House; there is a small display of memorabilia in the reception area. Novello won fame during the first world war as composer of the song 'Keep the Home Fires Burning' and for the rest of his life enjoyed immense success as actor and playwright. His greatest triumphs were the musical comedies *Glamorous Night* (1935), *Careless Rapture* (1936), *The*

Dancing Years (1939), *Perchance to Dream* (1945), and *King's Rhapsody* (1949).

The family of **Eric Linklater** (1899-1974), the Scottish writer, moved from Penarth in 1900 to live at 23 Fairoak Road, in the Roath area of the city. The first 23 years of his life were spent in Cardiff and he attended the Intermediate School which later became Cardiff High School. For more than 40 years Linklater fostered the notion that he was, like his father, an Orcadian, but the truth was finally disclosed in his third volume of autobiography, *Fanfare for a Tin Hat* (1970), in which he recalled Cardiff with affection.

The novelist **Maurice Edelman** (1911-75) was born at 26 Cowbridge Road, Canton, where his father kept a photographer's shop; he was educated at Cardiff High School. He was Labour MP for Coventry West from 1945 to 1950 and for Coventry North West from 1950 until his death. Most of his novels have parliamentary settings and are primarily concerned with the intrigues of political life. They include *A Trial of Love* (1951), *Who Goes Home* (1953), which is partly set in a Welsh constituency, *A Dream of Treason* (1955), *The Happy Ones* (1957), *A Call on Kuprin* (1959), *The Minister* (1961), *The Prime Minister's Daughter* (1964), *All on a Summer's Night* (1969) and *Disraeli in Love* (1972).

The poet **Alun Llywelyn-Williams** (1913-88) was born in Roath Park and brought up at 33 Ninian Road in that part of the city. He described his boyhood in his autobiography *Gwanwyn yn y Ddinas* (1975). While a student at the University College, he launched a magazine, *Tir Newydd*, which printed poems and prose by younger writers and grappled with issues of the day. His collected poems were published under the title *Y Golau yn y*

Gwyll (1974). A selection of his poetry and prose has been translated by Joseph P. Clancy as *The Light in the Gloom* (1998).

The English children's writer **Roald Dahl** (1916-90) was born at Villa Marie (now Tŷ Gwyn) in Fairwater Road. Three years later his family moved to Tŷ Mynydd in the northern suburb of Radyr; the house has been demolished and a housing estate occupies the gardens. In 1920 the Dahls moved to Llandaf, where they lived at Cumberland Lodge, now part of Howell's School, and where the boy was educated at the Cathedral School. His childhood is described in *Boy* (1984). Roald Dahl was christened at the Norwegian Church, a small arts centre situated in Cardiff Bay, where a portrait of him is kept.

In 1929 the novelist **Jack Jones** (1884-1970) came to Rhiwbina and lived above a boot shop on the junction of Heol-y-bryn and Heol-y-coed, where he wrote the novels *Rhondda Roundabout* (1934) and *Black Parade* (1935), the first part of his autobiography *Unfinished Journey* (1937) and a play, *Land of my Fathers* (1937). He moved to a house which he named Sarandai (after his parents, Saran and David) in 1938, living there until 1946 and writing the novels *Off to Philadelphia in the Morning* (1947), *Some Trust in Chariots* (1948) and *River out of Eden* (1951). His last home was at 57 Pen-y-dre, where the following novels were written: *Lily of the Valley* (1952), *Lucky Lear* (1952), *Time and the Business* (1953), *Choral Symphony* (1955) and *Come, Night; End Day!* (1956). He died at his home and was buried at Pantmawr Cemetery, a little to the N. There is a collection of his books and other materials at the public library in Rhiwbina.

In 1925 **Glyn Jones** (1905-95), poet and prose-writer, returned from college in Cheltenham to live with his parents, who had moved from Merthyr Tydfil, to 156 Donald Street, in the Roath district of the city; two years later the family made their home at 27 Pentyrch Street in Cathays. In the same year he was appointed to a teaching post at Wood Street School (gone), in a slum area of the city near what is today the Central Station. After his marriage in 1935 Glyn Jones lived with his wife at 65 Heol-y-deri in Rhiwbina and in 1937 they moved to Trawscoed in Heol-y-bryn; he lived the rest of his life at 158 Manor Way, Whitchurch; the house has a commemorative plaque placed there by the Rhys Davies Trust in the year of his death. In 1937 he began teaching at Allensbank School (now gone), but was dismissed in 1942 because he had registered as a conscientious objector to war. All his books were written in Cardiff; they include *The Dragon Has Two Tongues* (1968), a largely autobiographical account of Anglo-Welsh writing, and three novels: *The Valley, The City, The Village* (1956), *The Learning Lark* (1960) and, his most important work, *The Island of Apples* (1965). His *Collected Poems* appeared in 1996 and his *Collected Stories* in 1999.

The poet **Vernon Watkins** (1906-67) lived during the late 1920s in lodgings at 73 Connaught Road, while employed as a junior clerk in the Butetown Branch of Lloyds Bank. In 1927, deeply depressed by his daily routine and yearning for the Arcadian life of Repton School, where he had been exceedingly happy, he suffered a nervous breakdown after witnessing an accident in the street outside his lodgings for which he felt he was somehow to blame.

Lewis Jones (1897-1939), the novelist, died of a heart-attack at 12 Clare Road, a lodging-house where he stayed while on visits to Cardiff. He had spoken at some 30 street-meetings in favour of the Spanish Republic; Barcelona was to fall to the Fascist forces of Franco in the same week.

The novelist **T. Rowland Hughes** (1903-49) was a producer of feature programmes with the BBC in Cardiff from 1935 to 1945. He lived at 59 Windermere Avenue in Roath, and was buried in Cathays Cemetery, where his gravestone bears the inscription *'Y Dewraf o'n Hawduron'* (The bravest of our writers), a line from an *englyn* by **R. Williams Parry** (1884-1956).

The prose-writer **Aneirin Talfan Davies (Aneirin ap Talfan;** 1909-80) joined the BBC at the end of the second world war and became Head of Programmes with BBC Wales in 1966. He lived first at 13 Maesycwm Street in Barry and then at 98 Pencisely Road in Llandaf. He was the author of a substantial body of literary criticism in both Welsh and English. His book *Dylan: Druid of the Broken Body* (1964) was one of the first books to be published about the poet; he also wrote about T.S. Eliot, James Joyce and **David Jones** (1895-1974). With his brother Alun Talfan Davies, he founded the publishing house known as *Llyfrau'r Dryw* (Christopher Davies Ltd.), which published the monthly magazine *Barn* and many books. A cultured man, he made important contributions to the life of Wales, not least as a lay member of the Church in Wales and as a generous patron of writers during his time with the BBC. He is buried in the graveyard of Llandaf Cathedral.

The poet **Harri Webb** (1920-94) lived for several

years in Cardiff during the late 1940s and 1950s, first at 22 Kyle Crescent in Whitchurch, then at 38 Hamilton Street in Canton and then at 39 Fitzhamon Embankment. In his 'Answer from Limbo' he wrote:

> Where will you spend eternity?
> The posters question us.
> The answer comes quite readily:
> Waiting for a Cardiff bus.

The poet **John Tripp** (1927-86) is commemorated by a bench near Ararat Chapel on the common in the northern suburb of Whitchurch, where he lived for most of his life at 2 Heol Pen-y-fai. One of the poets associated with 'the second flowering' of Welsh writing in English during the 1960s, he published seven volumes of poetry, including *The Loss of Ancestry* (1969) and *The Province of Belief* (1971); a selection of his work appeared in the *Penguin Modern Poets* series in 1979 and his *Collected Poems* in1978.

His friend, the poet **John Ormond** (1923-90), lived from 1955 to his death at 15 Conway Road, off Cathedral Road, in the district of Pontcanna; the house is now marked by a commemorative plaque put up by the Rhys Davies Trust in 1996. A film producer with BBC Wales, he published three volumes of poetry: *Requiem and Celebration* (1969), *Definition of a Waterfall* (1973) and *Cathedral Builders* (1991); a selection of his work appeared in the *Penguin Modern Poets* series in 1978 and his *Selected Poems* in 1987.

The poet **Gilbert Ruddock** (1938-98) was born at 97 Arran Street, off City Road, and lived for many years at 91 Westville Road in Penylan. He learned Welsh at Cathays High School in Cardiff and took a degree in the language at the University College in the city. In 1969 he was appointed Lecturer in the Welsh Department at the College. His four volumes of verse are : *Y Funud Hon* (1967), *Cwysi* (1973), *Hyn o Iachawdwriaeth* (1986) and *Troad y Rhod* (1997). He was buried in Thornhill cemetery on the N side of the city.

The Arthurian scholar **A.O.H. Jarman** (1911-99), who was Professor of Welsh at the University, lived for many years at 4 Henllys Road in Cyncoed.

The prose-writer and Viking scholar **Gwyn Jones** (1907-99) lived for many years in Brynderwen Close, Cyncoed. He was Professor of English at the University College from 1964 to 1975. While in Cardiff he published his magisterial *History of the Vikings* (1968). He often gave Blackwood as the town of his birth but, shortly after his death, it was revealed that he had been born in New Tredegar in Monmouthshire.

From 1970 to 1989 the poet **T. Arfon Williams** (1935-98) lived at Penmaen, 31 Heol Don, in the N suburb of Whitchurch; he was a dental officer in the Welsh Office. He wrote almost entirely in Welsh but here is one of his *englynion* in English:

A bee in your flower bed, I alight
on the lips full-parted
of your fox-glove, beloved,
and am freely, fully fed.

In the New Theatre, just off Queen Street in the centre of the city, there are bronze busts of the playwrights **Gwenlyn Parry** (1932-91) and **Gwyn Thomas** (1913-81) by Jonah Jones and Robert Thomas respectively.

A bust of **Dylan Thomas** (1914-53) by David Slivka can be seen in the foyer of BBC Wales in Llandaf and one of **Saunders Lewis** (1893-1985) by

Kostek Wojnarowski in the Salesbury Library, part of the University Library, in Colum Road, on the E side of Cathays Park.

Llandaf, with its magnificent 12th-century cathedral, lies about 2 m NW from the centre of Cardiff and is now a suburb of the city. **Geoffrey of Monmouth** (1100?-54), chronicler and author of *Historia Regum Britanniae (c.1136;* trans. *History of the Kings of Britain)*, was made archdeacon of the cathedral *c.*1140.

William Morgan (*c.*1545-1604), first translator of the Bible into Welsh, was consecrated Bishop of Llandaf in 1595 but was translated to St Asaph six years later.

The village of St Fagans, 4 m W of Cardiff off the A4232, is the home of the Museum of Welsh Life, part of the National Museum of Wales, which was established here in 1948 in the castle donated by the third Earl of Plymouth. Its first Curator was **Iorwerth C. Peate** (1901-82), poet and essayist. His ashes, with those of his wife and son, are buried in the graveyard of Penrhiw Chapel which, with many other buildings, has been rebuilt in the Museum's grounds.

A selection of poetry and prose by writers connected with Cardiff will be found in *A Cardiff Anthology* (ed. Meic Stephens, 1991).

CARDIGAN (W. Aberteifi), Cardiganshire; market town on the estuary of the river Teifi on the A487.

The castle, built by order of Roger de Montgomery, Earl of Shrewsbury, during his occupation of Ceredigion in 1093, was captured by Rhys ap Gruffudd in 1165. In 1176 the Lord Rhys of Deheubarth presided over an assembly of poets and musicians here which is sometimes said to have

71

been the earliest recorded eisteddfod; this fact is recorded by a plaque on the castle wall, facing the bridge.

A plaque opposite the Midland Bank at 11 High Street commemorates the poets **Telynog (Thomas Evans**; 1840-65) and **Ossian Dyfed (John Davies**; 1852-1916), both natives of the town.

The town has a Welsh bookshop, *Canolfan Teifi*.

CARMARTHEN (W. Caerfyrddin), Carmarthenshire; county town off the A40 and A48 and on the estuary of the Towy.

Its name is connected with the legendary Myrddin, known in English as Merlin, who was first popularized by **Geoffrey of Monmouth** in his *Historia Regum Britanniae* (*History of the Kings of Britain*, c.1136).

The *Black Book of Carmarthen*, a collection of manuscripts probably written in the mid-13th century, was first printed in 1868; the original text is now kept in the National Library of Wales.

An important eisteddfod was held here about 1450, probably at Carmarthen castle, for the purpose of drawing up new rules for traditional prosody. **Tudur Aled** (*c.*1465-*c.*1525) was present and **Dafydd ab Edmwnd** (*fl.*1450-99) won a miniature silver chair. Tudur Aled is believed to have died here and to have been buried in the friars' graveyard in the habit of the Franciscan order; there is a commemorative plaque in the Lammas Street carpark next to the Falcon Hotel which was erected as part of the celebrations marking the National Eisteddfod held in the town in 1974.

Merlin's Oak, said to have been grown from an acorn planted on 19 May 1659 to mark the town's proclamation of Charles II as king, was poisoned by a local tradesman early in the 19th century because he disapproved of people gathering under it at all hours of the day and night. The old stump, reinforced by cement, used to stand at a road junction at the E end of the town, but as traffic increased it became a hazard and was moved to Abergwili. The prophecy traditionally ascribed to Merlin reads in English:

When Merlin's Tree shall tumble down,
Then shall fall Carmarthen Town.

The English essayist **Sir Richard Steele** (1672-1729) settled in Carmarthen in 1724 and lived in King Street, where he also died; he was buried in St Peter's churchyard and his grave has a memorial tablet. He also lived for a while at Tŷ Gwyn, a house near Afon Towy which was the home of Mary Scurlock, who later became his wife.

At the Ivy Bush Royal Hotel in Spilman Street, then a more modest tavern, **Iolo Morganwg (Edward Williams**; 1747-1826) held a session of the Dyfed Provincial Eisteddfod, after which the Gorsedd of Bards, Iolo's creation, became associated with the National Eisteddfod. A circle of stones in the garden and a stained glass window in the hotel, put in place in 1974, commemorate Iolo's initiative.

Sir Lewis Morris (1833-1907), best remembered for his *Epic of Hades* (1876-77), was born in Spilman Street. He was educated at the Queen Elizabeth Grammar School in the town. A popular poet in his day, but now almost wholly neglected, he was knighted in 1892 and began to entertain hopes of becoming Poet Laureate after the death of Alfred, Lord Tennyson, in the same year. But the offer was withdrawn, it is thought, as a consequence of

Queen Victoria's disapproval when she learned that he had a common-law wife and three children, a fact which he had hitherto managed to conceal from the world. It was during the delay over the appointment of Tennyson's successor, and having complained to Oscar Wilde that there seemed to be a conspiracy of silence against him, he asked, 'What shall I do?', to which Wilde made the famous reply, 'Join it, dear boy, join it'. His verse has seemed vapid, over-blown and long-winded to modern readers, yet his *Works* (1891) sold many thousands of copies and ran to many editions. Perhaps his best poem, 'Gwen', is set in the parish of Llangunnor, where he was buried.

Ernest Rhys (1859-1946), the editor of the *Everyman* series, spent holidays at his grandfather's house, 50 King Street, about which he wrote in his autobiography, *Wales England Wed* (1940); his father lived at 2 Nott Square. He was a well-known figure on the London literary scene and was among those, including W.B. Yeats, who founded the Rhymers' Club in 1891. He was also prominent in the 'Celtic Twilight' movement and was considered in England to be the representative Welsh poet of his day. But he has few readers nowadays, in either England or Wales.

The French scholar **Percy Mansell Jones** (1889-1968) was born at 15 King Street. He described his boyhood in the town in *How They Educated Jones* (1974). He was professor of French at the University College of North Wales, Bangor, before moving to the Chair of Modern French Literature at the University of Manchester, a post which he held from 1951 to 1956.

From 1910 until his retirement in 1946 **John Dyfnallt Owen** (1873-1956) was minister of the

Congregationalist chapel in Lammas Street (known in Welsh as Heol Awst), where there is a memorial window. He was an influential editor of the Independents' newspaper *Y Tyst* from 1927 to 1956, particularly in his emphasis on the importance of Christian nationalism as a prerequisite of internationalism. Dyfnallt won the Crown at the National Eisteddfod in 1907 and his essays, which display a vigorous prose-style and an attractive personality, were collected in the volumes *Rhamant a Rhyddid* (1952) and *Ar y Tŵr* (1953).

The maternal grandfather of **Vernon Watkins** (1906-67) lived at Goleufryn in Picton Terrace, a house celebrated in the poem 'Returning to Goleufryn'.

During the 1940s the magazine *Wales* was edited and published by **Keidrych Rhys** (1915-87), a local man, at the Druid Press from offices in Lammas Street. This was the leading English-language literary periodical in Wales and it published the work of many new writers, including **Dylan Thomas** (1914-53).

The poet **Harri Webb** (1920-94) worked briefly with Keidrych Rhys in 1949, living in lodgings at Brynderw in Wellfield Road and subsequently at 9 The Avenue.

The prose-writer **D. Tecwyn Lloyd** (1914-92) lived from 1955 to 1980 at Garth Martin, a house on the outskirts of the town, during which time he edited the literary magazine *Taliesin*. He was a witty and trenchant commentator on Welsh affairs and a staunch supporter of the Welsh language. From 1961 until his retirement he was a tutor with the Extra-Mural Department of the University College of Wales, Aberystwyth. His collections of essays, *Safle'r Gerbydres* (1970), *Lady Gwladys a Phobl Eraill*

(1971) and *Bore Da, Lloyd* (1980), all written at Garth Martin, display wide erudition and a mischievous sense of humour.

The bookshop known as *Siop y Pentan* is situated in the New Market.

CARMEL, Gwynedd; village on a minor road 2 m NW of Pen-y-groes and 1 m W of Groeslon.

The scholar and literary critic **Thomas Parry** (1904-85) was born at Bryn Awel and brought up at Gwyndy from the age of 13; the family later moved back to Bryn Awel. He was appointed Professor of Welsh at the University College of North Wales, Bangor, in 1947 and Librarian of the National Library of Wales in 1953; from 1958 until his retirement in 1969 he was Principal of the University College of Wales, Aberystwyth. His *magnum opus* is *Hanes Llenyddiaeth Gymraeg hyd 1900* (1945; trans. H. Idris Bell, *A History of Welsh Literature*, 1955). He also published, in 1952, a magisterial edition of the work of **Dafydd ap Gwilym** (*fl.*1315/20-1350/70) and edited *The Oxford Book of Welsh Verse* (1962). A selection of his prose-writings appeared posthumously under the title *Amryw Bethau* in 1996.

CASCOB (W. Casgob), Powys; village on a minor road off the B4372, about 4 m W of Presteigne.

The antiquary **W.J. Rees** (1772-1855), one of 'the old literary clerics' who kept alive an interest in the culture of Wales in the early 19th century, was vicar of the parish from 1806 until his death. He was enthusiastically involved in the Eisteddfod and the Honourable Society of Cymmrodorion and active with the Welsh Manuscripts Society.

CEFNDDWYSARN, Gwynedd; small village with Sarnau on the A494 about 3 m NE of Bala. On a farm known as Cynlas, 3 m E of Bala, the Liberal leader Thomas Edward Ellis (1859-99) was born. He was elected MP for Meirionnydd in 1886 on a platform unequivocally advocating Home Rule for Wales but his appointment to the office of Junior Whip in Gladstone's cabinet in 1892 and Chief Whip two years later advanced his parliamentary influence at the expense of his Radical appeal; his early death while on holiday in Egypt canonized him as the lost leader of Victorian Wales.

Robert Lloyd (Llwyd o'r Bryn; 1888-1961), a prominent adjudicator at the National Eisteddfod, who lived at Erwfeurig, is commemorated by a sculpture on the wall of the school at Sarnau. He was famous as a keen supporter of traditional Welsh culture and the literary tradition of the district. A selection of his writings appeared as *Diddordebau Llwyd o'r Bryn* in 1967.

The poet **Robert Williams Parry** (1884-1956) spent an idyllic year as schoolmaster in the village in 1913/14.

CELLAN, Cardiganshire; village on the B4343 in the Teifi Valley about 3 m NE of Lampeter.

The literary historian and scholar **Griffith John Williams** (1892-1963) was born at Cellan Court (later the post office), the son of the village blacksmith. The course of his career was set in 1917 when he began examining the manuscripts of **Iolo Morganwg (Edward Williams**; 1747-1826) which had been acquired by the National Library of Wales. He spent almost the rest of his life mastering the complexities of this archive and in his book *Iolo Morganwg a Chywyddau'r Ychwanegiad* (1926) he demonstrated that the poems added to the first edition of Dafydd's works which had been published in 1789 were, in fact, Iolo's own work. He went on to publish a magisterial study of the literary tradition of Glamorgan, *Traddodiad Llenyddol Morgannwg* (1948), and the first volume of his projected biography of Iolo (1956), in which he presented the poet as a romantic visionary as well as a gifted forger. His unmasking of the Gorsedd as Iolo's creation shocked many and had implications for the Welsh culture of the time. Of the Gorsedd, Williams wrote: 'They are not poets; they are not literary critics; they know little about the history of Wales and still less about its literature . . . They are merely useless members of an institution that was founded on deceit and maintained by arrogance and ignorance.'

His younger brother, **David Matthew Williams** (1900-70), was a playwright under the pseudonym Ieuan Griffiths.

CERRIGYDRUDION, Denbighshire; village on the junction of the A5 and B5105.

The poet **Edward Morris** (1607-89) was born at Perthillwydion, a farm in the vicinity, and was by trade a drover. He wrote love-songs which are among the best of their kind in Welsh, as well as poems in the strict metres and Christmas carols. He died while on a cattle-drive into England and was buried at an unidentified place in Essex.

The satirical poet **John Jones (Jac Glan-y-gors;** 1766-1821) was also born in the parish, at a farm from the name of which he took his *nom de plume*. He went to London about 1789, kept a tavern there and became prominent in the Welsh life of the city as secretary and official poet of the Gwyneddigion Society. Sharing the views of Thomas Paine on such issues as war, the monarchy, the Church and the Rights of Man, he published two pamphlets, *Seren Tan Gwmwl* (1795) and *Toriad y Dydd* (1797), which aroused the wrath of more conservative writers. He was famous in his day as the author of lampoons criticizing Welsh expatriates in London, especially on account of their tendency to turn their backs on the speaking of Welsh. The name Dic Siôn Dafydd, a character he created, has become synonymous with this kind of Welshman, whether in London or in Wales.

CHEPSTOW (W. Cas-gwent), Monmouthshire; old market town and former port on the A48, on the W bank of the Wye, 2 m above its junction with the Severn.

The English writer **Robert Bloomfield** (1766-1823), author of *The Farmer's Boy* (1800), stayed at the Beaufort Arms while touring along the Wye and into Wales in the summer of 1807. In *The Banks of Wye* (1811) he described the delightful social evening spent after visiting the castle by moonlight and hearing an owl hooting lustily from the battlements.

Edward Ernest Bowen (1836-1901), author of the Harrow School Song, was born just outside the town. The song, 'Forty Years On', which he wrote in 1872, is to be found in his only book, *Harrow Songs and Other Verses* (1886).

CIL-Y-CWM, Carmarthenshire; village on a minor road about 6 m N of Llandovery.

The hymn-writer **Morgan Rhys** (1716-79) was

born at Efail Fach, a remote cottage (long derelict). Fired by the spirit of the Methodist Revival which had swept through the district, between 1757 and 1775 he worked as a teacher in the Circulating Schools of Griffith Jones (1683-1761). He was not a prolific hymn-writer, but some of his work proved very popular in his day and is still sung by Welsh congregations. His hymns were first published in *Golwg o Ben Nebo* (1775), a title he gave to two further collections.

CLYDACH VALE, see under **BLAENCLYDACH**

CLYNNOG FAWR, Gwynedd; village on the A499 about 4 m N of Llanaelhaearn.

The ornate church dedicated to St Beuno in the 7th century was once an important place on the pilgrims' road to Bardsey.

The poet **Ebenezer Thomas (Eben Fardd**; 1802-63) lived at Bod Cybi, a fact recorded by a plaque on the house, situated on a path leading to the church of St Cybi.

At Pontllyfni, about 2 m from Clynnog Fawr, **Sir Ifor Williams** (1881-1965) lived for many years at Hafod-lwyd. He and his wife are buried at Capel Brynaerau; they are described on the gravestone as *'Cymro cadarn a'i gymar hynaws'* (A staunch Welshman and his charming companion). The gravestone also bears the inscription *'A gwedy elwch, tawelwch vu'* (And after merriment, there was silence), a line from *Y Gododdin*.

CLYRO (W. Cleirwy), Powys; village on the A438, 2 m NW of the Hay.

The English diarist **Francis Kilvert** (1840-79), while curate here, lived at Ashbrook House (formerly Tŷ Dulas), now an art gallery and private house, which bears a commemorative plaque. The seven years he spent here (1865-72) were the genesis and heart of the diary for which he is now famous. Of Clyro he wrote: ' To me there seems to be a halo of glory round this place . . . Many sweet and sacred memories hover about these hill homes and make the place whereon one stands holy ground.' There is a memorial to the diarist in the church. He is buried at Bredwardine, a little way into England, where he briefly held the living before his sudden death from peritonitis.

Sir Arthur Conan Doyle (1859-1930) stayed at Baskerville Hall, less than 1 m outside the village, and is thought to have used the family name in his novel *The Hound of the Baskervilles* (1902), drawing on a local tradition about the ghost of a ferocious black dog said to roam the countryside hereabouts; the figure of such a beast stands above the entrance to the Baskerville Arms opposite the Kilvert Gallery.

CORRIS, Gwynedd; former slate-quarrying village in a narrow valley on the A487 about 2 m SE of Tal-y-llyn Lake.

Here, in 1938, the prose-writer **Geraint Goodwin** (1903-41) lived in a cottage known as Pen-y-cwm in the upper part of the village. He was already seriously ill with tubercolosis and the dampness of the house aggravated his condition until he was obliged to return to Montgomery, where he died three years later.

CORWEN, Denbighshire; town on the A5, 11 m E of Llangollen.

The town is associated with Owain Glyndŵr

(*c.*1354-*c.*1416), the national hero of the Welsh, who had a home at Carrog, about 3 m to the E in the valley of the Dee. There is a statue of him on Corwen's square.

John Cowper Powys (1872-1963) moved here late in 1934 and lived at 7 Cae Cod. His novel *Maiden Castle* was published three years later; he also wrote *Owen Glendower* (1941) and *Porius* (1951) before moving to Blaenau Ffestiniog in 1955.

The Welsh-language writer **R. D. Rowland (Anthropos**; 1853?-1944) was brought up at Ty'n-y-cefn and was later, in *Y Pentref Gwyn* (1909), to write a vivid account of his childhood there.

The novelist **Elena Puw Morgan** (1900-73) was also born at Corwen, where after her marriage in 1931 her home became a centre of Welsh culture. She was the author of three novels for adults, namely *Nansi Lovell* (1933), *Y Wisg Sidan* (1939) and *Y Graith* (1943), and several tales for children. She gave up writing in 1939 to look after relatives suffering from ill health.

The prose-writer **D. Tecwyn Lloyd** (1914-92) was born at Penybryn in the district known as Llawr-y-betws between Corwen and Bala, and is buried in the churchyard there. His last years were spent at Maes-yr-Onnen, a former parsonage at Maerdy, about 4 m to the W on the A5.

The poet **W.D. Williams** (1900-85) was born at Llwyn Ithel in Llawr-y-betws, and lived in the village shop.

COWBRIDGE (W. Y Bont-faen), Vale of Glamorgan; market town on the junction of the A48 and the A4222.

A shop opposite the Town Hall bears a plaque

recording the fact that the poet and antiquary **Edward Williams (Iolo Morganwg;** 1747-1826) kept a bookshop there. It was unveiled on 17 December 1826, to mark the centenary of the writer's death, by the Glamorgan branch of the Union of Welsh Societies, and refers to Iolo (in Welsh) as 'Stonemason, Poet of Freedom, Antiquary, and one of the greatest benefactors of the literature and history of Wales.' The motto *'Gwir yn erbyn y byd'* (The truth against the world), devised by him as part of the neo-druidic ceremonies of the Gorsedd of Bards, which his fertile imagination invented, is

Plaque commemorating Iolo Morganwg,
in Cowbridge

inscribed on the plaque in ogham. The local Welsh School is named after him. In 1795 the first meeting of the Gorsedd of Bards to be held in Wales was organized by Iolo Morganwg at Stalling Down (Bryn Owen), less than 1 m to the E of the town off

83

the A48.

The poet **Alun Lewis** (1915-44) was a boarder at the Grammar School from 1926 to 1932, when he was already showing promise as a writer.

CRAIG-CEFN-PARC, Swansea; village on a minor road about 1 m NW of Clydach in the upper Clydach Valley, a side-valley of the Swansea Valley.

The poet **William Williams (Crwys;** 1875-1968) was born at 9 Fagwyr Road, the son of a shoemaker; he took the name by which he was generally known from the chapel, Pant-y-crwys, in the village. Archdruid from 1939 to 1947, he won the Crown at the National Eisteddfod on three occasions and published four collections of his poems between 1920 and 1944; some of his shorter lyrics, such as *'Dysgub y Dail'*, are among the best-known poems in the Welsh language. A bronze bust of the poet is kept in Swansea City Library.

CRICIETH, Gwynedd; small town on the A497 about 5 m W of Porthmadog on the Llŷn peninsula.

The prose-writer **John Griffith Williams** (1915-87) lived at Llysowain in the town. A native of Llangwnadl, he left school at the age of 14 to work as a carpenter on the Gwynfryn and Talhenbont estate, and later became a teacher of woodwork. He wrote two very fine volumes of autobiography, namely *Pigau'r Sêr* (1969), which describes his early years in the district, and *Maes Mihangel* (1974), which deals *inter alia* with his experiences as a conscientious objector on political grounds during the second world war. J.G. Williams also wrote a historical novel about the rising of Owain Glyndŵr, *Betws Hirfaen* (1978).

CROESOR, Gwynedd; hamlet on a minor road to the W of the A4085 between Aberglaslyn and Penrhyndeudraeth.

The book-collector and scholar **Bob Owen (Robert Owen**; 1885-1962), who was born at Pen-y-parc (Twllwenci) near Llanfrothen, lived for many years in Croesor and was generally known as Bob Owen Croesor. He was an authority on the history of Quakerism in Wales but was acquainted with almost all aspects of Welsh history. He amassed a huge library of books and maunuscripts, which filled his home. His knowledge was in great demand among Americans of Welsh extraction and his opinion was sought by many professional scholars. There is a chapter devoted to this extraordinary man in Philip O'Connor's book *Living in Croesor* (1962). The society for Welsh book-collectors, *Cymdeithas Bob Owen*, founded in 1976, is named after him. He was buried at Llanfrothen.

CWMAMAN, see under **ABERDARE**

CWMFELINFACH, Caerphilly; village in the Sirhowy valley, on the A4048 about 3 m W of Crosskeys.

The Calvinistic Methodist minister and poet **William Thomas (Islwyn**; 1832-78) began preaching at Y Babell, the chapel here, in 1854 and was ordained five years later. After his marriage in 1864 he lived at Green Meadow, close by the chapel, and then at Y Glyn, which he built himself; he lies in the chapel burial-ground. He was a prolific writer, most of his work being in the form of odes entered for competition at eisteddfodau, but he also wrote *Y Storm*, which he began at the age of 22 after the death of Anne Bowen, to whom he had been engaged. The death of Anne Bowen was the central experience of his life and cast a long shadow over his marriage to Martha Davies. According to one witness, the poet's dying words were (trans.): 'Thank you, Martha, for all you have done for me. You have been very kind. I am going to Anne now.'

CWM PENNANT, Gwynedd; valley on the W of Snowdon, reached from Garndolbenmaen off the road from Caernarfon to Porthmadog.

It was immortalized by **Eliseus Williams (Eifion Wyn**; 1867-1926) in the couplet (trans.):
Why, Lord, did you make Cwm Pennant so lovely
And the life of an old shepherd so short?

CYNWYL ELFED, Carmarthenshire; village 5 m NW of Carmarthen on the A484.

A signpost near the bridge points the way to Y Gangell, about 1 m to the W, near Blaen-y-coed, the birth-place of **Howell Elvet Lewis (Elfed**; 1860-1953), minister, poet and hymnwriter; the small cottage is preserved as a memorial to him. From 1898 to 1940 he was a Presbyterian minister in King's Cross in London. Some of his Socialist and patriotic poems brought him fame; his lyrics such as *'Gwyn ap Nudd'*, *'Pan Ddaw'r Nos'* and *'Y Ddau Frawd'* were even more popular. Among his hymns the most famous are *'Rho im yr hedd'* and *'Cofia'n Gwlad'*; the latter is so often sung at patriotic gatherings that it is considered almost as the second national anthem of Wales. Among his collections of verse in English were *My Christ and Other Poems* (1891), *Israel and Other Poems* (1930) and *Songs of Assisi* (1938). The writer's ashes were buried at Blaen-y-coed.

DEINIOLEN, Gwynedd; village off the A4086, 3 m N of Llanberis.

The playwright **Gwenlyn Parry** (1932-91) was born in a slate-quarryman's house known as Tan Post (gone) near the centre of the village. A commemorative plaque with a silhouette of the writer is to be seen on the wall of the village school. He discovered an interest in the theatre while living in London and, after his return to Wales to take up a teaching post at Bethesda, began winning prizes for his plays at the National Eisteddfod. Among his best plays are *Saer Doliau* (11966), *Tŷ ar y Tywod* (1968), *Y Ffin* (1973), *Y Tŵr* (1978) and *Sâl* (1982). All make use of the anti-naturalistic techniques of the post-war theatre and are enigmatic in their message. The writer is buried in Macpelah Cemetery at Pen-y-groes.

DENBIGH (W. Dinbych), Denbighshire; county town at the junction of the A525 and the A543, on a hill overlooking the Vale of Clwyd.

The writer of interludes **Thomas Edwards (Twm o'r Nant**; 1738-1810) is buried at Whitchurch in the town and there is a memorial plaque inside the church; his grave is located between two yews near the church tower. He was born at Penporchell Isaf, a farm in Llanefydd, on a minor road about 6 m to the NW, and brought up at Nant Isaf in Henllan, a farm from which he took his sobriquet, on the junction of the B5382 and B5428. He lived for a while in Dyffryn Street, where a plaque records the fact. His interludes (dramatic productions, often in verse) reflect a keen intelligence, fertile imagination and considerable technical skill. Among the best are *Pedair Colofn Gwladwriaeth* (1786) and *Tri Chryfion Byd* (1789). Because of the dearth of drama in Welsh before the 20th century, excessive claims have been made for Twm o'r Nant as 'the Cambrian Shakespeare'. The theatre in the town, opened in 1979, is named after him.

The journalist and printer **Thomas Gee** (1815-98) was born in Denbigh and Gwasg Gee, his publishing firm, is still located in Lôn Swan; he lived for many years at a house known as Bronallt. His press published a large number of magazines, newspapers, dictionaries, hymnals, theological works and books of poetry. Chief among them was the weekly newspaper *Baner ac Amserau Cymru*, launched in 1859, the most influential paper of its day. Among the Radical causes it promoted were the provision of non-sectarian education for Nonconformists, the widening of electoral suffrage and the Disestablishment of the Anglican Church in Wales. Thomas Gee's grave is in the New Cemetery in the town.

The explorer **Henry Morton Stanley** (1841-1904) was born John Rowlands in a cottage which used to stand within the precincts of Denbigh castle. An illegitimate child, he was brought up in the union workhouse at St Asaph, ran away at the age of 15 and took ship for the USA; in America he was befriended by one Henry Morton Stanley, from whom he took his new name. It was as a journalist he was to achieve distinction. In 1871 he set out in search of David Livingstone and, during the first of several expeditions across Africa, found him at Ujiji on 10 November 1871, greeting him with the famous words, 'Dr Livingstone, I presume?' His travels are recounted in *How I Found Livingstone* (1872), *Through the Dark Continent* (1878) and *In Darkest Africa* (1890).

The poet **Arthur Glyn Prys-Jones** (1888-1987) was born at 60 Love Lane in the town, but his family moved to Pontypridd when he was nine. In 1919 he was appointed Staff Inspector for Secondary Education in Wales. He edited the first anthology of Anglo-Welsh poetry, *Welsh Poets* (1917), and published six volumes of his own verse; the *Collected Poems* of A.G. Prys-Jones appeared in 1988. He excelled in the writing of light verse, as in 'Quite So':

> Within the whispering gallery of St Paul's
> The merest whisper travels round the walls;
> But in the parts where I was born and bred
> Folk hear things long before they're even said.

In 1935 the novelist **Kate Roberts** (1891-1985) and her husband Morris Williams bought Gwasg Gee, the printing-press founded by Thomas Gee which published the weekly newspaper *Baner ac Amserau Cymru*. After her husband's death in 1945 Roberts continued to run the business alone for another ten years, regularly contributing to the paper on a variety of subjects. The town is the background to many of her later books, including *Stryd y Glep* (1949), *Y Byw sy'n Cysgu* (1956; trans. Ll. Wyn Griffith, *The Living Sleep*,1978), *Te yn y Grug* (1959; trans. Ll. Wyn Griffith, *Tea in the Heather*, 1968), *Y Lôn Wen* (1960), *Tywyll Heno* (1962), *Hyn o Fyd* (1964) and *Tegwch y Bore* (1967). A selection of her prose-writings has been translated by Joseph P. Clancy, *The World of Kate Roberts* (1991).

The bookshop known as *Siop Clwyd* is at 33 High Street.

DINAS BRÂN, see under **LLANGOLLEN**

DINAS MAWDDWY, Gwynedd; small village off the A470, about 7 m E of Dolgellau.

In the 16th century the valley known as Cwm Dugoed, a little to the SE of the village, was plagued by a band of outlaws known as *Gwylliaid Cochion Mawddwy* (The Red Bandits of Mawddwy). The earliest reference to them occurs in **Thomas Pennant**'s *Tours of Wales* (1778) where it is said that 80 of their number were hanged by order of Judge Lewis Owen near the farm known as Collfryn. It is a historical fact that the judge, who made determined attempts to uphold the rule of law as Sheriff of Meirionnydd, was murdered in the district in 1555 while on his way home to Dolgellau from the Assizes at Dolgellau. The tale of the bandits has since been richly embroidered in popular tradition, as several local place-names testify; it is also said that the red hair of many local people was inherited from them.

In the churchyard is the grave of Llywelyn Thomas (Llywelyn Fawr o Fawddwy; d.1870), who was famous for his physical strength. He is immortalized in the folk-rhyme which begins *'Llywelyn Fawr o Fawddwy a aeth i foddi cath'* (Llywelyn Fawr of Mawddwy who went to drown a cat).

The parish was fortunate in the 19th century in having several cultured men as its rectors, including the antiquary **John Williams (Ab Ithel**; 1811-62) and the lexicographer **D. Silvan Evans** (1818-1903). On such men the survival of Welsh as a language of culture and learning largely depended.

About half way between Dinas Mawddwy and Dolgellau, in the valley known as Maesglasau, on the S side of the road, the hymn-writer **Hugh Jones** (1749-1825) was born; he wrote one of the greatest hymns in the Welsh language: *'O tynn y gorchudd yn y mynydd hyn'*.

DOLANOG, see under LLANFIHANGEL-YNG-NGWYNFA

DOLGELLAU, Gwynedd; town near the Mawddach estuary and at the junction of the A470 and the A494.

The district has strong associations with the Quakers, who established a meeting-place at Tyddyn-y-garreg, about 2 m outside the town, in 1657, and later at Tabor, near the cemetery.

Of Pentwr, where the Quaker leader **Ellis Pugh** (1656-1718), the author of *Annerch ir Cymru*, was born, only ruins remain.

In 1686 Rowland Ellis (1650-1731) of Bryn-mawr emigrated to Pennsylvania, together with about a hundred Friends, there to found the college known to this day as Bryn Mawr. The house can be reached by taking Ffordd y Gadair for about 1 m and then turning left near the farmhouse called Rhydwen; within less than a mile, Bryn-mawr can be seen to the right, on a rise in the midst of a wooded grove.

The history of the Quakers in Wales forms the background of two novels by Marion Eames, namely *Y Stafell Ddirgel* (1969; trans. *The Secret Room*, 1975) and *Y Rhandir Mwyn* (1972; *Fair Wilderness*, 1976).

Bryn Tynoriaid at Rhydymain, about 5 m to the NE on the A494, is the birthplace of **Evan Jones (Ieuan Gwynedd**; 1820-52), essayist and Radical pamphleteer; he was brought up at Tŷ-croes, Bontnewydd, on the Brithdir road, in a cottage which is now a ruin. He is remembered for his stout defence of the Welsh people against the strictures of the Blue Books of 1847.

There is a bookshop at 1 Eldon Terrace on the square in Dolgellau.

DOLWYDDELAN, Gwynedd; village on the A470 between Betws-y-coed and Blaenau Ffestiniog.

It is believed that Llywelyn Fawr, King of Gwynedd, was born in the castle in 1173.

Near by stands a farmhouse known as Tanycastell, the birth-place of **John Jones** (1796-1857) of Talsarn, the most famous Welsh preacher of the 19th century; a boulder on which he practised his sermons is inscribed with an *englyn*.

In the churchyard are the graves of the novelist and bookseller **Ellis Pierce (Elis o'r Nant**; 1841-1912) and the pacifist **George M.Ll. Davies** (1880-1949), who was a grandson of John Jones.

DOWLAIS, see under **MERTHYR TYDFIL**

DYFFRYN ARDUDWY, Gwynedd; small village on the A496 between Barmouth and Llanbedr.

In the nearby churchyard of Llanddwywe in the direction of Tal-y-bont the antiquary **John Williams (Ab Ithel**; 1811-62) is buried. He was one of the old literary clerics who kept alive an interest in Welsh literature during the first half of the 19th century when the Church of England disapproved of most things Welsh.

A little further S in the direction of Llanaber, stands Hendrefechan, the home of the poet **William Phylip** (1579-1669); the Sunnysands Caravan Park is now the dominant feature of the landscape hereabouts.

To the N, about 1 m from Llanbedr, is Y Faeldref,

the birth-place of **E. Morgan Humphreys** (1882-1953), journalist and writer of books for children. He wrote for the *Liverpool Daily Post* and the *Manchester Guardian* but is remembered for his detective stories, notably *Dirgelwch Gallt y Ffrwd* (1938), *Ceulan y Llyn Du* (1944) and *Llofrudd yn y Chwarel* (1951), and two volumes of articles about eminent Welshmen with whom he was acquainted, *Gwŷr Enwog Gynt* (1950, 1953). He was buried at Llanbeblig.

DYLIFE, Powys; hamlet 3 m SW of Pennant off the B4518.

On an unclassified road on the slopes of Moel Fadian there is a stone commemorating the writer and broadcaster **Wynford Vaughan-Thomas** (1908-87). This was his favourite spot and the view is memorable. The ground was acquired by the Council for the Preservation of Rural Wales, the work of which meant much to the writer. Born in Swansea, he was the author of books about the history and topography of Wales, and of a volume of autobiography, *Trust to Talk* (1980)

ELAN VALLEY (W. Cwm Elan), Powys; narrow valley SW of Rhayader, flooded to make a reservoir for the English Midlands.

In the summer of 1811 the English poet **Percy Bysshe Shelley** (1792-1822) spent some weeks at a house owned by his cousins, the Grove family; he returned the following year with his new wife Harriet. In a letter to William Goodwin, he wrote: 'Steal, if possible, my revered friend, one summer from the cold hurry of business, and come to Wales.' Thomas Grove helped the Shelleys try to buy a house, Nantgwillt, but the lease proved too expensive and they left. The poet is commemorated at the Elan Valley Visitors' Centre.

The English writer **Francis Brett Young** (1884-1954) was fascinated by the building of the reservoir and it became the inspiration for his novel *The House under the Water* (1932).

FISHGUARD (W. Abergwaun), Pembrokeshire; town at the end of the A40 and at its junction with the A487.

The prose-writer **D.J. Williams** (1885-1970), who

Memorial stone to D.J. Williams at
49 High St., Fishguard

taught at the Grammar School until his retirement in 1945, lived at the Bristol Trader (formerly a pub), 49 High Street, where a plaque records his long association with the town; the house's name was changed to The Old Pump House in 1982. The bookshop at 14 Y Wesh is known as *Siop D.J.*

His friend, the poet **Waldo Williams** (1904-71), lived at 3 Plasygamil Road in Goodwick; he taught at the Catholic primary school in the town.

Near Trefaser, 5 m W of Fishguard, on the coastal path above Pwllderi, there is a memorial to the poet **David Emrys James (Dewi Emrys**;1881-

Monument to Dewi Emrys at Pwllderi

1952). He won the Crown at the National Eisteddfod in 1926 and the Chair on four occasions between 1929 and 1948. His most famous poem is *'Pwllderi'*, written in the Welsh dialect of northern Pembrokeshire, and a couplet is inscribed on the stone:

A thina meddilie sy'n dŵad ichi
Pan foch chi'n ishte uwchben Pwllderi.

(Trans. And these are the thoughts that come to you / When you sit above Pwllderi).

FLEMINGSTON (W. Trefflemin), Vale of Glamorgan; village on a minor road above the Thaw valley, about 4 m SE of Cowbridge.

The poet and antiquary **Edward Williams (Iolo Morganwg**; 1747-1826) grew up here. He did not attend school but learnt to read by watching his father cutting inscriptions on gravestones, and was taught at home by his mother. At an early age he came under the influence of local poets, who encouraged him to learn the bardic craft and to study Welsh manuscripts. In 1773 he went to London, where he made contact with members of the Gwyneddigion Society, then returned to Wales, settling at Flemingston. The house where he lived, near the church, has gone and a farmhouse now occupies the site. He published two collections of English verse, both entitled *Poems Lyrical and Pastoral* (1794), as well as many poems and hymns in Welsh; he was also a masterly forger of poems which he attributed to such poets as **Dafydd ap Gwilym** (*fl.*1315/20-1350/70). Iolo Morganwg, who called himself 'The Bard of Freedom', is remembered as the man who invented the Gorsedd of Bards of the Isle of Britain, the rituals of which are a prominent part of the ceremonies of the

National Eisteddfod. In the church at Flemingston there is a memorial tablet to him and his son **Taliesin Williams (Taliesin ab Iolo;** 1787-1847).

GILFACH GOCH, Rhondda Cynon Taff; former mining village 2 m W of Tonyrefail off the A4093 and on the B4564.

The novel *How Green Was My Valley* (1939) by **Vivian Lloyd (Richard Llewellyn;** 1906-83) is thought to have been loosely based on the district, which he is known to have visited while writing it. It begins: 'I am going to pack my two shirts with my other socks and my best suit in the little blue cloth my mother used to tie around her hair when she did the house, and I am going from the Valley.' It ends with the words: 'How green was my Valley then, and the Valley of them that have gone.' This is the most famous novel ever written about industrial south Wales but it describes a society that never was, in a powerfully mythical way which has won the affection of generations of readers all over the world; its popularity was greatly enhanced by John Ford's film (1940) starring Roddy McDowall as the boy-narrator Huw Morgan. Recent research has shown that Lloyd's grandfather was not a miner here and that the author did not work in the local pits, as he often claimed; and that he was born in London. There is nothing in the village that can be recognized in the novel, but the book's association with Gilfach Goch is commemorated by a plaque on the wall of the Six Bells public house, now a ruin.

GLAIS, Swansea; village on the B4291 in the lower Swansea Valley.

The poet **Thomas Evan Nicholas** (1878-1971)

was minister of the Congregationalist chapel Seion from 1904 to 1914; although he spent only ten years here he was always associated with the village and was generally known as Niclas y Glais. A Marxist, he was the most eloquent spokesman for the Independent Labour Party in the Welsh language. The collections of poems which he wrote during his ministry at Glais were *Salmau'r Werin* (1909), *Cerddi Gwerin* (1912) and *Cerddi Rhyddid* (1914). A bardic chair won by T.E. Nicholas is kept in Seion.

Niclas y Glais baptized the infant **Thoms John Morgan** (1907-86), who was born in an unnamed house at Ynys-y-mwn near Seion Chapel. T.J. Morgan was Registrar of the University of Wales from 1951 to 1961, when he was appointed Professor of Welsh at the University College, Swansea. As an essayist he was fond of returning to his native district, delighting in its dialect, humour and popular culture. Among his collections are *Trwm ac Ysgafn* (1945), *Amryw Flawd* (1966), *Dydd y Farn* (1969) and *Hirfelyn Tesog* (1969).

GLASINFRYN, see under **BANGOR**

GLYN CEIRIOG, Denbighshire; village about 3 m S of Llangollen, reached by a minor road or by the B4500 from Chirk.

The Institute and Library, opened in 1911, are a memorial to the poet **John Ceiriog Hughes** (1832-87), who was born at Llanarmon Dyffryn Ceiriog. He was the author of the words beginning *'Ar D'wysog Gwlad y Bryniau'* which are sung to the tune 'God Bless the Prince of Wales'; the English words are by G. Linley. There is a memorial inscription to the poet in the Reading Room. Ceiriog is buried at Llanwnnog in Powys.

Also in the hall is a stained-glass window commemorating **William Morgan** (1545-1604), the first translator of the Bible into Welsh.

Next to the Institute there is a memorial to **George Borrow** (1803-81), who passed this way in 1854 and praised the valley in his book *Wild Wales* (1862).

GLYNLLIFON, Gwynedd, mansion on the A499 between Llandwrog and Pontllyfni, 6 m SW of Caernarfon.

In the house's grounds the Writers of Gwynedd scheme was inaugurated in 1990 by *Cywaith Cymru* (formerly the Welsh Sculpture Trust) in association with the County Council. The aim was to commission pieces of sculpture, to be set in the park, celebrating some of the major Welsh writers associated with the county. The writers thus commemorated include **O.M. Edwards** (1858-1920), **Saunders Lewis** (1893-1985) and **John Gwilym Jones** (1904-88). The house was recently bought from the County Council but the grounds can still be visited.

GOLDEN GROVE (W. Y Gelli Aur), Carmarthenshire; mansion about 4 m SW of Llandeilo, just S of the B4300; it is also signposted from the A40, 3 m W of Llandeilo.

The English writer **Jeremy Taylor** (1613-67), who as chaplain to Charles I had been imprisoned here after the Royalist defeat at Cardigan, retired to live in the house from 1645 to 1658. His wife, Joanna Bridges, was the heiress of Mandinam, a fine house perched on the hill above Glansefin, near

Llangadog. Many of Taylor's best works were written here, including *Holy Living* and *Holy Dying* (1650-51) and *The Golden Grove* (1655), a manual of daily prayers. The mansion is now owned by the Carmarthen Technical and Agricultural College, but can be visited by appointment.

GOODWICK, see under **FISHGUARD**

GRESFORD, see under **WREXHAM**

GROESLON, Gwynedd. Small village 4 m S of Caernarfon, just E of the A487.

John Gwilym Jones (1904-88), dramatist, novelist and literary critic, was born, grew up, lived and died in the house in Rathbone Terrace known as Angorfa, which has a commemorative plaque put up in 1990. After teaching in London (1926-30) and Wales (1930-49), he became a producer of radio plays with the BBC in Bangor. He was later a lecturer in Drama at the University College of North Wales. His first play, *Y Brodyr* (1934), was followed by many more, including *Y Tad a'r Mab* (1963) and *Ac Eto Nid Myfi* (1976). He also wrote two novels, *Y Dewis* (1942) and *Tri Diwrnod ac Angladd* (1979), and a volume of short stories, *Y Goeden Eirin* (1946). The writer was buried at Llanddwrog.

GROES-WEN, see under **CAERPHILLY**

GWAELOD-Y-GARTH, Rhondda Cynon Taff; village nestling under the Garth mountain about 2 m N of Cardiff on the A405 between Taff's Well and Nantgarw.

A meeting of the Gorsedd of Bards, at which its

creator **Iolo Morganwg (Edward Williams**; 1747-1826) presided, was held on the Garth mountain in 1797 under the watchful eye of the Glamorgan Yeomanry who suspected that Iolo was preaching the principles of the French Revolution of eight years before.

The playwright and short-story writer **R.G. Berry** (1869-1945) was an Independent minister at Bethlehem Chapel for about fifty years and lived in the adjacent manse. He wrote plays to be performed by amateurs in the chapel vestry, some of which have literary merit. They include *Ar y Groesffordd* (1914), *Noson o Farrug* (1915), *Y Ddraenen Wen* (1922) and *Yr Hen Anian* (1929). Like his short stories, collected under the title *Y Llawr Dyrnu* (1930), his plays have a strong element of satire. At his own request, there is no memorial to him in the village but on his grave in the cemetery of St Mary's Church at Pentyrch, a village a little to the W, he is described as *'Llenor coeth a gwas Crist'* (An accomplished writer and servant of Christ). One of the streets in Gwaelod-y-Garth, Heol Berry, is named in his honour.

The literary historian **Griffith John Williams** (1892-1963), Professor of Welsh at the University College, Cardiff, from 1946 until his retirement in 1957, lived at Bryn Taf in the village.

GWERNOGLE, Carmarthenshire; village on a minor road off the B4310 about 3 m N of Brechfa and in a side-valley of the Cothi valley.

Tomos Glyn Cothi (Thomas Evans; 1764-1833) was born at Capel Sant Silyn. Self-educated, he became a Unitarian in religion and a Radical in politics. He was imprisoned for two years in

Carmarthen on account of his support for the French Revolution of 1789; it seems that he had sung a Welsh version of *'La Marseillaise'* in public. About 1794 he became minister of the Cwm Cothi meeting-house, the first Unitarian chapel to be built in Wales. He was a prolific author and a competent poet in both the strict and free metres. His publication *Y Drysorfa Gymreig*, the first attempt to launch a Welsh periodical, was suppressed after only three numbers in 1795.

HANMER, Wrexham; hamlet off the A539 4 m W of Overton.

Here, at a house called Yr Owredd, was born the poet **Dafydd ab Edmwnd** (*fl.*1450-97). He belonged to a branch of the Hanmers, a gentry family descended from Sir Thomas de Macclesfield, one of Edward I's officials who had settled in NE Wales a century before. It was Dafydd ab Edmwnd who won the miniature silver chair at the eisteddfod held in Carmarthen about the middle of the 14th century and who was responsible for drawing up new rules governing the writing of Welsh poetry. Primarily a love-poet, he wrote many poems in praise of beautiful women, which are still admired for their technical skill and imagery.

HARLECH, Gwynedd; town on the A496 on Tremadoc Bay, dominated by its castle built by order of Edward I *c.*1283.

In **The Mabinogion**, Brân, king of Britain, has a court at Harlech. A sculpture by Ivor Roberts-Jones, entitled *Y Ddau Frenin* (The Two Kings), stands in front of the castle. It depicts Brân (Bendigeidfran) returning from Ireland with the body of Gwern,

Branwen's son.

Ellis Wynne (1670/1-1734), author of the prose-masterpiece *Gweledigaetheu y Bardd Cwsc* (1703; *Visions of the Sleeping Bard*), was born at Y Lasynys, a farmhouse now restored as a memorial to him, 2 m to the N. Wynne was incumbent of Llandanwg, a village on the coast some 2 m S of Harlech. In 1711 he moved to Llanfair-juxta-Harlech, a little further N, where he remained until his death; he is buried under the altar in the church, which has a memorial window.

The poet **Siôn Phylip** (*c*.1543-1620) is buried in the churchyard at Llandanwg; he was drowned while on his way home from one of his bardic itineraries. He earned a living by farming Mochres and supplemented his income as an itinerant poet. His patrons were the Wynn family of Gwydir and the Nannau family. His poems display the new learning of the day and are among the most sophisticated of the period.

The English poet **Robert Graves** (1895-1985) spent many childhood holidays in Harlech, at a house known as Erinfa, which his father, the Irishman Alfred Perceval Graves (1846-1931), owned. He found here, as he put it in his autobiography, *Goodbye to All That* (1929), 'a personal harmony independent of history or geography'.

Coleg Harlech was founded in 1927 at the instigation of **Thomas Jones** (1870-1955). It was born out of his commitment to the cause of adult education and his belief that it would produce a new generation of leaders from the Welsh working-class. Its motto is *A fo ben bid bont* (Let he who would be a leader be a bridge), which comes from the story of Bendigeidfran in **The Mabinogion**.

Among the writers who taught at Coleg Harlech was **T. Rowland Hughes** (1903-49); he lived at Bryn Twrog.

HAVERFORDWEST (W. Hwlffordd), Pembrokeshire; market town on the Western Cleddau, at the junction of the A40 and A4076.

The poet **Waldo Williams** (1904-71) was born at the School House of the Boys' School, which now bears a plaque, but his family moved to Mynachlogddu when he was seven. The move from Haverfordwest to a Welsh-speaking area proved crucial to his development as a poet.

HAY or **HAY-ON-WYE** (W. Y Gelli Gandryll), Powys; market town on the border between Wales and England and on the B4350.

The Hay (as older people still call it) is famous for its secondhand bookshops and for the Literary Festival which has been held there since 1988 but no writer of any note is associated with it, unless it is **Francis Kilvert** (1840-79), the diarist, who was curate of Clyro from 1865 to 1872.

HERGEST, Hereford and Worcester; hamlet off the A44 just on the English side of the border, 1 m. SW of Kington.

The Red Book of Hergest, a manuscript containing Welsh prose and verse, written between 1375 and 1425, was for many years in the possession of the Vaughan family at Hergest Court. It was given to Jesus College, Oxford, in 1701 and is now kept at the Bodleian Library. **Lady Charlotte Guest** (1812-95), who had learned Welsh after her marriage in 1833, translated some of the tales, together with others, and published them under the title *The Mabinogion* (1839-49).

The Hergest estate once belonged to the family of **Sir John Clanvow** (1341-91), to whom is attributed the poem known as 'The Cuckoo and the Nightingale' or 'The Boke of Love', once thought to be the work of Chaucer.

The Welsh writer **Ffransis G. Payne** (1900-92), author of *Crwydro Sir Faesyfed* (2 vols., 1966, 1968), a book about Radnorshire, was born at Kington. He also published a collection of fine essays, *Cwysau* (1980).

HOLYWELL (W. Treffynnon), Flintshire; town on the A55, 10 m E of St Asaph.

It was named after the holy well of St Winefride, a place of pilgrimage from the 7th century to the present day. According to legend, Prince Caradoc attempted to seduce Winefride and struck off her head when she tried to escape. She was miraculously restored to life by St Beuno, her uncle, and a spring of water gushed from where she had fallen.

In the 15th century a chapel was built over the well. Among visitors were Celia Fiennes, Daniel Defoe and Samuel Johnson; a poem by **Gerard Manley Hopkins** (1844-89) extols the medicinal power of the waters.

The English writer **Francis Thompson** (1859-1907), author of 'The Hound of Heaven', lived at Aloysius Cottage, Pantasaph, from 1893 to 1897 and wrote most of his *New Poems* (1897) here.

Frederick Rolfe (Baron Corvo; 1860-1913) lived in Holywell from 1895 to 1898; five of the banners he painted for the shrine may be seen at the

Presbytery on request. Rolfe's stormy years at Holywell are described in A.J. Symon's book, *The Quest for Corvo* (1934).

KNUCKLAS (W. Cnwclas), Powys; village on the B4355 about 3 m from Knighton.

The Puritan preacher and author **Vavasor Powell** (1617-70) was born near here in the parish of Heyop. He became an itinerant preacher, fought in the English Civil War and flung himself with enthusiasm into evangelical work after the passing of the Act for the Propagation of the Gospel in Wales in 1650. He was a staunch opponent of Cromwell against whose rule he wrote a manifesto, *A Word for God* (1655). After the restoration he suffered arrests and imprisonment, dying in the Fleet prison in London. His autobiography was published as *The Life and Death of Mr Vavasor Powell* in 1670.

LAMPETER (W. Llanbedr Pont Steffan), Cardiganshire; university and market town at the junction of the A482, A475 and A485, about 20 m NE of Carmarthen.

St David's University College, now a University in its own right, is the oldest in Wales. It opened in 1827 for the training of young men for the Anglican ministry but now teaches a wide variety of subjects.

The humourist **Idwal Jones** (1895-1937) was born at Rhoslwyn in Station Road, off College Road; the house, marked by a plaque, is now a hostel for students. It was his contention that Wales, 'our little country, does not take its humour seriously enough,' and he wrote verse, plays, and songs in Welsh which made many people laugh. They are to be found in the volumes *Cerddi Digri a Rhai Pethau Eraill* (1934), *Cerddi Digri Newydd a Phethau o'r Fath (1937)*, and *Ystorïau a Pharodïau (1944)*; his *Pobl yr Ymylon* (1927) is an argument against respectability. One of his plays, *My Piffle*, is a parody of *My People* (1915), a volume of short stories by **Caradoc Evans** (1878-1945). Jones is buried in the graveyard of Soar Chapel, which faces the common.

The offices of the weekly magazine *Golwg* are in Bridge Street and there is a Welsh bookshop, *Siop y Smotyn Du*, in the High Street.

LAUGHARNE (W. Lacharn or Talacharn), Carmarthenshire; small town on a minor road on the Taf estuary, reached on the B4312 from Carmarthen.

The writer **Richard Hughes** (1900-76) lived in a Georgian house in the grounds of the ruined castle from 1934 to the end of 1946. Here he completed his novel *In Hazard* (1938).

It was at Hughes's invitation that **Dylan Thomas** (1914-53) and his wife Caitlin, in 1938, came to live

The Boathouse, Laugharne

in a two-roomed cottage at 2 Gosport Street and then at Sea View, near the Town Hall and castle. They left in October of the same year but returned in 1949 to live at The Boathouse, a three-storey, whitewashed, slate-roofed cottage below the cliff, where the poet worked in a shed, formerly a garage, at the top of the garden. Both shed and house, which was opened as a museum in 1975, can be seen from the end of Cliff Road, renamed Dylan's Walk. Much of the writer's best work was done in Laugharne, including the greater part of his play for voices, *Under Milk Wood* (1954). The town of 'Llareggub' (a famous palindrome) is usually said to be Laugharne, where the play has been performed regularly since 1958. Its opening words are: 'To begin at the beginning. It is spring, moonless night in the small town, starless and bible-black, the cobblestreets silent and the hunched, courters'-and-rabbits' wood limping invisible down to the sloeblack, slow, black, crowblack, fishingboat-bobbing sea.' It also includes the oft-quoted verse, spoken by the Reverend Eli Jenkins:

> We are not wholly bad or good
> Who live our lives under Milk Wood,
> And Thou, I know, wilt be the first
> To see our best side, not our worst.

After the writer's death on a reading tour of the USA in November 1953, his body was brought home for burial in the annexe to the graveyard of St Martin's Church, where his grave is marked by a simple white wooden cross on which are painted his name and the date of his death, 9 November 1953. His parents were living at the time of his death at The Pelican, a house in King Street, and the poet's body rested there before his funeral. Among

Dylan Thomas' grave, Laugharne

the other buildings associated with Dylan Thomas is Brown's, also in King Street, which was one of his favourite drinking places; the pub has a 'Dylan Thomas Corner'. In *Quite Early One Morning* (1954) Laugharne is described as 'this timeless, beautiful, barmy (both spellings) town . . . a legendary lazy little black-magical bedlam by the sea'. Sir John's Hill stands less than 2 m to the S of Laugharne and is visible from the Boat House.

LLANARMON, Gwynedd; small village off the B4354 between Y Ffor and Llanystumdwy.

Here, at Plas Du, was born **John Owen** (1564?-1628?), known as 'the British Martial' on account of the biting wit of his epigrams. Educated at New

College, Oxford, he was a schoolmaster in Trelleck in Monmouthshire until 1595 and then became headmaster of Warwick School, after which nothing else is known about him. He wrote eleven collections of Latin epigrams, published between 1606 and 1613, some of which are anti-Catholic. Although placed on the *Index Expurgatorius*, they were very popular in his day and were translated into French, German and Spanish.

LLANARMON DYFFRYN CEIRIOG, Denbighshire; village in the Berwyn Mountains, about 6m SW of Llangollen, at the end of the B4500.

John Ceiriog Hughes (1832-87), the lyric poet who is commemorated at Glyn Ceiriog, was born at Penybryn, a long low farmhouse high above the bridge; the house has a plaque in his memory. His gift was that he could write singable words to old Welsh and English airs, and he produced some of the finest lyrics in the Welsh language on such subjects as nature, love and patriotism; they include *'Nant y Mynydd'*, *'Dafydd y Garreg Wen'* and *'Alun Mabon'*, the last of which includes the verse (trans.):

To the customs of old Wales
    Changes come from year to year;
Every generation fails,
    One has gone, the next is here.
After a lifetime tempest-tossed
    Alun Mabon is no more,
Yet the language is not lost
    And the old songs still endure.

Another of Ceiriog's poems, *'Ar Hyd y Nos'*, is known in English as 'All through the Night':

Every star in heaven is singing,
    All through the night;
Hear the glorious music ringing

> All through the night;
> Songs of sweet ethereal lightness
> Wrought in realms of peace and whiteness,
> See, the dark gives way to brightness,
> All through the night.

It is said that the English writer **Nicholas Monsarrat** (1910-79) wrote most of his novel *The Cruel Sea* (1951) in the West Arms, a pub in the village.

LLANARTH, Cardiganshire; village on the A487 about 5 m SW of Aberaeron.

The lexicographer **Daniel Silvan Evans** (1818-1903) was born at Bron Wilym Uchaf. Professor of Welsh at the University College of Wales, Aberystwyth, he had an ambition to compile a dictionary of Welsh comparable to the *Oxford English Dictionary* but published only four parts between 1887 and 1896; a fifth appeared posthumously in 1906. He also edited a number of scholarly editions of Welsh poetry and prose, and four volumes of his own verse. He was buried in Cemmaes churchyard near Llanwrin in Montgomeryshire.

LLANBADARN FAWR, see under **ABERYSTWYTH**

LLANBADRIG, Anglesey; village on a minor road on the N coast of the island, off the A5025 about 5 m from Amlwch.

The writer and historian **Gweirydd ap Rhys (Robert John Pryse;** 1807-89) was born at a farm known as Clegyrnog Uchaf. Orphaned at the age of 11, he had very little schooling but learned to read and write while working as a farm labourer. From 1828 to 1857 he kept a shop at Llanrhuddlad, a village on the A5025, while working as a weaver.

He made a substantial contribution to *Y Gwyddoniadur Cymreig*, an encyclopaedia published in ten volumes between 1854 and 1879, and won prizes for his history of Welsh literature, *Hanes Llenyddiaeth Gymreig, 1300-1650* (1885). He struggled against great poverty but was acknowledged in his day as an authority on the Welsh language and its literature. He died in Bethesda and was buried at Holyhead.

LLANBERIS, Gwynedd; town on the A4086 at the N end of Llanberis Pass.

Near the lake known as Llyn Padarn, at a house called Penllyn (gone), lived Margaret uch Ifan (1695-1801?), a woman of Amazonian reputation and build. In his *Tours of Wales* (1778-81) **Thomas Pennant** (1726-98) records how he called at her home and was disappointed not to find her in. She was, it seems, the greatest hunter, shooter and fisher of her time, a champion wrestler, a blacksmith, a boat-builder, a maker of harps and an excellent fiddler. 'At length,' Pennant wrote, 'she gave her hand to the most effeminate of her admirers, as if predetermined to maintain the superiority which nature had bestowed on her.'

The novelist **T. Rowland Hughes** (1903-49) was born at 20 Goodman Street and spent his first nine years there before moving to Angorfa, next to the Baptist chapel in Well Street; the house has a plaque and is now a small museum. A producer of feature programmes for the BBC in Cardiff, he turned to writing novels when his health began to fail; he suffered from multiple sclerosis. The novels were *O Law i Law* (1943, trans. *From Hand to Hand*, 1950), *William Jones* (1944, trans. *William Jones*, 1953), *Yr Ogof* (1945, trans. *The Story of Joseph of Arimathea*

1961), *Chwalfa* (1946, trans. *Out of their Night*, 1954), and *Y Cychwyn* (1947, trans. *The Beginning*, 1969); all five were translated by **Richard Ruck** (1887-1973). His only volume of verse was *Cân neu Ddwy* (1948). Much of his prose is set in the slate-quarrying district around Llanberis and *Chwalfa*, perhaps his best novel, is a tale told against the background of the Penrhyn Lockouts of 1896-1903.

LLANBRYN-MAIR, Powys; village 5 m from Cemmaes Road on the A470.

Samuel Roberts (1800-85) was born in the chapel house of Yr Hen Gapel and was brought up at a nearby farm known as Diosg. He had great influence among the Nonconformists of Wales as a journalist and editor, denouncing slavery, English imperialism, the war in the Crimea, landlordism and capital punishment, and advocating universal suffrage, including votes for women, and supporting the building of railways. In order to escape the hostility of the Wynnstay estate, to which his farm belonged, he emigrated to the USA in 1857, where he hoped to found a Welsh settlement in Tennessee. But the project failed and he was caught up in the American Civil War, in which his pacifism caused him to be vilified by both sides. Attacked even in the Welsh press, he returned to Wales for good in 1867.

The poet **Mynyddog (Richard Davies**; 1833-77) was born at Dôl Lydan. He was famous as a conductor and soloist; his simple verses were sung to popular English melodies.

The poet **Iorwerth Cyfeiliog Peate** (1901-82), who became the first Curator of the Welsh Folk Museum at St Fagans, near Cardiff, was born at

Glanllyn, Pandy Rhiwsaeson, 2 m N of the village; the house has a plaque put up by the Montgomeryshire Society. The district is lovingly evoked in many of his poems, which were published in the volumes *Y Cawg Aur* (1928), *Plu'r Gweunydd* (1933), and *Y Deyrnas Goll* (1947); a volume of his selected poems, *Canu Chwarter Ganrif*, appeared in 1957 and his autobiography, *Rhwng Dau Fyd*, in 1976. Peate was so insistent in his praise for the Radicalism and Nonconformity of the district that some writers have since referred to 'the Llanbryn-mair tradition'.

LLANCARFAN, Vale of Glamorgan; village on a minor road off the B4266 between Bonvilston and Penmarc and about 5 m NW of Barry.

The poet and antiquary **Edward Williams (Iolo Morganwg**; 1747-1826) was born at a farmhouse known as Pen-onn, the son of a stonemason. The house is no longer there but it is thought that a modern bungalow, Bryn Iolo, was built on the site. At an early age Iolo moved with his parents to the neighbouring village of Flemingston.

LLANDAF, see under **CARDIFF**

LLANDANWG, see under **HARLECH**

LLANDDERFEL, Gwynedd; village on the B4402 about 5 m E of Bala.

Edward Jones (1752-1824), harpist and antiquary, was born at Henblas. He was known as *Bardd y Brenin* (The King's Poet) because he went to London in 1775 and was appointed harpist to the Prince of Wales, later George IV. He was present at the first congress of bards held by **Iolo Morganwg (Edward Williams**; 1747-1826) on Primrose Hill in 1792. His major literary work was *The Musical and Poetical Relicks of the Welsh Bards* (1784); this book, together with *The Bardic Museum* (1802) and *Hen Ganiadau Cymru* (1820), contain a good deal of valuable information about early Welsh poetry and served the purpose of awakening the interest of antiquaries and writers in England.

The Radical writer **Robert Jones Derfel** (1824-1905) was a native of Llandderfel, from which he adopted his surname; he was born at a house known as Foty. For most of his life he was a commercial traveller in the Manchester area, but took a keen interest in Welsh affairs. His play *Brad y Llyfrau Gleision* (1854), about the Blue Books of 1847, did much to form public opinion against the calumny of the Welsh contained in the Report. He was above all concerned to integrate Christianity, Socialism and Nationalism in a Welsh context, and is considered to be one of 'the fathers of Welsh nationalism'.

The poet **Dewi Havhesp (David Roberts**; 1831-84), a native of Llanfor, near Bala, spent most of his life in Llandderfel, where he was a tailor, and is buried here. His only collection of verse was the very popular *Oriau'r Awen* (1876).

The poet **Ifan Rowlands** (1879-1977) was born at the smallholding known as Y Gistfaen.

LLANDDEUSANT, Anglesey; small village on a minor road about 4 m NE of Llanfachraeth and 1m from the Alaw reservoir.

The district is rich in associations with **The Mabinogion**. The story is told of how, after the slaughter in Ireland, Bendigeidfran and his sister Branwen returned, with only seven survivors, to the Island of the Mighty (Britain). The princess heaved a great sigh, lamenting that she had been the cause of so much suffering, and died on the banks of the Alaw and was buried in 'a four-sided grave'. It is not easy to find the spot reputed to be the grave, which is located on the land of Glan Alaw in the hamlet of Elim, but a rough track leads for about 1 m towards the farm; on the right, before reaching the farmhouse, a gate opens into a field where there is a large boulder, all that remains of the tomb. In 1813 the cairn was broken up by local farmers who found an urn containing human remains dating from *c.*1500 BC.

LLANDDEUSANT, Carmarthenshire; village on a minor road about 6 m S of Llandovery off the A4069.

The novelist **Richard Vaughan** (1904-83), whose real name was **Ernest Lewis Thomas,** was born at Blaenllechach, a farm in the upper reaches of the Llechach valley. His novels *Moulded in Earth* (1952), *Who Rideth So Wild* (1952), and *Son of Justin* (1955) are set in the district of the Black Mountain.

LLANDDEWIBREFI, Cardiganshire; village on the B4343 between Tregaron and Lampeter.

The place is associated with St David, known in Welsh as Dewi Sant, the patron saint of Wales. Many miracles were attributed to him, but perhaps the best-known is said to have taken place here: while preaching at the Synod of Llanddewibrefi, some time in the 6th century, the ground rose under him so that all could see and hear him. There is a memorial to St David in the church.

The manuscript known as *Llyfr Ancr Llanddewibrefi* (The Book of the Anchorite), transcribed in 1346 and now kept in the Bodleian Library, Oxford, is the earliest and most comprehensive collection of medieval religious texts.

In the Presbyterian chapel in the village there is a memorial to Mary Roberts of Foelallt in the parish, who emigrated to America in 1775; among her descendants was **Harriet Beecher Stowe** (1811-96), the author of *Uncle Tom's Cabin* (1852).

LLANDDOWROR, Carmarthenshire; village on the A477 about 3 m SW of St Clears.

Griffith Jones (1683-1761), a native of Penboyr, was given the living in 1716 and lived here for 45 years. He is remembered as the founder of the Circulating Schools which taught children and adults to read the Welsh Bible and to learn the Catechism of the Anglican Church. These schools were an important medium for the spread of literacy in the Welsh language.

LLANDDULAS, Conwy; village on the A547 and off the A55, about 4 m E of Colwyn Bay.

The English novelist **Evelyn Waugh** (1903-66) taught at Arnold House School, thinly disguised as 'Llanabba School' in his first novel *Decline and Fall* (1928). Waugh's dislike of the Welsh is put into the mouth of the ghastly Dr Fagin: 'From the earliest times the Welsh have been looked upon as an unclean people. It is thus they have preserved their racial integrity.' The building survives as Llanddulas Hall and Country Club.

LLANDDWYWE, see under **DYFFRYN ARDUDWY**

LLANDEGLA-YN-IÂL, Denbighshire; village about 10 m W of Wrexham at the junction of the A5104 and the A525.

The prose-writer **Edward Tegla Davies** (1880-1967) was born at Yr Hen Giât, in Pen Stryt, a house which now has a plaque. Tegla was a minister with the Wesleyans and a well-known broadcaster. Some of his books, such as *Hunangofiant Tomi* (1912) and *Nedw* (1922), are humorous tales about mischievous boys. His most important novel, *Gŵr Pen y Bryn* (1923, trans. Nina Watkins, *The Master of Pen y Bryn,* 1975), is about the spiritual conversion of a prosperous farmer during the Tithe Wars of the 1880s and is set in the district. His short stories were collected in the volume *Y Llwybr Arian* (1934) and selections of his essays and newspaper articles were published in *Rhyfedd o Fyd* (1950), *Y Foel Faen* (1951) and *Ar Ddisberod* (1954). He was a master of Welsh prose and although given to sentimental philosophizing, at his best could be an accomplished and entertaining writer.

LLANDEILO, Carmarthenshire; market town on the junction of the A483, B430 and A40.

The ruined monastery of Talley (W. Talyllychau), a Premonstratensian house, about 8 m N of the town in the valley of the Dulais, rivals Strata Florida in its claim to being the burial-place of the poet **Dafydd ap Gwilym** (*fl.*1315/20-1350/70). Some scholars believe that the claim of Strata Florida is based on a misunderstanding of a poem by **Gruffudd Grug** (*fl.*1357-70) which seems to suggest that the poet was buried there. They prefer to think that this poem belongs to a tradition of mock-elegy and that Gruffudd Gryg merely speculated as to the likely place of Dafydd ap Gwilym's burial-place, well before he died. The traditional belief that he was buried at Talley dates from about 1600 and was later accepted by **Iolo Morganwg (Edward Williams**; 1747-1826), but this view was discredited when many of Iolo's poems were shown to be forgeries and his claims groundless. A memorial stone to Dafydd ap Gwilym was erected in the churchyard in 1984.

The hymn-writer **Thomas Lewis** (1759-1842), a native of Llanwnda, lived for many years in Talley. His most famous hymn is *'Wrth gofio'i riddfannau'n yr ardd'*, which is still sung by Welsh congregations. He is the blacksmith mentioned in the famous poem by **D. Gwenallt Jones** (1899-1968), *'Sir Forgannwg a Sir Gaerfyrddin'*, which includes the famous lines (trans.):

The span of the Cross is greater by far
Than their Puritanism and their Socialism,
And the fist of Karl Marx has a place in his Church:
Farm and furnace are one together in his estate,
The humanity of the pit, the piety of the country:
Tawe and Tywi, Canaan and Wales, earth and
heaven.

The English novelist **Anne Beale** (1816-1900) lived for fifty years at Llwynhelig, about 1 m outside Llandeilo on the road to Carmarthen, where she was governess to the children of the perpetual curate of Llanddyfeisant. Among her novels set in Wales are *The Pennant Family* (1876), *Rose Mervyn of Whitelake* (1879) and *Old Gwen* (1890). But her most important book is *The Vale of the Towy* (1844), one of the earliest novels about Wales published in English.

The poet and novelist **W. Leslie Richards** (1916-

89) was born at Y Cwm in Capel Isaac, a hamlet on a minor road to the NW of the town, and was brought up in Llandeilo, where he was deputy headmaster of the Comprehensive School from 1975 until his retirement in 1981. The school, now known as Ysgol Tregib, has moved to Ffair Fach. The writer lived for some years at Brynawel in Rhosmaen, now a part of the town, and later at 12 Heol Thomas. He published several novels, including *Yr Etifeddion* (1956) and *Cynffon o Wellt* (1960), and five volumes of verse: *Telyn Teilo* (1957), *Bro a Bryniau* (1963), *Dail yr Hydref* (1968), *Adlodd* (1973) and *Cerddi'r Cyfnos* (1986).

There is a bookshop, *Llecyn Llyfre*, at 123 Rhosmaen Street.

LLANDOVERY (W. Llanymddyfri), Carmarthenshire; market town on the junction of the A40 and A483, 13 m NE of Llandeilo in the Vale of the Towy.

It is believed that **Rhys Prichard** (1579-1644), known as *'Yr Hen Ficer'* (The Old Vicar), was born at Old Neuadd, now 33 High Street. He built Neuadd Newydd (gone) on a site near the Blue Bell inn, later occupied by part of the Assembly Rooms. Having obtained the living of Llandovery in 1602, he lived in the town until 1614, when he became chaplain to the Earl of Essex. He wrote a large number of verses about the Christian life which were published under the title *Cannwyll y Cymry* (The Candle of the Welsh) in 1681. This book took its place in the affection of the common people with the Welsh version of Bunyan's *Pilgrim Progress*. There is a monument to the Old Vicar behind the altar in the church at Llandingat. The primary school in Llandovery is named after him and there is a memorial hall in the town.

The prolific hymn-writer **William Williams** (1717-91), generally known as **Pantycelyn**, was born at Cefn Coed, a farmhouse a little to the N of Pentre-tŷ-gwyn, a hamlet 3 m E of Llandovery. One of the leaders of the Methodist movement in Wales, and its major poet, he wrote about 90 works between 1744 and 1791. After his marriage *c.*1748, he came to live at his mother's old home, Pantycelyn, a farmhouse a little to the E of Pentre-tŷ-gwyn, now one of the most famous literary shrines in Wales. The English hymn for which Williams Pantycelyn is most famous is the one usually sung – more often at rugby matches than in chapel these days – to the tune 'Cwm Rhondda':

> Guide me, O Thou great Jehovah,
>> Pilgrim through this barren land;
> I am weak, but Thou art mighty,
>> Hold me with thy powerful hand.
> Bread of Heaven, bread of Heaven,
> Feed me till I want no more!

The William Williams Memorial Chapel (where the services are in English) stands in the High Street of Llandovery and the local Comprehensive School is named after him. Visitors to the Heritage Centre will find further information about the writer.

Llandovery became a centre for the printing of Welsh books and periodicals after **William Rees** (1808-73) set up a press in the town in 1829. Rees, a native of Tonn, printed the journals *Y Cylchgrawn* and *Yr Haul*, the publications of the Welsh Manuscripts Society and the three volumes of the famous translation by **Lady Charlotte Guest** (1812-95) of **The Mabinogion**. The Tonn manuscripts are now housed in Cardiff City Library but the press is featured in the exhibition in the Heritage Centre.

LLANDRE, Cardiganshire; village on the B4353 about 8 m N of Aberystwyth.

The writer **T. Ifor Rees** (1890-1977) was born at nearby Bow Street and lived for many years at Bron Ceiro, on the left of the road as it leaves Llandre. He spent most of his life in the Civil Service, retiring as British Ambassador to Bolivia in 1949. He translated novels from French and Spanish into Welsh and wrote two travel-books, *Sajama* (1960) and *Illimani* (1964).

LLANDUDNO, Conwy; seaside resort on the A496 and A546.

The English critic **Matthew Arnold** (1822-88), while on holiday here with his family in 1864, was inspired to write his essays *On the Study of Celtic Literature*, first published in book form in 1867. He stayed at 10 St George's Crescent and visited the Eisteddfod which was being held in the town.

In the same year **Lewis Carroll (C.L. Dodgson**; 1832-98) was visiting Dean Liddell of Christ Church, Oxford, at his summer residence, Pen Morfa, on the West Shore, now part of the Gogarth Abbey Hotel. It is believed that part of *Alice in Wonderland* (1865) was written at Pen Morfa. Carroll is commemorated by a statue of the White Rabbit at the end of the Model Yacht Pond and by a marble font in the Church of our Saviour.

The novel *The Card* (1911) by the English writer **Arnold Bennett** (1867-1931) is set in Llandudno in its Victorian heyday.

LLANDWROG, Gwynedd; small village off the A499 about 6 m SW of Caernarfon.

Ellis Roberts (Elis Wyn o Wyrfai; 1827-95), poet and editor, was born at Llwyn Gwalch. In Anglican

Statue of the White Rabbit commemorating
Lewis Carroll at Llandudno

orders, he witnessed some of the most vicious incidents in the Tithe Wars of the late 1880s in the district of Llangwm, Denbighshire, and as editor of the Church periodical *Yr Haul* from 1885 to1895, he condemned violence and called for moderation. He wrote hymns and poems in Welsh and two long poems in English, namely *The Wreck of the London* (1865) and *The Massacre of the Monks of Bangor Iscoed* (1876).

The writer **Glasynys (Owen Wynne Jones**; 1828-70), a native of Rhostryfan, Caernarfonshire, is buried in the churchyard at Llandwrog. He excelled in the depiction of Welsh rural life and in writing ghost-stories and fairy-tales. A selection of his poems appeared posthumously in 1898 and some of his stories were published under the title *Straeon Glasynys* (1943).

The playwright **John Gwilym Jones** (1904-88) is buried at Llandwrog; his tombstone bears the inscription *'Dyn drama, gŵr geiriau'* (A man of the theatre, a man of words.)

LLANDYSILIO, Pembrokeshire; village on the A478 about 3 m S of Efail-wen.

The carved stone near the village records that here the first gate was smashed in 1838, an event signalling the start of the Rebecca Riots.

The father of **Waldo Williams** (1904-71) was the village schoolmaster and the family lived at Elm Cottage, to which the poet returned after losing his parents; he was married at Blaenconyn chapel between Llandysilio and Clunderwen and was buried in the graveyard there.

LLANDYSUL, Cardiganshire; market town on the A486 about 16 m N of Carmarthen.

There is a memorial plaque to **Gwilym Marles (William Thomas**; 1834-79) at Myfyrgell in Heol Llyn-y-Frân near Seion Chapel. Unitarian minister, poet and Radical writer, he kept a school in the town for the last twenty years of his life. It was in honour of Gwilym Marles, his father's uncle, that **Dylan Thomas** (1914-53) was given his second name, Marlais. Some have seen in the effusions of the Reverend Eli Jenkins in *Under Milk Wood* (1954) a pastiche of the verse of Gwilym Marles.

The presses of Gwasg Gomer, one of the major publishers of books in Wales, are in the main street.

LLANEDI, Carmarthenshire; small village near the river Loughor and off the B4297 about 2m N of Pontarddulais.

The hymn-writer **Dafydd William** (1720/21-94) was born in the parish but lived for many years in the parish of Llandeilo-fach (also known as Llandeilo Tal-y-bont), now Pontarddulais. He was the author of more than a hundred hymns, most of which were imbued with a warm Evangelical fervour. The most popular are *'Yn y dyfroedd mawr a'r tonnau'*, *'Anghrediniaeth, gad fi'n llonydd'* and *'O Arglwydd, dyro awel'*. He began as an exhorter with the Calvinistic Methodists but in the 1770s he was baptized in the river Ely at Peterston-super-Ely in the Vale of Glamorgan as a prerequisite to joining the Baptists.

LLANNERCH-Y-MEDD, Anglesey; village on the junction of the B5111 and B5112 about 7 m S of Amlwch.

The poet **Richard Parry (Gwalchmai**; 1803-97) and the balladeer **Dic Dywyll (Richard Williams**; *c.*1805-*c.*1865) were born in the district. The latter was blind and used to put his finger to his eye while singing. He sang mainly in south Wales, where he witnessed the Merthyr Rising of 1831 and the Rebecca Riots of 1839-43. About 70 of his ballads are preserved in the National Library of Wales.

LLANFACHRETH, Gwynedd; village on a minor road between the A470 and A494 about 6m NE of Dolgellau.

The poet and antiquary **Rhys Jones** (1713-1801) lived at Y Blaenau near Rhydymain but later moved to Tyddyn Mawr. He is remembered mainly on account of his anthology *Gorchestion Beirdd Cymru* (1773); one of the most important collections of Welsh poetry ever made, it remained a standard anthology for more than a century. The book has a preface which is full of optimism about the future of the Welsh language for which, the compiler declared, 'Helicon is inexhaustible'. He is buried in the churchyard at Llanfachreth.

LLANFAETHLU, Anglesey; village on the A5025 about 5 m N of Llanfachraeth.

The scholar **Siôn Dafydd Rhys** (1534-*c*.1619) was born in this parish. After travelling in Europe, he returned to Wales in 1574 and was appointed headmaster of Friars School in Bangor. His most important work was the impressively entitled *Cambrobrytannicae Cymraecaeve Linguae Institutiones et Rudimenta* (1592), a grammar of the Welsh language together with material relating to Welsh prosody. As one of the leading humanists of his day he strove to present to the world, in Latin, the language of scholarship, some idea of the wealth of the Welsh language and its literature. There is a commemorative plaque on the wall of the Coffee House in Llanfaethlu.

LLANFAIR ARDUDWY, Gwynedd; village on the A496 about 1 m S of Harlech.

The writer **Ellis Wynne** (1671-1734), author of *Gweledigaetheu y Bardd Cwsg* (1703; *Visions of the Sleeping Bard*), is buried under the altar of the Church of St Mary the Virgin. Here in 1702 he married Lowri Llwyd of Hafodlwyfog, near Beddgelert; he was rector of the parish from 1711 until his death.

The S window of the church has a window in his memory and the E window is dedicated to **Edmwnd Prys** (1543/44-1623), the poet and humanist scholar.

LLANFAIR MATHAFARN EITHAF, see under BENLLECH

LLANFAIR PWLLGWYNGYLL, Anglesey; village on the A5, about 3 m W of Menai Bridge.

The full name of the village is a spoof meant to entertain visitors: Llanfairpwllgwyngyllgogerychwyrndrobwyllllantysiliogogogoch (trans. The church of St Mary in a hollow of white hazel near the rapid whirlpool and the church of St Tysilio near a red cave). The name, said to be the longest place-name in the countries of Britain, is thought to have been concocted by a tailor from Menai Bridge in the mid-19th century.

The scholar and poet **John Morris-Jones** (1864-1929), who was born at Trefor in Llandrygarn, came to live here as a child in 1868 when his parents opened a shop in the village; he attended the elementary school. After his marriage in 1897 he lived the rest of his life at Tŷ Coch, where there is a commemorative plaque; he is buried in the village cemetery, where his tombstone is topped by a Celtic cross. The first Professor of Welsh at the University College of North Wales, he was an authority on the orthography of the language and made a major contribution to the study of Welsh poetry with his book *Cerdd Dafod* (1925), in which the system of

Grave of John Morris-Jones, Llanfair Pwllgwyngyll

cynghanedd (traditional prosody) was definitively described. He published only one volume of his own verse, *Caniadau* (1907), which includes translations of Heine and Omar Khayyám and a poem, *'Cymru Fydd'*, which includes the verse (trans.):

> And yet I sing my country,
>   for Wales shall one day be
> the happiest and loveliest land
>   a time when we shall see
> no violent hand to waste her,
>   no coward to betray her,
> no quarrelling to weaken her,
>   and when Wales shall be free.

LLANFAIR TALHAIARN, Denbighshire; village at the junction of the A548 and A544, about 5 m S of Abergele.

The poet **John Jones (Talhaiarn**;1810-69) was born at the Harp Inn (later named Hafod-y-gân), which is near the church. He won fame as a writer of songs, many of which became very popular in his day and are still sung. Apprenticed in his youth to an architect, in 1851 he went to work as superintendent of the building of the Crystal Palace in London. Returning to Wales in 1865, he committed suicide in the tavern where he had been born. He is buried in the churchyard where, on his grave, there is a profile of him similar to the one above the door of Hafod-y-gân.

LLANFECHAIN, Powys; small village on the B4393 about 8 m SW of Oswestry off the A495.

The poet and editor **Walter Davies (Gwallter Mechain**; 1761-1849) was born at Y Wern, near Tomen y Castell in the parish. One of 'the old literary clerics', although with little formal education, he devoted his energies to editing Welsh manuscripts and writing parish histories.

Here the novelist **James Hanley** (1901-85) lived between 1940 and 1964; he had previously lived at Tŷ-nant in Meirionnydd. During his time in Wales, some 34 years in all, he wrote four novels with Welsh settings: *Don Quixote Drowned* (1953), *The Welsh Sonata* (1954), *Another World* (1971) and *A Kingdom* (1978). Although he spent his last years at his son's home in London, he chose to be buried in the churchyard at Llanfechain.

LLANFECHELL, Anglesey; village on a minor road off the A5025 about 2 m SW of Cemaes.

William Bulkeley (1691-1760), the squire of Brynddu in the parish, left a number of diaries which provide fascinating information about Anglesey life in his day. They were used by **Barbara Dew Roberts** (1885?-1963) as material for her book *Mr. Bulkeley and the Pirate* (1936). The squire is commemorated by a plaque on the village square.

LLANFERRES, Denbighshire; village on the A494 about 6 m SW of Mold.

Dr John Davies (*c.*1567-1644), one of the greatest Welsh scholars of the later Renaissance period, was born in this parish, although he is usually associated with Mallwyd, where he was appointed to the living in 1604. It is believed that he did most of the work of revising the Welsh Bible for the new version which appeared in 1620 and he may have revised the Welsh Prayer Book which was republished in 1621. His magisterial work, a Welsh grammar in Latin, *Antiquae Linguae Britannicae,* appeared in 1632. He was a zealous collector and copyist of manuscripts and his work in establishing bardic vocabulary formed the basis for a scientific study of the Welsh language by later scholars. A stone set in the E wall of the church is inscribed IDSTD 1650; this is meant to read *Iohannes Davies Sacrae Theologiae Doctor 1650,* probably in recognition of his legacy of ten pounds for the upkeep of the original building, which has been replaced by one of more recent date.

LLANFIHANGEL ABERCYWYN, Carmarthenshire; village on the A40 about 3 m from St Clears.

Thomas Charles (1755-1814), leader of the second generation of Welsh Methodists, is believed to have been born at Longmoor, near the village. He was a prolific writer but his *magnum opus* is his *Geiriadur Ysgrythyrawl*, published in four volumes between 1805 and 1811. As an editor, his principal achievement was to standardize the text of the first Welsh Bible to be published by the British and Foreign Bible Society which he did much to establish. After marrying a Bala woman in 1783, he left the Anglican Church and settled in that town, devoting himself to the work of the Methodists.

His brother, the hymn-writer **David Charles** (1762-1834), was born at Pant-dwfn in the same parish. Ordained a minister with the Calvinistic Methodists in 1811, he wrote 24 hymns which are among the finest in the Welsh language, notably *'O fryniau Caersalem ceir gweled'*, *'Rhagluniaeth fawr y nef'* and *'O! Iesu mawr, rho'th anian bur'*, which are still sung by Welsh congregations.

LLANFIHANGEL AR ARTH, Cardiganshire; village on the B4459, about 2 m E of Llandysul on the junction of the B4459 and B4336.

Caradoc Evans (1878-1945), novelist and short-story writer, sometimes said to be 'the father of modern Anglo-Welsh literature', was born at a smallholding known as Pantycroi. The district and that of Rhydlewis, about 8 m to the NW, where he grew up and attended the board school, were satirized in his writings, which offended many people in Wales. His first collection of stories, *My People* (1915), brought him immediate and lasting notoriety. It presents a merciless portrait of a brutish peasantry, a corrupt religion and a grudging soil, in which greed, lust and hypocrisy are amply featured. Hawen Chapel in Rhydlewis is the setting of the stories in his second collection, *Capel Sion* (1915). He also wrote four novels, of which the most powerful is *Nothing to Pay* (1930). Lanlas Uchaf, the family's smallholding, stands on an eastward rise above the village.

LLANFIHANGEL BRYN PABUAN, see **BUILTH**

LLANFIHANGEL TRE'R BEIRDD, Anglesey; hamlet on a minor road 2 m E of Llannerch-y-medd.

Here the four **Morris Brothers**, antiquaries and writers, were born in the first decade of the 18th century. The most gifted was the eldest, **Lewis Morris** (1701-65), who was born at the farm known as Tyddyn Melys, which has a plaque. Behind Pentre-eiriannell, another farm near by, there is a monument to the brothers, erected by the Honourable Society of Cymmrodorion, which was founded by **Richard Morris** (1703-79), in 1751. The third brother was **William Morris** (1705-63) and the youngest was **John Morris** (1707-40); the latter died in the attack on Cartagena in Spain. The letters of the Morris brothers, of which about a thousand have been preserved, are a rich source of information about the literary life of Wales in their day. **George Borrow**, who admired them, had much to say about their work in *Wild Wales* (1862), although some of it is not quite correct.

LLANFIHANGEL-YNG-NGWYNFA, Powys; village on the B4382, less than 1 mile S of the B4393 from Llanfyllin to Llyn Efyrnwy (Lake Vyrnwy).

In the churchyard there is a monument to the great hymn-writer **Ann Griffiths** (1776-1805), who lies buried here. She was born Ann Thomas at Dolwar Fach, about 3 m to the S, where her home is kept in its original state; the house cannot be seen from the road. The hamlet of Dolanog, about 1 m to the S, where she received elementary education, has a chapel dedicated to her memory. She was converted to the Calvinistic Methodist cause in 1796, a time of fervent religious feeling in the district. Dolwar Fach became a centre of Methodist preaching and was officially registered as a place of worship in 1803. In October 1804 Ann married Thomas Griffiths and bore him a daughter in the following July, but both child and mother died shortly afterwards. Ann is generally regarded, with **Williams Pantycelyn** (1717-91) as the greatest hymn-writer of the Methodist Revival in Wales, despite the fact that only about 74 of her verses have survived. They include the famous one beginning *'Wele'n sefyll rhwng y myrtwydd'*, which is often sung to the tune 'Cwm Rhondda' (trans.):

Lo, between the myrtles standing,
    One who merits well my love,
Though His work I guess but dimly
    High all earthly things above;
Happy morning, happy morning,
When at last I see him clear!

Only a few of her hymns were written down and only one verse has survived in her own hand. They were committed to memory by her maidservant Ruth Evans and later copied down by Ruth's husband, John Hughes; they were first published in

Casgliad o Hymnau in 1806. The two main features of Ann's religious life were the profound depth and intensity of her spiritual experience and a firm grasp of the essential tenets of Calvinistic theology. Her main theme is the person and sacrifice of Jesus Christ, her love for Him and her longing for heaven. Some critics have found mystical qualities in her work and praised her keen intellect and deep sensitivity.

LLANFIHANGEL-Y-PENNANT, Gwynedd; hamlet on a minor road off the B4405 about 3 m N of Abergynolwyn.

The lexicographer **William Owen Pughe** (1759-1835) was born at Ty'n-y-bryn, but did not remain long in the district. In 1776 he went to London and became an active member of expatriate Welsh societies such as the Gwyneddigion. Industrious and erudite, but also gullible, he was persuaded by **Iolo Morganwg (Edward Williams;** 1747-1826) to include some of Iolo's pastiches of **Dafydd ap Gwilym** in the first printed volume of that poet's works (1789) and in *The Myfyrian Archaiology of Wales* (1801-07). One of the more endearing aspects of his character was his devotion to Joanna Southcott, the prophetess, whose factotum he was from about 1803 until her death in 1814. But his best-known work is his *Welsh and English Dictionary* (2 vols., 1803*)*. Unfortunately, Pugh included many words of his own invention and tinkered with the orthography of Welsh according to his own ideosyncratic theories about the origin of the language. He believed that an analysis of Welsh would reveal the secrets of the primeval language of Mankind.

The home of Mary Jones (1784-1864), the 16-year-old girl who walked barefoot from Llanfihangel to Bala, a distance of 25 m, to buy a Bible from **Thomas Charles** (1755-1814) in 1800, is now a ruin near the river. It is said that she had saved the price of the Bible, which was three shillings and sixpence, over a period of six years, and that her zeal was in the mind of Thomas Charles, who gave her his own copy, when he set about establishing the British and Foreign Bible Society in 1802. Mary Jones is buried in the graveyard of Bryncrug chapel.

LLANFIHANGEL-Y-TRAETHAU, see under **TALSARNAU**

LLANFYNYDD, Carmarthenshire; village on a minor road between the B4310 and A40, about 5 m NW of Llandeilo, approached by narrow twisting roads through wooded country.

The poet **John Dyer** (1699-1757), who later lived at Aberglasne House, Llangathen, was born here and baptized in the parish church.

There is a memorial to the hymn-writer **Morgan Rhys** (1716-79) in the churchyard.

LLANGAIN, Carmarthenshire; village off the B4312 about 3 m SW of Llandeilo.

The farm known as Fernhill, situated nearly 1 m from the village and reached by turning right off the B4312 to Llanstephan, belonged to an aunt and uncle of **Dylan Thomas** (1914-53), who spent holidays here as a boy. Two of his most famous poems, 'After the Funeral', which was written in memory of his aunt, Ann Jones, and 'Fern Hill', together with the story 'The Peaches', are set here.

Now as I was young and easy under the apple boughs
About the lilting house and happy as the grass was
>green,
>>The night above the dingle starry,
>>>Time let me hail and climb
>>Golden in the heydays of his eyes,
And honoured among wagons I was prince of the
>apple towns
And once below a time I lordly had the trees and
>leaves
>>Trail with daisies and barley
>>Down the rivers of the windfall light.

LLANGATHEN, Carmarthenshire; village in the Vale of the Towy off the A40 about 3 m W of Llandeilo.

The poet **John Dyer** (1699-1757) lived at Aberglasne and in his poem 'Grongar Hill' (1726) celebrated the surrounding countryside. The house, believed to have been built around the ruins of a 16th-century mansion, has recently been restored, together with its gardens, and is open to the public. The hill of Dyer's most famous poem, which praises the landscape of the district, lies less than 1 m SW of Aberglasne, overlooking the valley of the Tywi. It includes the lines:
>Ever changing, ever new,
>When will the landscape tire the view?

LLANGEINOR, Bridgend; village on the junction of the A4064 and A4061 in Ogmore Vale about 6 m NW of Aberkenfig.

The philosopher **Richard Price** (1723-91) was born at Ty'n-ton, but spent most of his life in England. His first publication and main contribution to philosophical thought was *A Review of the Principal Questions and Difficulties in Morals*

(1758), a classic statement of rational intuitionism in ethics. He came to public attention with the publication of his pamphlets in defence of the American rebels: *Observations on the Nature of Civil Liberty* (1776), *Additional Observations* (1777) and *Two Tracts* (1778). His view was that every community conscious of itself had the right to self-government and that the authority vested in government derived solely from the consent of the governed. For his contribution to the debate about the American colonies he was awarded an honorary degree by the University of Yale but felt unable to accept an invitation to become an American citizen. He is also remembered for *A Discourse on the Love of our Country* (1789), a sermon in which he enthusiastically greeted the French Revolution, thus provoking Edmund Burke into writing *Reflections on the Revolution in France* (1790). The Leisure Centre in Llangeinor is named after him.

LLANGEITHO, Cardiganshire; village on the B4342 about 5 m W of Tregaron.

The village is inextricably linked with the name and work of Daniel Rowland (1713-90), one of the leaders of the Methodist Revival of 1762, to whom there is a monument outside Zion Chapel which bears the inscription (trans.): 'O Heaven, Heaven, your corners would be pretty empty were it not for the fact that Zion nurtures children for you here on earth.'

The scholar and bibliophile **John Humphreys Davies** (1871-1926) was born at Cwrt Mawr and educated at the village school and the University College of Wales, Aberystwyth, of which he was appointed Registrar in 1915 and Principal in 1919. He edited the letters of **Goronwy Owen** (1723-69) and the **Morris Brothers** of Anglesey, and owned a large collection now known as the Cwrtmawr Manuscripts and kept in the National Library of Wales.

LLANGERNYW, Denbighshire; village on the A548 about 6m NE of Llanrwst.

Robert Roberts (1834-85), known as *Y Sgolor Mawr* (The Great Scholar), was born at Hafod Bach in the parish and is buried in the churchyard. Ordained as an Anglican priest in 1860, he was obliged to give up his curacy and emigrated to Australia a year later. Returning to Wales in 1875, he worked as a private tutor at Betws, near Abergele in his native county, where he earned a reputation on account of his erudition. While in Australia he wrote his autobiography, *The Life and Opinions of Robert Roberts, a Wandering Scholar, as told by himself,* but it was not published until 1923. It draws a vivid picture of religious life in the Wales of his day, both Anglican and Nonconformist. The Great Scholar is buried in the churchyard at Llangernyw.

The philosopher **Henry Jones** (1852-1922) was born here, the son of the village shoemaker. He was a Lecturer in Philosophy at the University College of Wales, Aberystwyth, and then at the University College of North Wales, Bangor, before his appointment as Professor at St Andrew's University in 1891; he spent the rest of his life in Scotland. The most important of his many books on philosophical subjects was *A Faith that Enquires* (1922), a work that reflects many of the theological trends of the Wales of his day. His early struggle for education is described in his autobiography, *Old Memories* (1923).

LLANGOLLEN, Denbighshire; tourist centre in the valley of the Dee on the A5.

For some fifty years the town was the home of the eccentric 'Ladies of Llangollen': Lady Eleanor Butler (1739-1829) and the Hon. Sarah Ponsonby (1755-1831). Of aristocratic Irish connections, they had eloped to escape the conventions of provincial life in Ireland and set up a ménage, together with their faithful maid Mary Carryll, at Plas Newydd, an elaborately decorated house on a hillside above the town. For nearly half a century after their arrival in 1780 the place became a mecca for many

Plas Newydd, the home of the Ladies of Llangollen

distinguished visitors to north Wales in search of 'the picturesque', including Shelley, Byron and Sir Walter Scott. Most fulfilled their hosts' expectation that they should leave a tribute, preferably some curio in carved oak. Wordsworth, who visited in 1824, offered only a sonnet in which he referred to Plas Newydd as 'a low-roofed cot' – and was never invited again. The Ladies' life at the house was spent in gardening, reading, writing, conversing, playing backgammon, and dominating the life of Llangollen, which was only a village at the time. Unfortunately, despite the wide circle of their acquaintances, their journals are quite dull. There is a memorial to the Ladies in the church of St Collen.

On the Eglwyseg escarpment above Llangollen, about 3 m N of the town, on a mountain road known as Panorama Walk, there is a monument to **Isaac Daniel Hooson** (1880-1948), at a spot where his ashes were scattered. He was born, lived and died at Victoria House, which has a plaque, in Market Street in nearby Rhosllannerchrugog. His poems, written for children, are among the most delightful of their kind in Welsh and are still great favourites as pieces for recitation. They are to be found in *Cerddi a Baledi* (1936) and in the posthumous volume, *Y Gwin a Cherddi Eraill* (1948). The poet is described on the memorial, erected in 1948, as *'Cyfaill i Blant Cymru'* (A Friend to the Children of Wales).

Memorial to I.D. Hooson, near Llangollen

140

Since 1947 Llangollen has played host to the world-famous International Musical Eisteddfod. The festival's motto was composed by the poet **T. Gwynn Jones** (1871-1949):

> Byd gwyn fydd byd a gano,
> Gwaraidd fydd ei gerddi fo.

(Trans. 'Blessed is a world that sings / Gentle are its songs.')

The castle known as Dinas Brân, which overlooks the town, is the setting for a traditional belief that a young woman named Myfanwy lived here and was loved by the poet Hywel ab Einion. The story is the subject of the poem *'Myfanwy Fychan'* by **John Ceiriog Hughes** (1832-87) and the castle plays an important part in the early chapters of the novel *Owen Glendower* (1940) by **John Cowper Powys** (1872-1963).

At the abbey of Valle Crucis, on the A542 to the N of the town, the poet **Guto'r Glyn** (*c*.1435-*c*.1493) found sanctuary towards the end of his life.

LLANGRANNOG, Cardiganshire; small seaside village on the B4334 about 12 m SW of Aberaeron off the A487.

The early feminist writer **Cranogwen (Sarah Jane Rees**; 1839-1916) was born at Llangrannog, the daughter of a master mariner, and is buried here; her tombstone has two *englynion*. She was the editor of *Y Frythones* (1878-91), a magazine for women, and founder of the Temperance Union of the Women of South Wales. A collection of her verse was published under the title *Caniadau Cranogwen* in 1870.

A farm near the village, known as Y Cilie, is famous as the home of a family of country-poets.

The father, **Jeremiah Jones** (1855-1902), was a blacksmith and farmer, and his wife Mary bore him 12 children; six of their sons were poets in the traditional metres. The literary talent of this extraordinarily gifted family, known in Welsh as *Bois y Cilie*, has persisted into the fourth generation. The grave of Jeremiah Jones, together with those of 22 members of the family, are to be seen in the cemetery at Capel-y-wig. A selection of verse written by the Cilie poets is found in *Awen Ysgafn y Cilie* (1976) and a history of the family in *Teulu'r Cilie* (1999) by Jon Meirion Jones.

LLANGRISTIOLUS, Anglesey; village off the B5 and B4422 about 3 m SW of Llangefni.

Here the writer **Ifan Gruffydd** (1896-1971) was born and spent most of his life, latterly at Rhos-y-ffordd, a house which now has a commemorative plaque. His two volumes of autobiography, *Gŵr o Baradwys* (1963) and *Tân yn y Siambar* (1966), are vivid portraits of rural life in Anglesey during the early part of the 20th century.

LLANGUNNOR, Carmarthenshire; village about 1 m E of Carmarthen on the B4300.

The English writer **Richard Steele** (1672-1729) retired here and lived at a farmhouse called Tŷ Gwyn, a property belonging to his wife's family on a slope above the village; the house was demolished in the early 19th century but a farmhouse of the same name occupies the site. The writer is commemorated in the parish church by a tablet bearing an inscription which ends with the words:

Is there a heart that can't affection feel
For lands so rich as once to boast a Steele?

The poet **Sir Lewis Morris** (1833-1907) is buried in the churchyard, as was his wish:

> Let me at last be laid
> On that hillside I know, which scans the vale,
> Beneath the thick yew's shade
> For shelter, when the rains and winds prevail.

LLANGWM, Denbighshire; village on a minor road off the A5 between Cerrigydrudion and Corwen.

This village was the scene of some of the first disturbances in the Tithe Wars of the 1880s, and there is a plaque on the bridge to that effect.

The prose-writer and publisher **Hugh Evans** (1854-1934) was born at Ty'n Rhos in Cwm Main. In 1875 he went to Liverpool, where in 1897 he established a printing press known as *Gwasg y Brython* and launched the periodicals *Y Brython* in 1906 and *Y Beirniad* in 1911. But he is chiefly remembered for his book *Cwm Eithin* (1931), a thesaurus of information about rural life and crafts which is now regarded as a minor classic; it was translated and published as *Gorse Glen* in 1948.

Near the bridge stands Penyfed, the home of **David Ellis** (1893-1918), a young poet who disappeared from his army camp in Salonika during the first world war; his body was never found and his fate remains unexplained.

LLANGYBI, Gwynedd; small village on a minor road about 2 m N of the B4354 from Chwilog.

The poet **Dewi Wyn o Eifion (David Owen**; 1784-1841) is buried on the W side of the churchyard.

The poet **Eben Fardd (Ebenezer Thomas**; 1802-63) was born at Gelli-gron. A weaver's son, he received little education and took to a wanton, drunken life, losing his religious faith. He settled at Clynnog Fawr and there he was to spend the rest of his life as a schoolmaster and later as a grocer. In 1839 he rejoined the Calvinistic Methodists and his school became a preparatory school for the training of candidates for the ministry. Choosing to call himself *Cybi o Eifion* as a young man, he learned the craft of poetry from poets in the district of Eifionydd, and came to prominence by winning the Chair at the Powys Eisteddfod in of 1824. As a critic he did much to improve the standard of literary criticism at the Eisteddfod.

The literary cleric **Morris Williams (Nicander**; 1809-74), a native of Caernarfon, was brought up at Coed Cae Bach, a little to the N of the village. From 1859 until his death he held the Anglican living of Llanrhuddlad in Anglesey, where there is a tablet to his memory. He was zealous in the cause of the Oxford Movement and wrote *Y Flwyddyn Eglwysig* (1843), which is based on Keble's *The Christian Year* (1827). He excelled as a hymn-writer and still has more hymns in the Church in Wales hymnal than any other writer except **William Williams (Pantycelyn**; 1717-91)

Among others buried in the Capel Helyg graveyard are the poets **William Ambrose (Emrys**; 1813-73) and **Robert Evans (Cybi**; 1871-1956); the latter's gravestone has an *englyn* by **Cynan (Albert Evans-Jones**; 1895-1970).

LLANGYBI, Cardiganshire; village on the A485 in the Teifi Valley about 5 m NE of Lampeter.

The poet **David Davis** (1745-1827) was born at Goetre-isaf near the village. He opened his famous school at Castell Hywel, in the same county, in 1782, where a number of eminent men received a classical education. Among his best poems are his *englynion* to the ruined mansion of Peterwell, near Lampeter, the home of the wicked squire Herbert Lloyd. Among the English poems which he translated into Welsh was Gray's 'Elegy Written in a Country Churchyard' (1750). His collected works were published as *Telyn Dewi* in 1824. There is a commemorative plaque at Castell Hywel; the author is buried in the churchyard at Llanwenog.

LLANGYNFELYN, see under **ABERYSTWYTH**

LLANGYNHAFAL, Denbighshire; village on a minor road between Denbigh and Llanbedr Dyffryn Clwyd on the E side of the valley.

At Plas-yn-llan, next to the church, **William Wordsworth** (1770-1850) stayed with the family of Robert Jones, his fellow-student at St John's College, Cambridge, with whom he made a Grand Tour of Europe in 1790. In an essay now kept in the National Library of Wales, there is a reference to a local belief that Wordsworth, according to local gossip, was fond of one of the Jones sisters. Some critics have suggested that the English poet heard about Lleucu Llwyd (Gray Lucy), the woman loved by **Llywelyn Goch ap Meurig Hen** (*fl.*1350-90), from Robert Jones, and that her name inspired the enigmatic Lucy Gray poems. Wordsworth's *Descriptive Sketches* (1793) were dedicated to Robert Jones.

The cleric and antiquary **John Williams (Ab Ithel**; 1811-62) was born at Tŷ-nant. For many years he was rector of Llanymawddwy in Meirionnydd; he was buried in the churchyard at Llanddwywe.

LLANGYNWYD, Bridgend; village on a minor road off the A4063 about 1 m S of Maesteg.

The parish, with Betws, Kenfig and Margam, is known as *'Yr Hen Blwyf'* (The Old Parish), and is part of Tir Iarll (The Earl's Land), so called because it came into the possession of the Earl of Gloucester after the Norman Conquest. Its literary traditions can be traced to the 15th century, according to **Iolo Morganwg (Edward Williams**; 1747-1826), who was fond of embellishing what he found and then making exaggerated claims based on scanty and sometimes non-existent evidence. Iolo was not only concerned to bring the literary heritage of Wales to the attention of English antiquaries but also to show to his fellow-Welshmen that Glamorgan held a particularly glorious position in that heritage.

Among the poets of Tir Iarll was **Siôn Bradford** (1706-85), after whom the street known as Heol Bradford in Betws is named. By trade a weaver, he belonged to a family which had moved into the district from Bradford-on-Avon in the previous century. His verse is undistinguished but **Iolo Morganwg** (1826), who received bardic instruction from him, claimed Bradford as an heir to the druidic system which had persisted in Tir Iarll over the centuries. Iolo also claimed that it was among Bradford's manuscripts that he had found much of the material which was later shown to have been of his own invention.

The antiquary and folklorist **Thomas Christopher Evans (Cadrawd**; 1846-1918) was born in this district, the son of the parish clerk and by trade a blacksmith, and lived most of his life in the village, latterly near the church. He is buried in the churchyard and there is a memorial plaque in the church; the street Heol Cadrawd in the village is named after him. He was encouraged in his youth by Mary Pendrill Llewelyn (1811-74), the vicar's wife, whose championship of the traditional story of the Maid of Cefn Ydfa (Ann Maddocks; 1704-27) he was later to defend in his *History of the Parish of Llangynwyd* (1887). She was said to have married, at the age of 21, a rich lawyer named Maddocks and from this recorded fact a romantic tale has been spun. Ann, so the story goes, was in love with a young poet, **Wil Hopcyn** (1704-41), and soon after her marriage to Maddocks she died of a broken heart. The tale, for which there seems to be no foundation, is the setting of the novel *The Maid of Cefn Ydfa* (1881) by **Isaac Craigfryn Hughes** (1852-1928). Wil Hopcyn, who is buried at Llangynwyd, is often associated with the folk-song *'Bugeilio'r Gwenith Gwyn'* (Watching the White Wheat).

The son of T.C. Evans, **Frederic Evans** (1881-1958), who wrote under the pseudonym **Michael Gareth Llewelyn,** was the author of five novels: *Sand in the Glass (1943), Angharad's Isle* (1944), *The Aleppo Merchant* (1945), *White Wheat* (1947) and *To Fame Unknown* (1949); the fourth of these retells the story of Ann Maddocks. He too is buried in the churchyard. These books can usually be found in second-hand bookshops.

The poet and Archdruid **Brinley Richards** (1904-81), who lived all his life in the Llynfi Valley, where he practised as a solicitor, is also buried at Llangynwyd.

LLANIDLOES, Powys; market town on the A470 about 10 m NE of Llangurig.

The poet **Gwilym R. Tilsley** (1911-97) was born

at Tŷ Llwyd in Y Fan, less than 2 m out of town in the direction of Llyn Clywedog.

LLANLLYFNI, Gwynedd; village on the A47 about 9 m S of Caernarfon.

The poet **Robert Silyn Roberts** (1871-1930) was born at a house known as Bryn Llidiart (now a ruin). A Socialist, he was a prominent figure in the Welsh literary revival of the early 20th century. After working as a quarryman, he was educated at the University College of North Wales, Bangor, and in 1925 established the North Wales Branch of the Workers' Educational Association. As a poet Silyn is often associated with **W.J. Gruffydd** (1881-1954), with whom he collaborated in the writing of the poems in *Telynegion* (1900). At the National Eisteddfod of 1902 he won the Crown for a poem later published in *Trystan ac Esyllt a Chaniadau Eraill* (1904); a selection of his verse was published posthumously under the title *Cofarwydd* (1930).

The poet and journalist **Mathonwy Hughes** (1901-99) was a nephew of Silyn's, and he too was born at Bryn Llidiart. From 1949 to 1977 he was assistant editor of the newspaper *Baner ac Amserau Cymru*. He won the Chair at the National Eisteddfod in 1956 and published four volumes of poems: *Ambell Gainc* (1957), *Corlannau* (1971), *Creifion* (1979) and *Cerddi'r Machlud* (1986), as well as four collections of essays and a volume of autobiography, *Atgofion Mab y Mynydd* (1982).

LLANOVER (W. Llanofer), Monmouthshire; village on the A4042 about 4 m S of Abergavenny.

Lady Llanover (Augusta Waddington Hall; 1802-96) of Llanover Court was a generous patron of Welsh folk-culture, especially music, dance and 'the

Welsh costume' which she did much to invent and promote. Known as *Gwenynen Gwent* (The Bee of Gwent) she lent her support to many Welsh causes, notably the Welsh Manuscripts Society and, unusually for one of her class, Nonconformity. The collection known as the Llanover Manuscripts, deposited in the National Library of Wales in 1916, was formed by **Edward Williams (Iolo Morganwg;** 1747-1826) and came into her possession on the death of Iolo's son, **Taliesin Williams,** in 1847. Her husband, Sir Benjamin Hall (1802-67), whom she married in 1823, was a champion of the Welsh people's right to have religious services in their own language and the first industrialist to disassociate himself from the Established Church on that account. During his term of office as Commissioner of Works, the hour-bell of the House of Commons was named Big Ben after him.

LLANPUMSAINT, Cardiganshire; village on junction of minor roads off the A484 about 5 m NE of Cynwil Elfed.

David Owen (Brutus; 1795-1866) was born in the parish, the son of a shoemaker. The most notable work of this prolific Anglican writer was *Wil Brydydd y Coed* (1863-65) in which he castigated Nonconformity and the 'noisy, ill-mannered Jacks' who were its ministers. As he himself had been a 'Jack', with the Baptists and Independents, and had been dismissed by both, it was widely believed that his attacks were motivated as much by pique as by his concern for religious standards. Nevertheless, he wrote eloquently and was a biting satirist.

LLANRHAEADR DYFFRYN CLWYD, Denbighshire; village on the A525 about 3 m SE of Denbigh.

The poet and hymn-writer **Edward Jones** (1761-1836) was born at Tan-y-waen at Prion in this parish, but lived from about 1796 at Maes-y-plwm, and is usually associated with the latter place. A popular poet in his day, he wrote carols, hymns and elegies which were collected after his death in the volume *Caniadau Maes-y-plwm* (1857). Many of his hymns, such as *'Mae'n llond y nefoedd, llond y byd'* and *'Pob seraff, pob sant'*, are still sung by Welsh congregations. He worked as a farmer and teacher, and is buried in the churchyard at Llanrhaeadr Dyffryn Clwyd.

LLANRHAEADR-YM-MOCHNANT, Denbighshire; village at the junction of the B4580 and B4396 about 4 m N of Llanfyllin.

William Morgan (1545-1604), the first translator of the Bible into Welsh, was vicar here from 1578 to 1595, a fact recorded in the church by a tablet to the left of the altar; another plaque on the organ states that the instrument was presented in his memory in the early years of the 20th century. There is a local tradition that he used to work while sitting on a large boulder at a spot known as Pen-y-walk, on the other side of the river from the church, which can be reached by a footpath and where a plaque can be seen. On the wall, there is a profile of the vicar which was placed there in 1988 to mark the fourth centenary of the Welsh Bible. Morgan's translation was published in London in 1588, an event of major significance for the language and literature of Wales.

Gwallter Mechain (Walter Davies; 1761-1849) held the living from 1807 until his death.

LLANRHYSTUD, Cardiganshire; village on the A487 about 8 m S of Aberystwyth.

The poet **J. M. Edwards** (1903-78) was born at a house known as Royal Diadem on the B4337; there is a commemorative plaque. He was a teacher in Barry, Glamorgan, from 1935 until his retirement but his poetry is rooted in country life, though reflecting also his concern with modern science and industrial society. Among the writers who influenced him were the Belgian Emile Verhaeren, the American Robert Frost and **Robert Williams Parry** (1884-1956). He published nine volumes of verse, notably *Peiriannau* (1947), *Cerddi Hamdden* (1962) and *Cerddi Ddoe a Heddiw* (1975). A collection of his essays, *Y Crefftwyr*, appeared in 1976 and his collected poems were published posthumously under the title *Y Casgliad Cyflawn* in 1980.

LLANRUG, Gwynedd; village on the A4086 about 4 m E of Caernarfon.

The poet **Dafydd Ddu Eryri (David Thomas;** 1759-1822) spent the last years of his life here and is buried in Llanfihangel churchyard. He is remembered as a teacher of poets rather than for his own writing. His pupils, known as *Cywion Dafydd Ddu* (Dafydd Ddu's chicks), included many of the leading poets of his day; he published a selection of their work in the volume *Corph y Gaincg* (1810). He died while returning from a visit to friends in Bangor: he slipped when crossing the river Cegin near Bach Riffri and was drowned. The tombstone erected by his friends is inscribed with six *englynion*.

LLANRWST, Conwy; market town on the E bank of the Conwy, on the A55.

William Salesbury (*c.*1520-1584?), scholar and chief translator of the first version of the New Testament in Welsh, lived here for most of his life. The ruins of his home, Plas Isaf, were formerly to be seen near the station, but nothing now remains.

The poet and humanist **Edmwnd Prys** (1543/44-1623) also belonged to the family of Plas Isaf, but his birth-place is unknown. He was a unique figure among Welsh poets of his day, steeped in both the humanistic learning of the Renaissance and in the traditional culture of Wales. He is remembered as the author of metrical psalms intended to be sung by Church congregations.

Gwydir, the home of **Sir John Wynn** (1553-1627), stands less than 1 m from the town across the bridge and is open to the public. He was a fine example of the rumbustious, greedy and litigious gentry of early modern Wales, and is remembered as the author of *The History of the Gwydir Family* (not published until 1770), in which he noted what 'a great temporal blessing it is . . . to a man to find that

Gwydir, Llanrwst, the home of Sir John Wynn

he is well descended'.

The grave of the poet **Trebor Mai (Robert Williams**; 1830-77) is near the main door of the church; his bardic name spells 'I am Robert' backwards. A tailor in the town, he excelled as a writer of *englynion*. Among his more curious poems is an eulogy of his fellow-poets which has rhyming lines set in the shape of an oak-tree, an early example of 'visual' poetry. Two collections of his work were published during his lifetime, namely *Fy Noswyl* (1861) and *Y Geninen* (1869), and another appeared posthumously.

The playwright and short-story writer **Robert Griffith Berry** (1869-1945) was born, the son of a postman, at London House.

The poet **Gwilym R. Tilsley** (1911-97) lived at Llys Myfyr in Station Road while writing *'Cwm Carnedd'*, the poem with which he won the Chair at the National Eisteddfod in 1957.

The poet and novelist **T. Glynne Davies** (1926-88) was born at 64 Denbigh Street and brought up from the age of five at 3 School Bank Terrace. He was a journalist and broadcaster. His important novel *Marged* (1974) traces the history of his family over the span of a hundred years. He also published three volumes of poetry, *Llwybrau Pridd* (1961), *Hedydd yn yr Haul* (1969) and *Cerddi T. Glynne* (1987), and a collection of short stories, *Cân Serch* (1954).

The short-story writer **Alun T. Lewis** (1905-86) was a teacher in Llanrwst for some thirty years; he lived in Llanddoged Road.

The publishing house *Gwasg Carreg Gwalch* is situated in Iard yr Orsaf, near the old railway station, and the bookshop known as *Bys a Bawd* is in Denbigh Street.

LLANSANNAN, Denbighshire; village on the A544 in the valley of the Aled.

The major poet **Tudur Aled** (*c*.1465-*c*.1525) was born in this parish. He is commemorated, together with **William Salesbury** (*c*.1520-1584?), the first translator of the New Testament into Welsh, who was born at a house known as Cae Du, by a memorial in the middle of the village, the work of Goscombe John (1860-1952), which was unveiled in 1899; the memorial features a girl with a posy of flowers. Tudur Aled was one of the commissioners

Memorial to Tudur Aled et al at Llansannan

of the bardic gathering held at Caerwys in 1523. He wrote in praise of prominent families of Norman and English origin who had become integrated into the society of the Vale of Clwyd, notably the Salesburys of Llewenni, near Llansannan, and genealogy was one of his favourite subjects. From the nine elegies written for him, it seems that he was a well-dressed gentleman, physically strong, a good horseman and an athlete. In his work the bardic tradition reached its climax and after his death there was a rapid deterioration of the Welsh poet's craft.

The writer **Gwilym Hiraethog (William Rees;** 1802-83) was born at Chwibren-isaf, a farmhouse nestling at the foot of the Hiraethog Mountain in the parish of Llansannan. Independent minister and Radical, he was a prolific writer. His verse was collected in the substantial volume *Gweithiau Barddonol* (1855). His vast epic *Emmanuel* (1861, 1867), which runs to more than 20,000 lines, has the distinction of being the longest poem in the Welsh language; that is perhaps its only distinction. Rees was more influential as a journalist: he edited *Yr Amserau* from 1843 to 1859, in which he argued in favour of social justice, including the abolition of slavery. He also corresponded with Garibaldi and supported the campaign of Kossuth in Hungary.

LLANSANFFRAID, Powys; village off the A40, 6 m SE of Brecon.

The poet **Henry Vaughan** (1621-95) was born in the parish at a house called Newton (shown on some maps as Trenewydd, the Welsh version of its name), near Scethrog, about 2 m to the NW in the direction of Brecon. The present-day Newton farm is believed to have been built on the site of the old house. The poet lived here for most of his life, practising medicine. In his book *Silex Scintillans* (1650;1655) he called himself 'The Silurist' in homage to his beloved county of Brecon, which he believed to have been formerly inhabited by the Silures. Among his best-known verses is this from his poem 'Peace':

My Soul, there is a Countrie
    Far beyond the stars,
Where stands a wingèd Centrie
    All skilful in the wars;
There above noise, and danger,
    Sweet Peace sits crown'd with smiles,
And One born in a manger
    Commands the beauteous files.

The poet is buried outside the E wall of the church, with a tombstone bearing a Latin inscription which he composed. Inside the church, rebuilt in the 19th century, there is a memorial tablet. The poem 'At the Grave of Henry Vaughan' by **Siegfried Sassoon** (1886-1967) ends with the line, 'And here stand I, a suppliant at the door'.

LLANSAWEL, Carmarthenshire; village at the junction of the B4310 and B4337 to the W of the Llandovery-Lampeter road, about 4 m NW of Talley.

The prose-writer **D.J. Williams** (1885-1970) was born at Penrhiw, a farm in the parish which is now an inaccessible ruin on forestry land.When he was six his family moved to Abernant, a smaller farm near Rhydcymerau, a few miles to the NW, and he lived there till he left at 16 to work in the mines of the Rhondda; the house has a plaque. The countryside hereabouts. together with its inhabitants, are immortalized in his two volumes of autobiography, *Hen Dŷ Ffarm* (1953; trans. Waldo Williams, *The Old Farmhouse*, 1961) and *Yn Chwech ar Hugain Oed* (1959). He was one of the early members of Plaid Cymru and in 1936, with **Saunders Lewis** (1893-1985) and **Lewis Valentine** (1893-1986), was gaoled for nine months for his part in a token act of arson at the RAF bombing-school at Penyberth on the Llŷn peninsula. At the time he was English master at the Grammar School in Fishguard. The vision which inspired him in his political work and all his writing was that of 'the square mile' around Llansawel, a small close community where human values exalted the individual and the spirit of co-operation was a natural instinct. He had a gift for gentle satire and a beguiling prose-style which was not afraid to digress, often to cunning effect. He published three volumes of short stories under the collective title *Storïau'r Tir* (1936, 1941, 1949), and a memoir of the early days of Plaid Cymru, *Codi'r Faner* (1968). In most of his stories he portrayed human nature in all its complexity, but especially that of people who exemplified ideals about Welsh nationhood. He won the affection of all who knew him by both the quality of his writing and the example of his devotion to Welsh culture in all its forms. He died in the chapel at Rhydcymerau while exhorting his own people to remain loyal to Wales and was buried in the adjacent graveyard where a memorial stone marks his grave.

The poem *'Rhydcymerau'* by **D. Gwenallt Jones** (1899-1968) commemorates the culture of the district, from which his family came, and its destruction by afforestation; the family farm, Esgeir-ceir, is now inaccessible, deep within the forest (trans.):

> On the land of Esgeir-ceir and the fields of Tir-
> bach,
> They have planted the saplings to be trees for the
> third war.

LLANSILIN, Denbighshire; village on a minor road about 5 m N of Pen-y-bont and very close to the border with England.

The writer **Charles Edwards** (1628-91?) was born at Rhydycroesau in the township of Lledrod, a little to the N. He is remembered as the author of *Y Ffydd Ddi-ffuant* (1667), one of the classics of the Welsh language, which gives a general history of the Christian faith and its history in Wales. Nothing is known about him after 1691 and the place of his burial has not been identified.

LLANSTEPHAN, Carmarthenshire; village on the Towy estuary and on the B4312 about 14 m SW of Carmarthen.

This is the village in *The Valley, The City, The Village* (1956), the first novel of **Glyn Jones** (1905-95), and in several of his poems. The writer's family came from this district and it held an important place in his affections; his ashes are buried near the W door of the church under a slate tombstone which bears his name, dates and the word *'Llenor'* (Man of Letters).

LLANTHONY (W. Llanddewi Nant Hodni), Monmouth-shire; small village in the Honddu valley, 9 m N of Abergavenny, reached by turning off the A465 at Llanfihangel Crucorney.

The ruined Augustinian priory, now in the care of the Department of the Environment, was bought by the English playwright **Walter Savage Landor** (1775-1864), a man of intractable temper, in about 1807. When he was refused permission to restore it he quarrelled with his neighbours and left the district.

LLANTRISANT, Rhondda Cynon Taff; large village on the A4119, on the N side of the M4, about 7 m SW of Pontypridd.

The people of Llantrisant are sometimes called 'the Black Army' because they sent a contingent of archers to fight for the Black Prince at the battle of Crécy in 1346. The claim of the village's television and electrical goods shop to have been established in the same year can be safely disregarded.

On the square stands a large statue of Dr William Price (1800-93), eccentric, Chartist, nudist, pagan, vegetarian and pioneer of cremation. When his infant son, whom he had named Iesu Grist (Jesus Christ), died in 1883, he had the corpse burned in a public ceremony at Llantrisant, where he lived, and was acquitted at the Cardiff Assizes in the following year; the verdict established the legality of cremation. The writer **Rhys Davies** (1901-78) was a great admirer of Dr Price and there is a bawdy ballad about his exploits which is often heard at folk clubs in south Wales:

> There once was a man called Dr Price
>> Who lived on lettuce, nuts and rice,
> His idols were the moon and sun
>> And he walked the hills with nothing on
>> Singing, 'I don't care a bugger
>> What anyone thinks of me!'

There is a memorial window to Dr Price in the crematorium at Glyntaf, near Trefforest.

LLANTWIT MAJOR (W. Llanilltud Fawr), Vale of Glamorgan; town on the junction of the B4265 and B4270, about 5 m S of Cowbridge.

The hymn-writer **Thomas William** (1761-1844) was for 38 years minister at the Independent chapel known as Bethesda'r Fro, near the town, which he and his congregation built; he was born at Trerhedyn in Pendoylan. He composed some of the best-known hymns in the Welsh language, including *'Adenydd fel c'lomen pe cawn'* and *'O'th flaen, O Dduw, 'rwy'n dyfod'*. His grave is near the wall of Bethesda Chapel.

LLANUWCHLLYN, Gwynedd; village on the A494 near Bala, 1 m SW of Llyn Tegid.

Rowland Vaughan (*c*.1587-1667) was the son of a lesser gentry family who lived at Caer-gai, a house on the N side of the A40 between Llanuwchllyn and Bala which had also been the home of the poet **Tudur Penllyn** (*c*.1420-*c*.1485). The building was burned down by Parliamentarian forces in 1645 and Vaughan was imprisoned, but eventually regained his property and built a new house on the site. Some of his poems were published in 1729 under the title *Carolau a Dyriau Duwiol* (1729). It is, however, as a translator that he is usually remembered, in particular for his *Yr Ymarfer o Dduwioldeb* (1630), a translation of Lewis Bayly's *The Practice of Piety* (1611).

The writer **Robert Thomas (Ap Vychan**; 1809-80) was born at Tŷ Coch, Pennantlliw-bach and is buried in the churchyard. He was ordained a Congregationalist minister in 1835 and appointed Professor of Divinity at Bala Independent College in 1873. His autobiography, published in the series *Llyfrau Deunaw* (1948), is a valuable account of the suffering caused by landlordism in Wales during the 19th century.

Owen Morgan Edwards (1858-1920), prose-writer and scholar, was born at Coed-y-pry, in the entrance to Cwm Cynllwyd, on the right under the road. He was educated at the village school now named after him, where he experienced the use of the Welsh Not, a device meant to prevent pupils from speaking their native language, and at the Calvinistic Methodist College in Bala, the University College of Wales, Aberystwyth, and Lincoln College, Oxford. He returned to Wales in 1907 on his appointment as Chief Inspector of Schools and made his home first at Tremaran and then at Neuadd Wen (the Welsh for White Hall), a large house in the village, where he died. His extensive literary output was written in Welsh for the benefit of the ordinary people of Wales, whom he tended to idealize. Besides his many books, he founded the influential periodicals *Cymru* and *Cymru'r Plant*, a magazine for the children of Wales.

Statue of Owen M. Edwards and son at Llanuwchllyn

He was buried at Pandy cemetery in the village. A statue to him and his son, Ifan ab Owen Edwards (1895-1970), the founder of *Urdd Gobaith Cymru*, the Welsh League of Youth, a movement launched in 1922, stands at the roadside a little outside the village where the B4403 joins the main road A494; the Red Dragon flag usually flies overhead. The movement has a recreation centre at Glan-llyn, on the shore of Llyn Tegid between Llanuwchllyn and Bala.

About 3 m further up Cwm Cynllwyd, in the valley of the Twrch, is Ty'n-y-fedw, on the hillside to the left. Here the poet **Eos Glan Twrch (John Edwards**; 1806-87) was born, a fact recorded by a plaque put up by the house's present owners. Edwards emigrated to the USA in 1828 and farmed near the town of Floyd in New York State and later near Rome in the same state. Active in the Welsh American community as a competitor at eisteddfodau, he was the author of only one collection of poems, *Llais o'r Llwyn*, which was published in Utica in 1854. The steep track from the road up to Ty'n-y-fedw is unsuitable not only for heavy goods vehicles but also for motor-cars with loose exhausts.

The poet **Euros Bowen** (1904-88) was vicar of Llanuwchllyn and Llangywair until his retirement from the Church in Wales in 1973, when he returned to live in Wrexham; it was during the heavy snow of 1947, when he was confined to the vicarage, that he began writing poetry. He was a prolific and erudite poet whose work many readers have found difficult in its imagery, but he is highly regarded by those who have taken the trouble to study his work, particularly on account of his experiments with *cynghanedd* (traditional Welsh prosody). A selection of his poems in his own translation was published in 1974; another selection will be found in Cynthia and Saunders Davies, *Euros Bowen: Poet-Priest* (1993).

LLANWINIO, Carmarthenshire; hamlet on a minor road off the B4299 about 7 m N of St Clears.

The poet **Wil Ifan (William Evans**; 1883-1968) was born at Yetygarn, Cwmbach. A prolific writer in both Welsh and English, he won the Crown at the National Eisteddfod on three occasions (1913, 1917 and 1925) and served as Archdruid from 1947 to 1950. Among his collections of poems in Welsh are *O Ddydd i Ddydd* (1927), *Y Winllan Las* (1936) and *Difyr a Dwys* (1960), while his English books include *A Quire of Rhymes* (1943), *Where I Belong* (1946) and *Here and There* (1953).

LLANWRTYD, Powys; former spa town 12 m W of Builth on the A483.

The farmhouse known as Cefn-brith, about 3 m to the SE on the N slope of the Epynt mountain, was the birthplace of **John Penry** (1563-93), the Puritan pamphleteer and martyr, and has a plaque to that effect. He was suspected of being the author of the Martin Marprelate tracts (1588-9), an attack on the institution of episcopacy, which also mocked the foibles and corruption of the bishops of the Church of England. Betrayed and arrested in London, Penry was indicted under the Act of Uniformity and executed at the age of 30.

LLANYBYDDER, Carmarthenshire; large village on the A485 about 6 m SW of Lampeter.

The poet **Lewys Glyn Cothi** (*c.*1420-89), also known as **Llywelyn y Glyn,** took his name from the forest of Glyn Cothi near the village. The absence of any facts about his life has given rise to several traditions about him, but it is known that he became an outlaw on the slopes of Pumlumon in 1461. His elegy for his son, Siôn y Glyn, who died at the age of five, is one of the most moving poems in the Welsh language.

The paleographer **John Gwenogvryn Evans** (1852-1930) was born at Ffynnon Felfed, but his family moved after about a year to Llanwenog in Cardiganshire; he coined his middle name in honour of that parish. He is remembered as the editor of some of the most important Welsh manuscripts, such as *The Text of the Mabinogion from the Red Book of Hergest* (1887), *The Book of Llandav* (1893), *The Black Book of Carmarthen* (1906), *The Book of Aneirin* (1908) and *The Book of Taliesin* (1910).

The historian and prose-writer **Gomer M. Roberts** (1904-93) was born at Cwm-bach in the vicinity. He started work as a collier at the age of 13 but local people collected money for him to receive an education and he entered the Calvinistic ministry in 1930. He was an authority on Welsh hymnology and the history of his denomination. He also published two collections of essays, *Cloc y Capel* (1973) and *Crogi Dic Penderyn* (1977).

LLANYSTUMDWY, Gwynedd; village on the A497 about 3 m from Cricieth.

The poet **Robert ap Gwilym Ddu (Robert Williams**; 1766-1850) was born at Betws Fawr, a farmhouse in the parish.

Dewi Wyn o Eifion (David Owen; 1784-1841)

was born at Y Gaerwen in the same parish and remained there for most of his life. Both Robert ap Gwilym Ddu and Dewi Wyn are commemorated by a tablet at the Baptist Chapel known as *Capel y Beirdd* (The Poets' Chapel). Like **Goronwy Owen** (1723-69), Dewi Wyn had an ambition to write a successful epic in the Welsh language, and this accounts for the tiresome length of his poems, but he was a master of *cynghanedd*. A selection of his poems was published as *Blodau Arfon* in the year after his death.

The writer and church historian **R. Tudur Jones** (1921-98) was born at Tyddyn Gwyn at Rhoslan. He was Professor of Church History and later Principal of Bala-Bangor Theological College until his retirement in 1988. Besides substantial works on the history of Protestantism in Wales, works characterized by wide-ranging scholarship, he published two volumes of essays, *Darganfod Harmoni* (1982) and *Ffydd yn y Ffau* (1993).

The writers' centre at Tŷ Newydd was opened in 1991 in the last home of David Lloyd George (1863-

Tŷ Newydd, the writers' centre at Llanystumdwy

1945); it stands off a lane near the river Dwyfor, where the statesman is buried. There is a Lloyd George Museum in the village.

LLAWR-Y-BETWS, see under **CORWEN**

LLAWR-Y-GLYN, Powys; small village on a minor road off the B4569 about 12 m W of Newtown.

The literary historian **Charles Ashton** (1848-99) was born at Ty'nsarn. An illegitimate child, he received little formal education before being put to work in the lead-mines at Dylife. Eventually, after much hardship, he joined the police force. The most important of his books on literary and historical subjects are *Hanes Llenyddiaeth Gymreig* (1893), a history of Welsh literature from 1651 to 1850, and *Llyfryddiaeth y 19fed Ganrif* (1908), a bibliography of Welsh books in the 19th century.

LLEDROD, Cardiganshire; village on the A485 about 8 m SE of Aberystwyth.

The poet **Evan Evans (Ieuan Fardd; Ieuan Brydydd Hir;** 1731-88), one of the great classicists of the 18th century, was born at Cynhawdref, a farm in the parish where he spent the last ten years of his life, 'incorrigibly addicted to drink' according to Samuel Johnson. He was a patriot and scholar who tried to rouse his countrymen to a greater awareness of the literary treasures of their land, for which reason he never found preferment in the Anglican Church; he was particularly incensed by the Church's policy of appointing English bishops in Wales. In a letter to **Lewis Morris** (1701-65), the antiquary, he wrote (trans.): 'Our bishops look upon me . . . with an evil eye because I dare have any affection for my country, language and antiquities, which in their opinion had better been lost and forgotten.' His book *Some Specimens of the Poetry of the Ancient Welsh Bards* (1764) was the first substantial selection of early Welsh poetry and it brought him immediate and lasting fame. It also satisfied the desire of English antiquaries for reliable information about Welsh literature. One of his best-known couplets is (trans.):

A good book, remember,
Is a man's best friend and a lantern.

There is a memorial tablet to Ieuan Fardd in the church at Lledrod but his burial-place is unknown.

MAESTEG, Bridgend; industrial town on the A4063 in the Llynfi Valley.

The poet **Vernon Watkins** (1906-67) was born at Lloyds Bank House, where his father was bank manager. Two years later the family moved back to Bridgend, where they made their home at Quarella, a house on the outskirts of the town which was demolished during the 1970s. In 1912 they left Bridgend for Llanelli and, after about a year, moved to Swansea, where the father took charge of the Wind Street Branch of Lloyds Bank.

MALLWYD, Gwynedd; village near the junction of the A458 and the A470 between Dinas Mawddwy and Cemmaes Road.

Here **Dr John Davies** (*c*.1557-1644), one of the greatest Welsh scholars of the later Renaissance period, was rector; there is a memorial to him on the N wall of the church. He did most of the work of revising the Welsh Bible for the new version which appeared in 1620. He also published a Latin grammar and dictionary of the Welsh language, *Antiquae Linguae Britannicae* (1621), in which he wrote (trans.): 'It is impossible to believe that God would have seen fit to keep this language until these days, after so many crises in the history of the nation . . . had He not intended His name to be called and His great work to be proclaimed in it.'

MANORBIER (W. Maenorbyr), Pembrokeshire; seaside village on the B4585 just S of the A4139.

The ruined castle was the birthplace of the chronicler **Giraldus Cambrensis (Gerald de Barri;** *c.*1146-1223). His most important works were *Itinerarium Kambriae* (*The Journey through Wales*) and *Descriptio Kambriae* (*The Description of Wales*); in the former he referred to his native district as follows (trans.): 'As Dyfed with its seven cantrefs is the fairest of all the lands of Wales, as Pembrokeshire is the fairest part of Dyfed, and this spot the fairest of Pembrokeshire, it follows that Manorbier is the sweetest spot in Wales.'

MENAI BRIDGE (W. Porthaethwy), Anglesey; small town off the A5 at the Anglesey end of Telford's suspension bridge.

The monumental lions on the Britannia Bridge, built by Stephenson, which carries both a road and a railway, were celebrated by **John Evans** (1826-88), a rhymester known as **Y Bardd Cocos** (The Cockle Poet) because he earned a living selling cockles and gathering chaff. He was famous for the unintentional humour of his doggerel in which he neglected meaning for the sake of rhyme. He described the lions thus (trans.):

> Four fat lions
> Without any hair,
> Two on this side
> And two over there.

Disappointingly, the lions – some 25 feet long and weighing 80 tons and made in 1848 by John Thomas who worked as a monumental sculptor for the railway companies – cannot be seen from either of the roads over the Menai Straits, but they can be glimpsed from the railway on the Britannia Bridge or from the lane that leads down the lane past St Mary's church and the entrance to the Carreg Brân Hotel. Evans, who lived at Pen Clip, was a figure of fun among his contemporaries, who invested him in a long coat and a hat crowned with coloured beads, in which he used to appear at the National Eisteddfod. He used to say that he did not know the year of his birth but that he was sure his name was John Evans because he had heard his mother calling him thus on many occasions. His high opinion of his verses led him to believe that Queen Victoria was interested in marrying him, a delusion in which his acquaintances encouraged him. He had no schooling and was of the opinion that other poets of his day had too much. He is buried in the graveyard of St Tyssilio's Church on Church Island, reached by a causeway from the Holyhead road. This cemetery, surrounded by the waters of the Straits, has been described as the healthiest spot in the whole of Wales in which to be buried.

Also buried here, under a very wide slate slab, is **Albert Evans-Jones (Cynan;** 1895-1970), a poet and eminent public figure. He lived in Menai Bridge from 1937 until his death at Penmaen in a road now called Ffordd Cynan.

There is a commemorative plaque on Wenllys, the house where **Sir Ifor Williams** (1881-1965) lived for many years. He was Professor of Welsh at the University College of North Wales, Bangor.

St Tysilio's church, the burial-place of Cynan,
on an island in the Menai Straits

A bookshop known as *Awen Menai* is situated in Bridge Street.

MERTHYR TYDFIL (W. Merthyr Tudful), Merthyr Tydfil; large industrial town on the A470 in the valley of the Taff and once the largest town in Wales.

In 1831 the town was the scene of a workers' insurrection now called the Merthyr Rising, during which the Red Flag was used as a symbol of working-class solidarity and militancy. The rioters took over the town for several days until the militia were called in to restore order. During a confrontation in the High Street a soldier was stabbed and Richard Lewis (1807-31), a miner known as Dic Penderyn, was accused of the assault. Found guilty and hanged in Cardiff on 13 August 1831, he is generally considered to be the first martyr of the Welsh working-class. His grave and monument are in St Mary's Church at Aberafan.

The novels *All Things Betray Thee* (1949) by

Gwyn Thomas (1913-81), *The Fire People* (1972) by **Alexander Cordell** (1914-97) and *The Angry Vineyard* (1975) by **Rhydwen Williams** (1916-97) take place against the background of the Rising.

Lady Charlotte Guest (1812-95), the first translator of the medieval Welsh tales known as **The Mabinogion** (3 vols., 1846), lived at Dowlais House after her marriage in 1835 to Sir Josiah John Guest, the ironmaster. The house has been demolished but the stables, now converted into flats, can still be seen.

Thomas Stephens (1821-75), the literary critic and author of *The Literature of the Kymry* (1849), kept a chemist's shop at 133 High Sreet, near Hope Chapel. He is generally considered to have been the first Welsh literary critic to adopt a scientific method and to have done more, as an adjudicator, to raise the standards of the National Eisteddfod and to win for it the confidence of scholars than any other Welshman of his time. In his book *Madoc* (1893), originally an essay submitted for a competition at the Eisteddfod of 1858, he refuted the widely cherished notion that America had been reached by Prince Madoc ab Owain Gwynedd in the 12th century.

The satirical poet **Sarnicol (Thomas Jacob Thomas**; 1873-1945) taught at Cyfarthfa School (the former home of the Crawshay family) and was appointed headmaster of Quaker's Yard Secondary School, near Treharris to the S of the town, in 1922.

The playwright **John Oswald Francis** (1882-1956) was born at 15 Mary Street in Twynyrodyn and lived as a boy at 41 High Street, next door but one to Howfield's baker's shop which is still there. He became a civil servant in London but kept in close touch with the amateur dramatic movement in

Wales. His play *Mrs Howells Intervenes*, later retitled *The Bakehouse*, was performed in London in 1912. It was followed by the specifically radical play *Change*, about the railwaymen's strike at Llanelli in 1911. Perhaps his most popular plays were *The Poacher* (1914), *The Little Dark People* (1922) and *Birds of a Feather* (1927), all comedies in a rural setting. J.O. Francis also wrote a collection of essays, *The Legend of the Welsh* (1924).

The novelist **Jack Jones** (1884-1970) was born at Tai Harri Blawd, a row of cottages (gone) near Pontmorlais at the top end of the High Street. After serving in the army, he returned to Merthyr, married and lived for a time in Park Place and Milton Place. He did not begin writing until he was in his forties but his first novel, *Black Parade* (1935), is set in Merthyr and deals with four generations of a mining family. It contains much action and a gallery of colourful characters, including a portrait of Saran, the matriarchal figure who was based on the author's own mother. His novel *Bidden to the Feast* (1938) is also set partly in the town, while *Some Trust in Chariots* (1948) is about 'Pontyglo', a thinly disguised Pontypridd.

The writer **Glyn Jones** (1905-95) was born at 16 Clare Street, off Plymouth Street just before the railway bridge over the road into the S side of the town. Although he never lived in Merthyr again after finishing his studies at St Paul's College, Cheltenham, he wrote about the town in many of his poems, stories and novels. It is the valley in *The Valley, The City, The Village* (1956) and the town in which *The Learning Lark* (1960) and *The Island of Apples* (1965) are set. His most explicit and affectionate tribute to his native place is to be found in his poem 'Merthyr':

Lord, when they kill me, let the job be thorough
And carried out *inside* that county borough
Known as Merthyr, in Glamorganshire,
A town easy enough to cast a slur
Upon, I grant.

One of the most provocative references to the
town is to be found in *'Y Dilyw, 1939'* by **Saunders
Lewis** (1893-1985) who, during the inter-war years
of economic depression, held classes for the
unemployed in Dowlais; it begins (trans.):

From Merthyr to Dowlais the tramway climbs,
A slug's slime-trail over the slag-heaps.
What's nowadays a desert of cinemas,
Rain over disused tips, this once was Wales.

The poet and prose-writer **Dyfnallt Morgan**
(1917-94) was born at 27 Haydn Terrace in Pen-y-
darren but moved with his family while still a child
to the house next door, number 28; his father
worked in the steelworks at Dowlais. In 1954 he
joined the staff of the BBC as a producer of radio
programmes and was appointed lecturer in the
Department of Extra-Mural Studies at the
University College of North Wales, Bangor, in 1964.
He won the Crown at the National Eisteddfod of
1957 with *'Y Llen'*, a poem written in the Dowlais
dialect of Welsh; it is to be found in his collection, *Y
Llen a Myfyrdodau Eraill* (1967).

The historian **Gwyn A. Williams** (1925-95) was
born at 11 Lower Row, Penywern, Dowlais. He was
appointed Lecturer in Welsh History at the
University College of Wales, Aberystwyth, in 1954
and Professor of History at University College,
Cardiff, in 1974. His books on specifically Welsh
subjects are: *The Merthyr Rising* (1978), *Madoc: the
Making of a Myth* (1979), *The Search for Beulah Land*
(1980), *The Welsh in their History* (1982) and *When*

Was Wales? (1985). He saw himself as 'a people's remembrancer' who tried to influence contemporary opinion by dramatic presentations of Welsh history in his books and television programmes. His work is characterized by passion, a colourful prose-style and wide erudition.

The poet **Harri Webb** (1920-94) was librarian at Dowlais from 1954 to 1964, living first in lodgings at 9 Dane Place. While a member of the Labour Party and one of the leaders of the Welsh Republican Movement, he published a pamphlet, *Dic Penderyn and the Merthyr Rising of 1831* (1956). In 1960, after rejoining Plaid Cymru, he moved into Garth Newydd, a large ramshackle house at the bottom of Brecon Road on a site now occupied by flats. The house became a centre for Nationalist activity in the town and Webb edited the party's newspaper *Welsh Nation* from there. The first number of the magazine *Poetry Wales* was published from Garth Newydd in 1965. Many of Webb's poems in his first collection, *The Green Desert* (1969), are about the town and people of Merthyr Tydfil. Although he wrote mainly in English, his most famous poem is *'Colli Iaith'*, a litany of the many defeats and losses suffered by the Welsh people, which ends with the defiant verse:

> Cael yn ôl o borth marwolaeth
> Cân a ffydd a bri yr heniaith
> Cael yn ôl yr hen dreftadaeth
> A Chymru'n dechrau ar ei hymdaith.

(Trans. To win back from the gate of death / Song and faith and the lustre of the old language / To win back the old heritage / And Wales setting out on her journey.)

The books of Wales are sold in the Welsh Centre at Soar Chapel Hall in Pontmorlais.

MOELFRE, Anglesey; seaside village at the end of the A5108 about 7 m SE of Amlwch.

At Porth Helaeth in 1859 the *Royal Charter*, an emigrant ship plying between Liverpool and Australia, was wrecked by a storm with the loss of 452 lives and a cargo of bullion. The desperate attempts by local people to rescue survivors (and find gold) made the shipwreck one of the most famous in the maritime history of north Wales. The part played by Stephen Roose Hughes, the rector of Llaneugrad and Llanallgo, in burying the victims and helping their grief-stricken relatives, was praised in *The Uncommercial Traveller* (1861) by Charles Dickens, who visited the village two months after the disaster.

MOLD (W. Yr Wyddgrug), Flintshire; county town on the river Alyn on the A494 and A541.

The poet **John Blackwell (Alun**; 1797-1841) was born at Ponterwyl near the town. He is remembered as the author of a number of delightful lyrical poems such as *'Doli'*, *'Cân Gwraig y Pysgotwr'* and *'Abaty Tintern'*. Apprenticed as a child to a shoemaker, he was provided with an education with the help of local clergymen and gentry, and was educated at Jesus College, Oxford. He was appointed curate at Holywell in 1829 and, four years later, was preferred to the rectory of Manordeilo in Pembrokeshire, where he remained until his death. No volume of his verse appeared during his lifetime, but *Ceinion Alun* was published in 1851. This book contains a number of the writer's letters in Welsh and English, which are redolent of a more leisurely age. A local school is named after him and there is a commemorative plaque near the entrance to Tesco's Supermarket in the town.

The composer John Ambrose Lloyd (1815-74) is commemorated by a plaque on Barclay's Bank in the High Street.

The novelist **Daniel Owen** (1836-95) was born at Maes-y-dref, a house on the road to St Asaph; the house has gone but a commemorative stone marks the site. He received only a little elementary education and was apprenticed to a tailor at the age of ten. His novels, which first appeared in periodicals, are mainly studies of Welsh life as it revolved around the Nonconformist chapel, and are famous for their humour and wealth of detail. His major works are *Rhys Lewis* (1865), *Enoc Huws* (1891), *Gwen Tomos* (1894) and *Straeon y Pentan* (1894). The author is buried in the public cemetery. The Daniel Owen Centre in Earl Street contains a small museum and a statue of the author stands outside the library; it bears the inscription (trans.): 'I wrote not for the intellectual, but for the ordinary man. If there is any merit in the book, it is in the Welshness of its characters, and in the fact that the portraits in it owe nothing to strangers.'

A bookshop known as *Siop y Siswrn* is situated at 6-8 New Street.

MONTGOMERY (W. Trefaldwyn), Powys; large village, formerly the county town of the old county of Montgomeryshire, on the B4385 and B4386, some 10 m S of Welshpool.

The prose-writer **Geraint Goodwin** (1903-41) lived here towards the end of his life at Bowling Green Cottage, Church Bank. He is buried in the parish churchyard of St Nicholas.

MORFA NEFYN, Gwynedd; village on the N side of the Llŷn peninsula on the junction of the B4417 and B4412.

Here the poet and prose-writer **R. Gerallt Jones** (1934-99) was born and brought up. He wrote a good deal about his childhood in the village and district, where his father was a clergyman with the Church in Wales, notably in *Gwared y Gwirion* (1966), a collection of stories which was adapted for television as *Joni Jones*. The family moved to Felin Fadryn, near Dinas, when he was seven, and later to Plas Gelliwig.

Nant Gwrtheyrn, the centre for the teaching of Welsh, is 1 m to the N off the B4417 down a very steep minor road from the village of Llithfaen.

MOSTYN, Flintshire; coastal village on the A548 some 3 m NW of Holywell.

The playwright **Emlyn Williams** (1905-87) was born at 1 James Terrace, Pen-y-ffordd, and christened at Gwynfa Chapel. He was brought up at the White Lion Inn, known locally as Pen-y-maes, at the top of the low hill in the nearby village of Glanrafon. When he was ten his family went to live at 1 Mainstone Cottages, Berthengam, Trelogan, another village in the same district, where he went to school. In 1917, when his father found employment at Summers' steelworks, they moved again, to 314A High Street, very close to the railway in Connah's Quay. The play *The Corn is Green* (1938) is based on the author's experiences while a pupil at Holywell County School and *The Druid's Rest* (1944), set in the fictional village of Tan-y-maes, is a dramatic re-creation of Glanrafon.

In the nearby village of Whitford, less than 2 m to the S, the naturalist and antiquary **Thomas**

Pennant (1726-98) was born and died in a house (destroyed by fire in 1922) known as Downing and still shown on maps. He is remembered as the author of *Tours in Wales* (3 vols., 1778, 1781, 1783), one of the earliest and best surveys of north Wales.

MOUNTAIN ASH (W. Aberpennar), Rhondda Cynon Taff; former mining town in the Cynon valley on the junction of the A4224 and A4059 about 5 m S of Aberdare.

The poet **Telynog (Thomas Evans**; 1840-65) is commemorated by a plaque at 18 Bridge Street, near the Royal Oak, in Cwmbach, a village between Mountain Ash and Aberdare on the A4059, and in the name of some council houses called Tre Telynog. He came from Cardigan to work in a coal-mine in the village and was prominent in the literary life of Aberdare, but died of consumption at the age of 25. A collection of his poems, *Barddoniaeth Telynog*, which includes a biographical sketch, was published posthumously in 1866.

The novelist **Joseph Keating** (1871-1934) was born in Mountain Ash but the exact place is not known. He was the son of Irish immigrants to Wales and worked in the local colliery until 1904, when he went to work for the *Western Mail* in Cardiff. Among his novels the only one with literary merit is *Maurice: the Romance of a Welsh Coalmine* (1905). His autobiography, *My Struggle for Life* (1916), has moments of genuine pathos. After the failure of his play in London, he returned to Mountain Ash and became involved in political life: he was elected a Labour councillor in 1923.

The poet and prose-writer **Pennar Davies** (1911-96) was born, a collier's son, at 11 Dyffryn Street. In

1952 he was appointed Principal of the Memorial College in Brecon and remained in that post after its removal to Swansea. His early verse was written in English under the name Davies Aberpennar, a pseudonym he relinquished in 1948, when he turned to Welsh as the medium of his literary work. He became known to Welsh readers as a member of the Cadwgan Group, among whom were **Rhydwen Williams** (1916-97) and others. He published five collections of poetry, notably *Y Tlws yn y Lotws* (1971) and *Llef* (1987), which include a number of love-lyrics and religious poems shot through with passionate imagery. His prose, including a collection of stories, *Caregl Nwyf* (1966), combines mythical symbolism and personal tenderness.

The poet **Tom Earley** (1911-98) was born at 8 Copley Street, but his family moved to 19 Lyndhurst Street, Caegarw, when he was a baby and it was there he grew up. He spent most of his adult life in London, where he was a teacher of English. A lifelong pacifist, he published four collections of verse, notably *The Sad Mountain* (1970), *Rebel's Progress* (1979) and *All These Trees* (1992), all of which reflect his upbringing in Mountain Ash and his interest in the Welsh language, which he learned. In his poem 'Rebel's Progress' he contemplates a return to the valley of his birth after a lifetime's political militancy:

> So now I'll leave the politics to others
> And not be an outsider any more;
> I'll go back to the valley, to my mother's,
> And never set my foot outside the door
>
> Except to go to chapel on Bryn Sion
> And maybe join the Cwmbach Male Voice
> Choir,

I'll sit at home and watch the television
And talk about the rugby by the fire.

The poet's ashes were scattered by his daughters on the mountain above the town.

The poet **Robert Morgan** (1921-94), born at 9 Gilfach Street in Bargoed, was brought as a baby to live at 27 Penrhiw-ceibr Road, part of Mountain Ash. He left school at 14 to work with his father in the local colliery. In 1947, after winning a short-story competition at the South Wales Miners' Eisteddfod, he trained as a teacher and for many years taught at schools in the Portsmouth area. He published several collections of poetry, notably *The Night's Prison* (1967), a verse-play, *Voices in the Dark* (1976), and a volume of autobiography, *My Lamp Still Burns* (1981). His *Selected Poems* appeared in three volumes in 1993 and a posthumous collection of his stories, *In the Dark*, in 1994. Almost all his writing, like his painting, is concerned with mining or with his experiences as a teacher of boys with special needs.

The poet **Harri Webb** (1920-94) lived from 1972 to 1985 at 2 Rose Row in Cwmbach. In 1985 he moved to sheltered accommodation at 41, and then 103, Bryn-hir in the same village. From 1964 to 1974 he had been Librarian of Mountain Ash; a commemorative plaque inscribed in Welsh and English was put up in the foyer of the library by the Rhys Davies Trust in 1996.

MUMBLES (W. Y Mwmbwls), Swansea; seaside resort on the Gower about 3 m W of Swansea on the A4067.

Here, on 27 January 1883, Maggie and Jessie Ace, daughters of the lighthouse-keeper, waded into the stormy sea during the shipwreck of the *Prinz Albert* and pulled some of the crew to safety with their scarves. This act of bravery was celebrated in a stirring ballad by the English writer **Clement Scott** (1841-1904), 'The Women of Mumbles Head', which became a favourite piece for recitation in school and music-hall:

> Bring, novelists, your notebook, bring, dramatists,
> your pen
> And I'll tell you a simple story of what women do
> for men;
> It's only a tale of a lifeboat, the dying and the dead,
> Of a terrible storm and shipwreck that happened
> off Mumbles Head.

The Antelope Hotel on Mumbles Road was a favourite haunt of **Dylan Thomas** (1914-53).

MYDDFAI, Carmarthenshire; village on a minor road off the A4069 about 4 m S of Llandovery.

It is famous as the home, from the 13th to the 18th century, of a family of country doctors known as the **Physicians of Myddfai**. Their manuscripts contain collections of medical material of a type common to the whole of Europe in the Middle Ages, such as instructions for diagnosis, prognosis and treatment by drugs, blood-letting and cauterizing. The family is associated with the folk-tale of Llyn y Fan Fach, near Llanddeusant in the same county, in which a young man falls in love with a beautiful maiden who lives in the lake. After being offered three kinds of bread, she agrees to marry him but warns that she will leave him if he strikes her 'three causeless blows'. They live happily for many years at Esgair Llaethdy but after her husband accidentally strikes her three times, she returns to the lake, calling all their cattle to follow her. Rhiwallon, their eldest son, became physician

181

to Rhys Gryg, the son of Rhys ap Gruffudd (1132-97), Lord of Dinefwr, and thus established the famous line.

MYNACHLOG-DDU, Pembrokeshire; small village in the Preseli hills about 12 m S of Cardigan and to the W of the A478.

The poet **Waldo Williams** (1904-71) lived here as a boy when his father was headmaster of the village school. The fact that Welsh was the first language of the inhabitants proved a decisive influence on his later writing. Most of his poetry, collected in the volume *Dail Pren* (1956), was written during the 1940s and was inspired by the district. He is one of the greatest Welsh poets of the 20th century. Pacifist and mystic, he wrote on universal themes such as the brotherhood of all men and women, but his work is rooted in the Preseli hills and in a vision of

Memorial to Waldo Williams on the Preseli hills

a free, Welsh-speaking, unbelligerent and Christian Wales. In his poem *'Pa beth yw Dyn?'* he asks and answers a number of fundamental questions about society and the individual, such as (trans.):

> What is being a nation? A talent
>   Springing from the heart.
> And love of country? Keeping house
>   Among a cloud of witnesses.

A commemorative stone was erected near the village in 1978. Waldo taught at a number of primary schools in Pembrokeshire between 1928 and 1942, including those at Dinas, Solva, Camrose, Dale, Cresselly, Carew, Redberth, Rudbaxton and Cas-mael. The poet is buried at Blaenconin, where his tombstone bears the words, *'Gwyn eu byd y tangnefeddwyr'* (Blessed are the peacemakers).

MYNYDD BACH, Cardiganshire; a bleak, hilly area to the NW of Tregaron and SE of Llanrhystud.

Near Llyn Eiddwen, on a minor road between Trefenter and Blaenpennal, there is a memorial to three poets associated with the district: **J.M. Edwards** (1903-78), **B.T. Hopkins** (1897-1981) and **E. Prosser Rhys** (1901-45). The second of these lived at Blaenafon, Chapel House; he is remembered as the author of *'Rhos Helyg'*, a poem which celebrates the wild scenery hereabouts. Prosser Rhys was born at Pentre Mynyd', Trefenter.

The writer **Gwyn Williams** (1904-90) lived at a house known as Treweithian before moving to Aberstwyth in 1983; his father's family was from this district. He describes what the district meant to him in his autobiography, *ABC of (D)GW* (1981).

MYNYTHO, Gwynedd; village on the B4413 about 2 m SW of Llanbedrog on the Llŷn peninsula.

The village hall, paid for by contributions from a poor community in 1935, is one of the most famous in Wales – not for its architecture, which is very plain, but for the englyn by **R. Williams Parry** (1884-1956) which is inscribed on its wall:

Adeiladwyd gan dlodi, – nid cerrig
Ond cariad yw'r meini;
Cydernes yw'r coed arni,
Cyd-ddyheu a'i cododd hi.

(Trans. It was built out of poverty, the stones are not stones but love; its wood is a pledge, it was raised out of yearning.) The poet had an evening class in the village during the 1930s.

The poet **Moses Glyn Jones** (1913-94), a native of the district, lived for many years at Llwydiarth in the village; he was a teacher. He published four volumes of poetry: *Y Ffynnon Fyw* (1973), *Mae'n Ddigon Buan* (1977), *Y Sioe* (1984) and *Y Dewin* (1993); he won the Chair at the National Eisteddfod in 1974.

NANMOR, Gwynedd; small village about 2 m S of Beddgelert on the E side of the A4085.

This was the birthplace of **Dafydd Nanmor** (*fl.*1450-90). His love-poems addressed to a married woman, Gwen o'r Ddol, caused his banishment from the district at an early age and he spent the rest of his life in south Wales.

On the road that passes the chapel stands Carneddi, the home of the poet **Richard Griffith (Carneddog;** 1861-1947). He and his wife were obliged by ill health to leave their home in 1945 and go to live with their son at Hinkley near Leicester. Their departure was the subject of a moving article and photograph in *Y Cymro* (14 Sept.1945) which caused a good deal of public emotion.

NANTGAREDIG, Carmarthenshire; village off the A40 about 5 m E of Carmarthen.

The poet **J. Eirian Davies** (1918-98) was born at Y Llain, a smallholding on the N bank of the river Teifi. He was a minister with the Calvinistic Methodists and lived after his retirement in Llangunnor. He was the author of five volumes of poetry: *Awen y Wawr* (1947), *Cân Galed* (1974), *Cyfrol o Gerddi* (1985), *Darnau Difyr* (1989) and *Awen yr Hwyr* (1991). His wife, **Jennie Eirian Davies** (1925-82), was editor of the weekly newspaper *Y Faner* from 1979 until her death.

NANT-Y-GLO, see under **PONTYPOOL**

NELSON, Caerphilly; village on the A472 about 2 m E of Abercynon on the road to Ystrad Mynach.

The playwright **Eynon Evans** (1904-89) was born at his grandmother's house in Wern Crescent, near the post office. He lived as a boy at 12 Station Road, but later moved to Bryngolau in Tŷ-du Road.

NEWCASTLE EMLYN (W. Castellnewydd Emlyn), on the border between Cardiganshire and Carmarthenshire; small town on the A472 about 10 m E of Cardigan.

The historian and man of letters **Theophilus Evans** (1693-1767) was born at Pen-y-wenallt near the town. He is remembered as the author of *Drych y Prif Oesoedd* (1716), an account of the early history of Wales which is regarded as a classic of Welsh prose. It has a robust style and was significant in that it was the first book for two hundred years to present a view of Wales as a country with a history distinct from that of England.

At Atpar (also called Trerhedyn), in 1718, **Isaac Carter** (d.1741) established the first permanent printing-press in Wales, a fact recorded by a plaque. The village is now part of Newcastle Emlyn, on the B4571 on the N side of the town. Carter began by printing ballads but moved on to more substantial works. The press was moved in 1725 to Carmarthen, where he continued to print books of a religious nature.

The romantic novelist **Allen Raine (Anne Adaliza Evans**; 1836-1908) was born in Bridge Street. At the age of 40 she married Beynon Puddicombe at Penrhyn Church, Tresaith, a seaside village 12 m to the N. From 1900 they lived at Bronmor, a large house above the village, and there she wrote the immensely popular novels *A Welsh Witch* (1902), *Hearts of Wales* (1905), and *Queen of the Rushes* (1906). Her grave is at the top end of Penrhyn churchyard.

The prose-writer and poet **Aneirin Talfan Davies (Aneirin ap Talfan**; 1909-80) was born at Pant-y-barcud in Cwm Hiraeth near Drefach Felindre, a village about 3 m S of Newcastle Emlyn.

Also in Drefach Felindre, at a house known as Tŷ Dyffryn, lived the historian **Gwyn A. Williams** (1925-95); after his cremation at Narberth Crematorium, at which 'The Internationale' and a Welsh hymn were sung, his ashes were buried in the garden.

NEW CROSS, Cardiganshire; small village on the B4340 about 5 m SE of Aberystwyth.

The writer **Caradoc Evans** (1878-1945) is buried

in the cemetery of Horeb Chapel, above Brynawelon, his last home. The gravestone, near the top wall and a little to the right, has an inscription of his own composition: 'Bury me lightly that the small rain shall reach my face and the fluttering of the butterfly shall not escape my ear.'

NEWPORT (W. Casnewydd), Newport; large industrial town on the estuary of the Usk.

About 2 m to the W and 1 m from Bassaleg can be seen the few remains of Gwern-y-clepa, the home in the 14th century of Ifor ap Llywelyn (Ifor Hael), the patron of the great poet **Dafydd ap Gwilym** (*fl.*1315/20-1350/70). Four centuries later **Iolo Morganwg** (**Edward Williams**; 1747-1826) visited the spot with **Ieuan Brydydd Hir (Evan Evans**; 1731-88) who was inspired to write his famous poem '*Llys Ifor Hael*' in which he lamented the loss of patronage to Welsh poets (trans.):

> A poor sight the hall of Ifor Hael – mounds
> In a swamp are lying.
> Thorn and blasted thistle own it,
> Bramble where once was greatness.

In 1839 the town of Newport was the scene of a Chartist demonstration led by John Frost (1785-1877) and Zephaniah Williams (1795-1874) when on 4 November a crowd of perhaps 20,000 workers from all over SE Wales, many armed, marched down Stow Hill calling for electoral reform. After a confused confrontation with the authorities inside the Westgate Hotel, fighting began in the street outside and troops opened fire, killing some two dozen people and wounding many demonstrators. For their part in what has come to be known as the Newport Rising, Frost and Williams were condemned to death but the sentences were commuted to transformation to Van Diemen's Land. John Frost Square is in the centre of town and there is a commemorative sculpture by Christopher Kelly outside the Westgate Hotel.

The poet **W.H. Davies** (1871-1940) in *The Autobiography of a Super-tramp* (1908) records that he

W.H. Davies' memorial, Newport

was born at the Church House Inn, 14 Portland Street, off Commercial Street and near the docks, and in 1938 he attended the unveiling of a plaque on the house. In 1941, however, soon after his death, it was discovered that he had been born at 6 Portland Street (gone). He had been taken to live at Church House after the death of his father in 1874 and been brought up by his grandparents there; they later lived at 38 Raglan Street and then in Upper Lewis Street. Walks in rural Gwent fired in him a love of nature and he recalled his boyhood in his poem 'Days that have been':

> Can I forget the sweet days that have been,
> When poetry first began to warm my blood;
> When from the hills of Gwent I saw the earth
> Burned into two by Severn's silver flood.

After the death of his grandfather, a former sea-captain, he was apprenticed to a picture-framer but became restless and left Newport for Bristol; he set sail for America in 1893. On the junction of Hill Street and Commercial Street in the town's shopping-centre there is an allegorical sculpture by Paul Bothwell-Kincaid, erected in 1990, which is inscribed with the famous couplet from Davies's poem 'Leisure':

> What is this life if, full of care,
> We have no time to stand and stare.

The *Selected Poems* of W. H. Davies were published in 1985. Epstein's bronze bust of the poet can be seen by prior arrangement in the Newport Museum.

St Julian's Parish Church, on the Caerleon side of the town, was built on a site given by the English novelist **Ronald Firbank** (1886-1926), who had visited Newport in 1904 in search of the former home of his paternal grandparents, only to find that it had fallen into disrepair. The grounds of the ruined house have been developed as St Julian's Estate. On the E wall of the church is a large crucifix which Firbank, a convert to Catholicism, presented in memory of his parents, and beneath it a memorial stone inscribed with a request for prayers for the donor. Dandy, aesthete, exotic, homosexual and habitué of the Café Royal, Firbank received little encouragement as a writer during his lifetime but some recent critics have seen in him an innovator whose prose-style prefigures that of James Joyce.

NEW QUAY (W. Y Cei Newydd), Cardiganshire; coastal town at the end of the A486 on Cardigan Bay.

The poet **Dewi Emrys (David Emrys James;** 1881-1952) was born at Majorca House but his father, an Independent minister, took the family to Pen-caer in Pembrokeshire soon afterwards.

Dylan Thomas (1914-53) lived briefly during the second world war at a small bungalow known as Majoda; it can be found about 1 m from the town, down a left turn off the Aberaeron road opposite the Cambria Hotel. Here, in 1945, there occurred an incident which nearly caused the death of the poet, his wife and children, when a Captain William Killick, drunk and jealous of his wife's close friendship with the Thomases, fired at the house with a sten-gun and threatened to throw in a hand-grenade, shouting, 'You're nothing but a lot of egoists!'. He was later charged with attempted murder but the case against him was dropped 'for lack of evidence'. The bullets went through the bungalow's walls and could still be seen years later.

NEWTOWN (W. Y Drenewydd), Powys; market town at the junction of the A483 and A489 in the valley of the Severn.

Robert Owen (1771-1858), the Utopian Socialist and author, was born here and returned to the town to die. The Robert Owen wing of the public library was built by the Co-operative Union in 1903, the statue in the town centre was erected in 1956, and a museum devoted to his memory was opened in 1983. Owen's best-known work, *A New View of Society* (1813), dedicated to William Wilberforce, was the last influential statement of a rationalist doctrine to be published in England and his autobiography (1857) is valuable for its account of working-class movements. His grave is in the old churchyard where the Co-operative Movement erected a monument in 1902.

The novelist and short-story writer **Geraint Goodwin** (1903-41) was born at 43 Commercial Street in the parish of Llanllwchaearn but which is now part of the town. He spent his boyhood at Forest Villa in New Road and also lived there in the early 1920s while working for the *Montgomeryshire Express* before leaving for London. Newtown is the setting for his novels *The Heyday in the Blood* (1936), *Watch for the Morning* (1938) and *Come Michaelmas* (1939) and most of his stories are rooted in the surrounding countryside.

NOTTAGE (W. Nottais), Bridgend; large seaside village now part of Porthcawl off the A4106.

The English novelist **R. D. Blackmore** (1825-1900), author of *Lorna Doone* (1869), spent much of his childhood at Nottage Court and was a regular visitor in later life. He trained as a lawyer but poor health prevented him from practising law and a legacy from his uncle, who was vicar of Neath, allowed him to take up writing instead. His Welsh connections are evident in his early novels, *Clara Vaughan* (1864) and *Cradock Nowell* (1866), but are reflected most clearly in *The Maid of Sker* (1872), perhaps his best work. Although set mainly in Glamorgan, it does not refer to the traditional tale of Elizabeth Williams (*c*.1747-76), who was known as the Maid of Sker, but is, rather, an informed and patriotic portrait of Welsh life in the latter part of the 18th century. Sker House, a tall, gaunt building, is visible across marshland from the carpark of the Maid of Sker Hotel. The author's father, the Reverend John Blackmore, is buried in the churchyard.

OLD RADNOR (W. Pencraig), Powys; village on a minor road on the S side of the A44, very near the border with England and about 5 m N of Gladestry and 9 m E of Llanfihangel Nant Melan.

The historian **John Lewis** (1548?-1616?) was born at Harpton Court (Tre'r Delyn). His only published work, *The History of Great Britain . . . till the Death of Cadwaladr* (1792), was dedicated to James I and written to refute Polydore Vergil, in vindication of **Geoffrey of Monmouth** (*c*.1090-1155), in praise of the House of Stuart and in defence of the traditional history of Wales. Lewis, who was a barrister, lived at Llynwene near Llanfihangel Nant Melan.

The political writer and statesman **George Cornewall Lewis** (1806-63) lived at Harpton Court while MP for Radnor Boroughs. He had a distinguished parliamentary career under Lord Palmerston: he was Chancellor of the Exchequer

(1855-58), Home Secretary (1859-61) and Secretary of State for War (1861-63). His literary interests included the editorship of *The Edinburgh Review* (1852-55); his *Letters* were edited by G.F. Lewis in 1870. A scholarly man, he was noted for his sardonic wit: to him is attributed the remark, 'Life would be tolerable but for its amusements.' There is a very large monument to Lewis in the centre of Old Radnor.

OYSTERMOUTH (W. Ystumllwynarth), Swansea; village about 5 m SW of the city of Swansea on the road to Mumbles.

On the W side of All Saints' churchyard is the grave of **Thomas Bowdler** (1754-1825), whose *Family Shakespeare* (1818), an expurgated edition of the plays 'in which those words and expressions are omitted, which cannot with propriety be read aloud in a family', gave rise to the verb 'to bowdlerize'. He spent the last 15 years of his life at Rhyddings House in Brynmill.

The house had previously been occupied by **Walter Savage Landor** (1775-1864) who, while living there, met Rose Aylmer, one of his early loves and about whom he wrote a famous poem (1806).

In the same churchyard is the grave of the composer Morfydd Llwyn Owen (1891-1918), the first wife of the psychoanalyst **Ernest Jones** (1879-1958), a native of Gowerton and the biographer of Freud. Their marriage, which lasted only a year, was marred by the tension between her religious faith and his atheism. On her gravestone is inscribed a quotation from Goethe's *Faust*: *'Das Unbeschreibliche, hier ist's getan'* (Here the indescribable consequences [of love] have been fulfilled). Jones is commemorated by a plaque inscribed in Welsh at his home, 12 Woodlands, Gowerton.

The folk-poet **Cyril Gwynn** (1897-1988) was brought up in Newton and at Langland Bay Farm on the S side of Mumbles Head; the farmhouse was removed to make way for a golf-course. Although he was born in Briton Ferry, his mother's home-town, Gwynn was closely associated with Gower because he lived on the peninsula for many years, earning a reputation as a writer and reciter of verses celebrating rural communities and chronicling a society which has now nearly disappeared. In 1906 the Gwynns took over a butcher's shop at Southend and the poet lived thereafter at various places, including Llanrhidian and Newton; after his marriage in 1922 he made his home in what is now the post office at Parkmill. In 1946 he bought Hills Farm, at Port Eynon, but four years later moved to Three Crosses. In 1964 he and his wife emigrated to Australia to be near two of their seven children who lived there, and it was there he died. A selection of his verse had been published as *Gower Yarns* in 1928 and, in 1975, during a return visit to his native patch, the Gower Society brought out a new, augmented edition which has continued to sell ever since; curiously, the photograph on the cover is not of Cyril Gwynn but of Phil Tanner (1862-1950), the Gower folk-singer. Many of Gwynn's poems and stories were read at weddings, ploughing match dinners, wakes, Christmas parties, and at Court Leet and harvest-suppers. Known as 'The Bard of Gower', he influenced the young **Harri Webb** (1920-94), to whom he was distantly related.

PANDY, Monmouthshire; village on the A465 about 6 m N of Abergavenny and very near the border with England.

Raymond Williams (1921-88), the social historian, critic and novelist, was born at Llwyn Derw, situated behind Glannant House in the old part of the village on the other side of the road from the Lancaster Arms; a plaque was put up by the Rhys Davies Trust in 1997. The signal-box where his father worked no longer exists. From 1932 to 1939 Williams attended the King Henry VIII Grammar School in Abergavenny. His novel *Border Country* (1960) is set in his native district, as is the posthumous *People of the Black Mountains* (2 vols., 1989 and 1990). Among his many books of cultural analysis the following are most noteworthy: *Culture and Society* (1958), *The Long Revolution* (1966), *May Day Manifesto* (1968), *The Country and the City* (1973), *Keywords* (1976), *Marxism and Literature* (1977) and *Politics and Letters* (1979). His growing identification with Wales in the 1960s is reflected in his novels *The Fight for Manod* (1979) and *Loyalties* (1985). For many years the writer and his wife had a small house at Craswall, on a minor road at the head of the Monnow valley. The writer was buried at Clodock in the churchyard of St Clydawg, on the other side of the road from the church, on the way to Longtown at the junction of the rivers Olchon and Monnow, about 1 m over the border into England.

PANDY RHIWSAESON, see under **LLANBRYN-MAIR**

PENARTH, Vale of Glamorgan; town on the A4160 about 3 m S of Cardiff, for which it serves as a dormitory.

The writer **Saunders Lewis** (1893-1985) lived at Bryn-y-môr in Westbourne Road after his appointment to a lecturer's post in the Welsh Department of University College, Cardiff, in 1952. Poet, literary historian, dramatist and critic, he is generally regarded as the outstanding Welsh literary figure of the 20th century. In 1925 he was the founder of the Welsh Nationalist Party (later Plaid Cymru) and, in 1936, was gaoled for his part in a token act of arson at the RAF bombing-school at Penyberth on the Llŷn peninsula. He wrote some

Grave of Saunders Lewis in Penarth, near Cardiff

20 plays, notably *Buchedd Garmon* (1937), *Blodeuwedd* (1948) and *Brâd* (1958), as well as two novels and a substantial body of literary criticism. The play *Buchedd Garmon* contains the well-known passage (trans.):

> Garmon, Garmon,
> A vineyard placed in my care is Wales, my country,
> To deliver unto my children
> And my children's children
> Intact, an eternal heritage;
> And behold, the swine rush on her to rend her.
> Now I will call upon my friends,
> Both scholars and simple folk,
> 'Stand with me in the breach
> That the age-old splendour be kept for ages to come.'
> And this, Lord, is the vineyard of your beloved, too;
> From Llan Fair to Llan Fair, a land where the Faith is
> established.

All Lewis's writings are informed by a love of Wales seen in the context of European Catholic Christendom. His plays and poetry have been translated by Joseph P. Clancy and his novel *Monica* by Meic Stephens (1997). He and his wife are buried in the Roman Catholic cemetery at Penarth, where their grave bears the inscription *'Sanctaidd Fair, Fam Duw: gweddïa drosom'* (Holy Mary, Mother of God: pray for us).

PENCADER, Carmarthenshire; village on the B4459 about 14 m N of Carmarthen.

In his *Descriptio Kambriae* (1193) **Giraldus Cambrensis (Gerald de Barri;** *c*.1146-1223) described how Henry II, during the English king's progress through Wales in 1163, questioned an old Welshman on whether he thought the Welsh would continue to resist the power of England. Speaking in Welsh, he gave this reply: 'This nation, O King, may now, as in former times, be harassed, and in a great measure weakened and destroyed by your and other powers, and it will often prevail by its laudable exertions, but it can never be totally subdued through the wrath of man, unlkess the wrath of God shall concur. Nor do I think that any other nation than this of Wales, or any other language, whatever may hereafter come to pass, shall on the day of severe judgement before the Supreme Judge, answer for this corner of the earth.' The old man's defiant but dignified reply, one of the classic statements of Welsh patriotism, is inscribed on a memorial which was erected in the village under the auspices of Plaid Cymru in 1952.

Nearby is the ruin of the farmhouse Lletherneuadd Uchaf, the home of Sarah Jacob (1857-69), known as 'The Welsh Fasting Girl'. Her parents' claim that she had lived for two years without food or drink aroused widespread curiosity but, under closer surveillance, the child died; the parents were sentenced to terms of hard labour for the crime of manslaughter. Further details of this macabre case will be found in John Cule, *Wreath on the Crown* (1967); it is also the subject of the play *Sàl* (1982) by **Gwenlyn Parry** (1932-91) and the novel *Sarah Arall* (1982) by Aled Islwyn.

The poet and hymn-writer **Nantlais (William Nantlais Williams**; 1874-1959) was born at Llawr-y-cwrt, Gwyddgrug, near the village. He published two collections of his poems, namely *Murmuron y Nant* (1898) and *Murmuron Newydd* (1926), and a collection of hymns, *Emynau'r Daith* (1949). Among his most familiar hymns, which are still popular among children, are *'Plant bach Iesu Grist ydym ni bob un '*, *'Draw draw yn China'* and *'Uno wnawn â'r* *nefol gôr'*. He was buried in the graveyard of Bethany chapel in Ammanford.

PENISA'R-WAUN, Gwynedd; village near Deiniolen on a minor road off the A4086 about 5 m E of Caernarfon.

The playwright **Huw Lloyd Edwards** (1916-75) was born at Siop Gron in the village. After teaching for 15 years at Dyffryn Nantlle, he was appointed Lecturer in the Drama Department at the Normal College, Bangor. He lived at Sŵn y Gwynt in Hen Lôn, Penygroes. Among his most memorable plays are *Ar Ddu a Gwyn* (1963), translated into English as *Salvador*, about racial prejudice in South Africa, *Pros Kairon* (1967) and *Y Llyffantod* (1973). He is buried in the cemetery at Llanbeblig, near Caernarfon.

PENMACHNO, Gwynedd; village on the B4406 on the S side of the A5 and about 6 m S of Betws-y-coed.

Tŷ Mawr, a remotely situated house in Gwybrnant on a minor road (unsuitable for buses) was the birth-place of **William Morgan** (1545-1604), the first translator of the Bible into Welsh. Now restored and open to visitors during the summer months, the house has a small exhibition illustrating the life and work of the great man. There is also a memorial window in the church at Penmachno. **D. Gwenallt Jones** (1899-1968) wrote of William Morgan (trans.):

Let us celebrate him for his diligence, his daring, and his
holiness,
And for helping to keep alive the learned language of the
nation,
Conferring dignity on Welsh and giving it the highest
honour

By converting it to one of the dialects of God's
revelation.

PENMAENPOOL (W. Llynpenmaen), Gwynedd; small village on the A493 and the Mawddach estuary about 1 m from Dolgellau.

The English poet **Gerard Manley Hopkins** (1844-89), while visiting the George III Hotel in 1876, wrote some verses in the visitors' book which end:

> Then come who pine for peace or pleasure
> Away from counter, court, or school,
> Spend here your measure of time and treasure
> And taste the treats of Penmaen Pool.

PENMYNYDD, Anglesey; hamlet on the B5420 to the N of the A5 between Llanfair Pwllgwyngyll and Llangefni.

The hamlet takes its name from the home of Catrin of Berain (1534-91), who was connected by descent and marriage with many of the leading families of north Wales. The granddaughter of an illegitimate son of Henry VII, she was married four times and her numerous descendants formed an intricate web of influence throughout north Wales; she had children by her first three husbands and marriages took place between her children and step-children. Among the poets who sang in her praise was **Wiliam Cynwal** (d.1587/88) who described her as (trans.): 'Splendid Catrin, like the brightness of foam, fine her aspect, the candle of Gwynedd'. The life and times of this remarkable woman are the subject of three novels by R. Cyril Hughes: *Catrin o Ferain* (1975), *Dinas Dihenydd* (1976) and *Castell Cyfaddawd* (1984).

PENNAL, Gwynedd; village on the A493 on the N side of the Dyfi estuary between Machynlleth and Aberdovey.

The village is famous because here, in 1406, Owain Glyndŵr held an assembly from which he despatched a letter, known as the Pennal Policy, to Charles VI of France which contained proposals that the Welsh should recognize the Avignon Pope on terms which would have severed the connection between the Welsh Church and Canterbury and established two universities in Wales. The letter contained the sentence (trans.): 'My nation has been trodden underfoot by the fury of the barbarous Saxons.'

Lleucu Llwyd, in the 14th century, the woman loved adulterously by the poet **Llywelyn Goch ap Meurig Hen** (*fl*.1350-90) lived in Pennal. His elegy for her is one of the finest love-poems in the Welsh language.

PENTRE, Rhondda Cynon Taff; industrial village on the A4058 in the Rhondda Fawr between Ystrad and Treherbert.

The poet and novelist **Rhydwen Williams** (1916-97) was born at 41 Treharne Street but on his fifteenth birthday his family left for Chester, an uprooting which marred his adolescence. His ashes were scattered from the mountain above Rhigos at a spot overlooking the Rhondda and Cynon Valleys.

Rhydwen Williams was a member of *Cylch Cadwgan,* a literary group which took its name from the home of J. Gwyn Griffiths and his wife **Kate Bosse-Griffiths** (1910-98) in St Stephen's Avenue; **Pennar Davies** (1911-96) was also among the group's members.

PENTRE-TŶ-GWYN, see under **LLANDOVERY**

PEN-Y-BONT-FAWR, Powys; village on the junction of the B4391 and the B4396 between Llangynog and Llanrhaeadr-ym-mochnant.

The poet **Robert Ellis (Cynddelw**; 1812-75) was born at Ty'n-y-meini near the village. He was a Baptist minister and edited several of his denomination's periodicals. His poems were collected after his death in the volume *Barddoniaeth Cynddelw* (1877).

PENYSARN, Anglesey; village on the A5025 about 3 m SE of Amlwch.

The poet and journalist **Llew Llwyfo (Lewis William Lewis**; 1831-1901) is commemorated by a plaque on the village hall; he was born at Y Gwynfa in Penysarn. As a boy he worked in the copper-mines at Parys, near Amlwch, but turned to journalism about 1850, founding newspapers in Wales, Liverpool and America. Paralyzed at the age of 47, he ended his life in poverty, living for a while in the workhouse at Llangefni. He was described by **D. Tecwyn Lloyd** (1914-92) as 'an artist in Philistia', because the materialism and respectability of the times in which he lived all but stifled his vivacious spirit.

On the wall of the village school there is a plaque in memory of **Bedwyr Lewis Jones** (1933-92), who was brought up and is buried at nearby Llaneilian. He was Professor of Welsh at the University College of North Wales, Bangor, from 1974 until his death. As a critic he specialized in the work of **R. Williams Parry** (1884-1956) and in the study of place-names and the lives of eminent Anglesey people.

PONTARDAWE, Swansea; large industrial village on the junction of the A474 and A4067, 8 m NE of Swansea.

The poet **David Gwenallt Jones** (1899-1968) was born in Wesley Terrace, a fact recorded by a plaque, but moved at an early age with his family to the nearby village of Alltwen, on the other side of the Tawe and overlooking the Swansea Valley. It was from Alltwen that he took his middle name, by which he is generally known. His early years were treated fictionally in an unfinished novel, *Ffwrneisiau* (1982) and in many of his poems. In rebellion against the callousness of industrial capitalism – his father was killed by molten metal in an accident at work – and against a religion lacking in social commitment, he moved first to Christian Socialism, then to Marxism, before returning to Christianity and nationalism in a Welsh context. During the first world war he was a conscientious objector and served a prison sentence in Wormwood Scrubs. His poems were published in the collections *Ysgubau'r Awen* (1939), *Eples* (1951), *Gwreiddiau* (1959), and the posthumous *Coed* (1969). For many years Gwenallt was a member of staff of the Welsh Department at the University College of Wales, Aberystwyth.

In the open-air theatre at Ynysderw there is a memorial fountain commemorating, besides Gwenallt, **T.J. Morgan** (1907-86) and **Tom Ellis Lewis** (1900-78), both of whom were prominent literary figures born in the Swansea Valley.

PONTARDDULAIS, on the boundary between Carmarthenshire and Swansea; industrial town off the M4 and on the A48 about 4 m NE of Llanelli.

At Hendy, on the Carmarthenshire side of the

town, the poet and theologian **Gwili (John Jenkins**; 1872-1936) was born. His main contribution was *Hanfod Duw a Pherson Crist* (1931), a history of theology in Wales. He won the Crown at the National Eisteddfod and served as Archdruid from 1932 to 1936. He published only one volume of poems in Welsh, namely *Caniadau* (1934) and one, *Poems* (1920), in English. A jovial man, much liked by his contemporaries, he was a friend of the poet **Edward Thomas** (1878-1917), who relied on him for information about the history and literature of Wales. In his poem 'Roads' Thomas wrote:

Helen of the roads,
The mountain ways of Wales
And the Mabinogion tales
Is one of the true gods.

PONTERWYD, Cardiganshire; village on the A44 about 13 m E of Aberystwyth near the upper reaches of the river Rheidol.

George Borrow (1803-81), author of *Wild Wales* (1862), stayed at the inn, now named after him, during his tour of Wales in the summer and autumn of 1854; the inn-sign bears a portrait of him.

The Celtic scholar **John Rhŷs** (1840-1915) was born at Aberceiro-fach, on the left about 1 m after leaving the village and in Cwm Rheidol in the direction of the Nant-y-moch reservoir; there is a plaque on the house. He became the first Professor of Celtic at Oxford in 1877 and Principal of Jesus College in 1895. Primarily a philologist, he published a number of important articles and books about the Celtic languages, including *Lectures on Welsh Philology* (1877), and edited the texts of the *Mabinogion* (1887), *The Red Book of Hergest* (1890) and *The Book of Llandaf* (1893). He also had an interest in archaeology, mythology, folk-literature and ethnology, publishing many books on these subjects, notably *Celtic Folklore, Welsh and Manx* (2 vols., 1901).

PONTLLYFNI, see under **CLYNNOG FAWR**

PONTNEWYNYDD, Torfaen; industrial village on the A403 about 3 m from Pontypool.

The poet **Myfanwy Haycock** (1913-63) was born at Glyndwr in the Mount Pleasant part of the village. She published four volumes of verse: *Fantasy* (1937), *Poems* (1944), *More Poems* (1945), and the posthumous collection, *Mountain over Paddington* (1964). A selection of her work, which is steeped in the landscape of her native Gwent, was published as *Hill of Dreams* in 1987.

William Williams (1850-1917) was known as 'The Poet of Mount Pleasant' on account of his lifelong adherence to the Congregationalist chapel of that name. For nearly fifty years he was employed as a clerk by the Great Western Railway at Pontypool. His only volume of poems was *Songs of Siluria* (1916).

PONTRHYDFENDIGAID, Cardiganshire; village on the B4343 about 7 m NE of Tregaron.

The ruined abbey of Strata Florida (W. Ystrad Fflur) was once one of the most celebrated in Wales; it was the burial-place of the Princes of the House of Dinefwr. There is a splendid memorial inside the walls, inscribed in Welsh and Latin and erected by the Honourable Society of Cymmrodorion in 1951, to the memory of the great poet **Dafydd ap Gwilym** (*fl.*1315/20-1350/70). He is traditionally said to be

The remains of Strata Florida abbey,
the burial-place of Dafydd ap Gwilym

buried under a yew-tree at the front of the church; the spot is marked by a very shabby stone with painted lettering and is easily missed. It should be noted – without, of course, taking sides in the argument – that the abbey at Talley near Llandeilo also has a claim to being the poet's last resting-place.

Also in the churchyard is a large memorial to Sir David James (1887-1967), a native of the village who spent some of his immense wealth in supporting local culture such as the Eisteddfod held annually at Pontrhydfendigaid, and other good causes. The close proximity of his grave to that of the poet drew from **Harri Webb** (1920-94) the squib entitled 'Lines written in a Country Churchyard':

Who says that our nation
Does not honour its poets?
Is not Dafydd ap Gwilym
Buried in the same sacred spot
As Sir David James?

PONTYPOOL, Torfaen; large industrial town at the junction of the A4043, A472 and A4042 about 7 m N of Newport.

Edmund Jones (1702-93), known to his contemporaries as *Yr Hen Broffwyd* (The Old Prophet) and to later generations as Edmund Jones the Transh, built an Independent chapel at Tranch, on the W side of the town on the A472. He was said to have sold his library for £15 in order to complete the work which his congregation, which paid him only £3 a year, were too poor to afford. He is remembered as the author of *An Historical Account of the Parish of Aberystruth* (1779) and *A Relation of Apparitions in Wales* (1780). A tireless recorder of religious events, he kept voluminous diaries, some of which were rescued from use as wrapping paper in a Pontypool shop after his death. He was born at Penllwyn Uchaf (now a ruin) in the parish of Aberystruth, near what later became Nant-y-glo, at the top end of the valley of the Ebbw Fach on the A467.

The district around Blaenafon, on the A4043 to the N of Pontypool, has recently come to be called 'Cordell Country' because it is the setting for some of the novels of **Alexander Cordell (George Alexander Graber**; 1914-97).

PONTYPRIDD, Rhondda Cynon Taff; industrial town at the confluence of the rivers Taff and Rhondda on the A470.

Here, in 1856, the words of *'Hen Wlad fy Nhadau'*, which later became the Welsh national anthem, were written by **Evan James (Ieuan ap Iago**; 1809-78); his son James James (Iago ap Ieuan;1833-1902) composed the music. The anthem is sung wherever Welsh people gather:

> Mae hen wlad fy nhadau yn annwyl imi,
> Gwlad beirdd a chantorion, enwogion o fri,
> Ei gwrol ryfelwyr, gwladgarwyr tra mad,
> Dros ryddid collasant eu gwaed.

*Monument to Evan and James James
in Ynysangharad Park, Pont y pridd*

(Trans. The old land of my fathers is dear to me / Land of poets and singers, men of renown / Her brave warriors, excellent patriots / Shed their blood for freedom.)

The plaque which commemorates them is on the gable-end of the last building in Mill Street, but it can be seen only from Sardis Road. The nearby Welsh primary school is known as Ysgol Evan James. A bronze monument to father and son, the work of W. Goscombe John, was erected in Ynys Angharad Park, on the E bank of the Taff near the Old Bridge, in 1930.

The poet **Brynfab (Thomas Williams**; 1848-1927), a native of Cwmamman, Aberdare, settled at the age of 25 at Hendre, a farm on the hillside above Glyntaf to the S of the town opposite Trefforest, and remained there for the rest of his life. He was a prominent member of the literary circle known as *Clic y Bont*, a group of poets who met regularly in Pontypridd; none wrote verse of any lasting merit but their group was typical of the many bardic circles which flourished in the industrial parts of south Wales during the 19th century. His verse has not been collected but his novel, *Pan oedd Rhondda'n bur* (1912), gives a vivid account of life in the Rhondda before the discovery of coal.

The University of Glamorgan, established in 1992 and before that the Polytechnic of Wales, occupies a hillside site off Llantwit Road on the W side of the Taff at Trefforest.

PORTH, Rhondda Cynon Taff; industrial town at the confluence of the Rhondda Fawr and Rhondda Fach on the A4225 about 3m NW of Pontypridd.

Gwyn Thomas (1913-81), novelist and playwright, was born and brought up at 196 High Street, Cymmer, in the direction of Trebanog; the house has a plaque. He attended Porth County School and, after studying at St Edmund Hall, Oxford, taught Spanish and French at Cardigan and Barry. But Porth remained the centre of his world and Rhondda society is vividly and sometimes hilariously portrayed in his novels and stories. They include *The Dark Philosophers* (1946), *The Alone to the Alone* (1947), *The World Cannot Hear You* (1950), *A Frost on my Frolic* (1953) and *A Point of Order* (1956). Many of his *bons mots* are memorable, for example: 'There are still parts of Wales where the only concession to gaiety is a striped shroud' and 'I am a true Welsh aristocrat: in a good light I can trace my ancestry all the way back to my father'. The writer's ashes were scattered at Llanwynno on the hill between the rivers Rhondda Fach and Cynon, near the Brynffynnon Arms, one of his favourite spots.

The poet and novelist **Rhydwen Williams** (1916-97) lived, after marrying, at Pleasant Hill, 104 Cemetery Road. He wrote mainly in Welsh but a selection of his English poems will be found in *Rhondda Poems* (1987).

PORTHMADOG, Gwynedd; small town and seaside resort on the estuary of the river Glaslyn at the junction of the A487 and A497.

According to tradition, it was from here that Prince Madoc ab Owain Gwynedd set sail in the 1170s for America. This tale, for which there is no firm evidence, gave rise to the belief that the Mandans were the descendants of the Welshman and his crew. Encouraged by the fabrications of **Iolo Morganwg (Edward Williams**; 1747-1826), the myth caught the imagination of Welsh Radicals in the 18th century and became an incentive for emigration to America among impoverished Welsh people awakening to a new sense of nationhood.

The story has nothing to do with William Madocks (1773-1828), the English industrialist who built much of Porthmadog and neighbouring Tremadog, about 1m to the N, which were named after him. He spent a fortune on the construction of a road from London to Holyhead and, between 1808 and 1811, completed the embankment later known as the Cob across Traeth Mawr, the delta of the Glaslyn river. A detailed account of his life and work is to be found in *Madocks and the Wonder of Wales* (1967) by Elizabeth Beazley.

Madock's philanthropy inspired the English poet **Percy Bysshe Shelley** (1792-1822) to help him raise money for the project. The Shelleys rented Tan-yr-allt, a house belonging to Madocks, from the autumn of 1812 to February 1813, when intruders fired shots at the poet one evening and they were obliged to leave the district. The reasons for the attack remain obscure but may have arisen out of local resentment at his Radical political views.

The English writer **T.E. Lawrence** (1888-1935), who became known as Lawrence of Arabia after his exploits during the first world war, recounted in his *Seven Pillars of Wisdom* (1926), was born at Gorphwysfa, Tremadog, where this fact is recorded by a plaque.

The poet **William Jones** (1896-1961), author of the poem 'Y Llanc Ifanc o Lŷn', translated by **Harri Webb** (1920-94) as 'Young Fellow from Llŷn', lived at 14 Church Street in Tremadog. He published two collections of poems, *Adar Rhiannon* (1947) and *Sonedau a Thelynegion* (1950). His grave is in the cemetery adjoining Bethel Chapel above Penmorfa.

The poet **Eifion Wyn (Eliseus Williams;** 1867-1926) was born at 10 Garth Terrace, a house which now has a plaque, and at 28 Heol Newydd, where he lived, the mystic mark of the Gorsedd of Bards can be seen above the door. He was a teacher in the town and later clerk and accountant to the North Wales Slate Company. His reputation as a lyricist is based on his book *Telynegion Maes a Môr* (1906), which contains a number of poems still popular as recitation pieces. For example, in *'Y Llanw'* he wrote (trans.):

> It's worth turning exile now and again
> And from little Wales to go,
> If only to come back to Wales
> And be able to love her more.

The local primary school is named after Eifion Wyn. He was buried in the village of Chwilog about 9 m to the E on the B4354, where the monument on his grave was unveiled by David Lloyd George in 1934.

Siop Eifionydd, a Welsh bookshop, is at 115 High Street, Porthmadog.

PORTMEIRION, Gwynedd; village off the A487 to the S of Minffordd and on the estuary known as Traeth Bach.

In 1925 the mansion formerly known as Aber Iâ became the property of the architect **Clough Williams-Ellis** (1883-1978) who transformed it into the focal point of a village rebuilt in an Italianate style, for which reason it has been called 'the Xanadu of Wales'. The English writer **Noël Coward** (1899-1973) is said to have written *Blithe Spirit* while staying at Portmeirion in 1940. Williams-Ellis wrote two volumes of autobiography, *Architect Errant* (1971) and *Around the World in Ninety Years* (1978), as well as *Portmeirion, the Place and its Meaning* (1963).

His wife, **Amabel Williams-Ellis** (1894-1984), wrote a collection of short stories, *Volcano* (1931), and four novels: *Noah's Ark* (1926), *To Tell the Truth* (1933), *The Big Firm* (1938) and *Learn to Love First* (1939); she also collaborated with her husband in the writing of a short novel, *Headlong down the Years* (1951), which was intended to combat what they considered to be the despoiliation of the north Wales countryside by the building of a hydro-electric power station.

PRESTATYN, Flintshire; seaside resort on the junction of the A548 and the A547 about 5 m E of Rhyl.

The poet **Gwilym R. Tilsley** (1911-97) lived for some twenty years after his retirement from the Wesleyan ministry at Estyn in Pen Dyffryn Road.

PWLLHELI, Gwynedd; market-town on the A497 on the N coast of Cardigan Bay.

The poet **Albert Evans-Jones (Cynan**;1895-1970) was born at Liverpool House (now council offices) in Penlan Street. He attended the local primary school before going to college at Bangor. He won the Crown at the National Eisteddfod in 1921 with his poem *'Mab y Bwthyn'*. There is a commemorative tablet on Ffynnon Felin Bach, a well where as a boy he used to draw water for his grandmother; it is on the left as one leaves the town along Lôn Llŷn.

Also in Penlan Street is the home, marked by a plaque, of the philosopher **John Robert Jones** (1911-70). He began his academic career in 1937 as a lecturer at the University College of Wales,

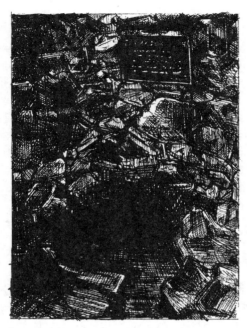

*Ffynnon Felin Bach and a plaque in memory of
Cynan's poem, near Pwllheli*

Aberystwyth, and was appointed Professor of
Philosophy at the University College, Swansea, in
1952. He is remembered in Wales as the author of
essays on the crisis of Wales in the 20th century,
notably *Prydeindod* (1966), *A Raid i'r Iaith ein
Gwahanu?* (1967), *Gwaedd yng Nghymru* (1970) and
Ac Onide (1970); the last-named is his most
substantial work. For him community meant the
Welsh language and his emphasis on the
interconnection between land and language helped
to fuel the campaigns of *Cymdeithas yr Iaith Gymraeg*
(The Welsh Language Society). J.R. Jones is buried
in Pwllheli.

At Penyberth, a farmhouse near Penrhos about 2

m W of Pwllheli on the A499, there is a memorial to **Saunders Lewis** (1893-1985), **D.J. Williams** (1885-1970) and **Lewis Valentine** (1893-1986), the three Welsh Nationalists who committed a token act of arson at an RAF bombing-school that was being built here in 1936. The house was significant in the Welsh literary tradition in that it had been the home of a Recusant family in the 16th and early 17th centuries. There was widespread opposition to the bombing-school in Wales and the incident had a deep influence on many writers, including **Robert Williams Parry** (1884-1956). When the three appeared at Caernarfon the jury failed to reach a verdict but at the Old Bailey in the following year they were found guilty and sent to prison.

The bookshop known as *Llên Llŷn* is situated on Pwllheli square.

RESOLVEN (W. Resolfen), Neath Port Talbot; former mining village 6 m NE of Neath off the A465 and on the B4434.

Bert Lewis Coombes (1894-1974) came here from Madley, Herefords., in 1912 and spent the rest of his life in the village, working as a collier in the local pit. His books, *These Poor Hands* (1939), *Those Clouded Hills* (1944) and *Miners' Day* (1945), describe the harsh conditions prevailing in the mines of south Wales during the years between the world wars. He and his wife lived first at 10 New Inn Place, then at Oak Lodge, Rheola, then at Ynys-gron in Glyn Neath and finally at Nant-y-fedwen, a smallholding near Onllwyn. He is buried in the graveyard of St Mary's Church, Resolven.

RHEWL, Denbighshire; village 2 m NW of Ruthin on the A525.

The patriotic writer **Robert Ambrose Jones (Emrys ap Iwan**; 1848-1906), spent the last six years of his life here and is buried in the graveyard. He was a tireless, prolific writer and an influential literary critic.

RHOSGADFAN, Gwynedd; village about 2 m S of Caernarfon, between the A487 and A4085.

The writer **Richard Hughes Williams (Dic Tryfan**; 1878?-1919) was born at Hyfrydle, near the village square. After working in local quarries, he went to Liverpool and London and took up journalism, but returned to Wales to work on newspapers in Caernarfon, Aberystwyth and Llanelli. His ambition was to be a novelist but his health was ruined while he was employed in a munitions factory at Pembrey during the first world war, and he died soon afterwards. Two volumes of his stories, which are mostly about quarrymen and

Cae'r Gors, the home of Kate Roberts, at Rhosgadfan

their families, appeared during his lifetime, namely *Straeon y Chwarel* (n.d.) and *Tair Stori Fer* (1916), and a selection was published posthumously in 1919.

The novelist and short-story writer **Kate Roberts** (1891-1985) was brought up at Cae'r Gors, a croft now partially restored as a monument, from the age of about five; she was born at Bryngwyrfai. The author of some 15 novels and collections of stories, notably *Traed mewn Cyffion* (1936; trans. Idwal Walters and John Idris Jones, *Feet in Chains*, 1977), *Y Byw sy'n Cysgu* (1956; trans. Ll. Wyn Griffith, *The Living Sleep*, 1978) and *Te yn y Grug* 1959 (trans. Ll.Wyn Griffith, *Tea in the Heather*, 1968) she is generally considered to be the 20th century's finest writer of fiction in Welsh. Much of her early work deals with her native district at a time when the slate-quarrying industry was in its heyday, while her later novels, written in Denbigh, often portray old people living alone in a harsh modern world. On the moorland road above the village, known as Y Lôn Wen, there is a memorial to her at a spot often mentioned in her writing, with splendid views to the N and NW.

RHOSLLANNERCHRUGOG, see under **LLANGOLLEN**

RHOSTRYFAN, Gwynedd; village on a minor road off the A487 between Bontnewydd and Groeslon.

The poet and novelist **Glasynys (Owen Wynne Jones**; 1828-70) was born at Ty'n-y-ffridd, a small-holding between Rhostryfan and Glanrhyd, where there is a plaque. He is remembered mainly as the author of books about the pre-Methodist traditions of Wales, including ghost-stories and fairy-tales.

RHYDARGAEAU, Carmarthenshire; village on the A485 about 5 m N of Carmarthen.

The prose-writer **David Davies** (1849-1926) was born at a house known as Penstâr, but moved with his family to Trefforest, near Pontypridd, when he was nine. He became a staunch opponent of the Established Church and joined the Baptists, and the last years of his life were spent at Penarth, near Cardiff. The contrast between life in industrial Glamorgan and the green arcady of Rhydargaeau, and his antipathy towards the Anglican Church, animate his books *Echoes from the Welsh Hills* (1883), *John Vaughan and his Friends* (1897) and *Reminiscences of my Country and People* (1925).

RHYDCYMERAU, see under **LLANSAWEL**

RHYD-DDU, Gwynedd; village on the A4085 in the upper valley of the Gwyrfai at the W foot of Snowdon.

The poet and essayist **T.H. Parry-Williams** (1887-1975) was born at Tŷ'r Ysgol, the school house

Tŷ'r Ysgol, Rhyd-ddu, where T.H. Parry-Williams was brought up

where his father was headmaster and where an exhibition illustrating his life and work can now be visited. The plaque on the house bears the inscription *'Mae darnau ohonof ar wasgar hyd y fro'* (Pieces of me are scattered throughout the district). He first won recognition as a poet when he won both Chair and Crown at the National Eisteddfod in 1912 and again in 1915. He was Professor of Welsh at the University College of Wales, Aberystwyth, from 1920 to 1952. A volume of his collected essays, *Casgliad o Ysgrifau*, was published in 1984 and his collected poems, *Casgliad o Gerddi*, in 1987. Some of his poems are among the finest ever written in Welsh and he was the first Welsh writer to use the essay form, of which he was a master. The influence of the district of Rhyd-ddu is to be seen in both his verse and prose, as in his poem *'Hon'*, translated here by the American poet Joseph P. Clancy:

Why should I give a hang about Wales? It's by a
mere fluke of fate
That I live in its patch. On a map it does not rate

Higher than a scrap of earth in a back corner,
And a bit of a bother to those who believe in order.

And who is it lives in this spot, tell me that,
Who but the dregs of society? Please, cut it out,

This endless clatter of oneness and country and race:
You can get plenty of these, without Wales, any place.

I've long since had it with listening to the croon
Of the Cymry, indeed, forever moaning their tune . . .

Here's Snowdon and its crew; here's the land, bleak
and bare,
Here's the lake and river and crag, and look, over there,

The house where I was born. But see, between earth and
heaven,
All through the place there are voices and apparitions.

I begin to totter somewhat, and I confess,
There comes over me, so it seems, a sort of faintness;

And I feel the claws of Wales tear at my heart.
God help me, I can't get away from this spot.

A small selection of the essays of T.H. Parry-Williams was translated by Meic Stephens as *The White Stone* (1987).

RHYDLEWIS, Cardiganshire; village on the B4334 between Brynhoffnant and Hawen.

The novelist **Moelona (Elizabeth Mary Jones**; 1878-1953) was born at Moylon in the centre of the village on the road to Brynhoffnant; the house has a commemorative plaque. By profession a teacher, she was the author of about thirty books for adults and children, notably her most famous novel, *Teulu Bach Nantoer* (1913). Patriotic and progressive in her view of the social status of women, she championed women's rights in her novels *Cwrs y Lli* (1927) and *Ffynnonloyw* (1939). She also translated the stories of Alphonse Daudet into Welsh under the title *Y Wers Olaf* (1921).

The mother of **Caradoc Evans** (1878-1945) brought him here as a boy to live at a house known as Lonlas, near Twrgwyn Chapel.

RHYMNEY (W. Rhymni), Caerphilly; former colliery and iron-working town on the A469 at the head of the Rhymney Valley.

The civil servant and author **Thomas Jones** (1860-1932) was born at 100 High Street, the son of a shop manager. After a distinguished academic career, he became in 1910 Secretary of the National Health Insurance Commissioners and, in 1916, Deputy Secretary of Lloyd George's cabinet. He wrote his autobiography under the title *Rhymney Memories* (1938) and published a collection of essays, *Leeks and Daffodils* (1942), in one of which he suggested, not altogether sardonically, that the valleys of south Wales should be used for bombing practice.

The poet **Idris Davies** (1905-53) was born at 16 Field Street (gone) into a mining family and went to work underground at the age of 14. He left the mines at the beginning of the General Strike of 1926 and trained as a teacher at Loughborough College and the University of Nottingham. He taught at various schools in England and Wales, latterly at Cwmsyfiog Primary School, a little to the S. The poet of industrial south Wales *par excellence*, he drew inspiration from the inter-war years of economic decline and social deprivation. Among his most famous poems is 'The Bells of Rhymney', which was set to music by Pete Seeger; it begins:

> O what can you give me?
> Say the sad bells of Rhymney.

His main collections were *Gwalia Deserta* (1938), *The Angry Summer* (1943) and *Tonypandy and Other Poems* (1945); his selected poems appeared in 1953 and his complete poems in 1994. The poet died at 7 Victoria Road and was buried in the public cemetery in Rhymney; the commemorative plaque describes him as *'Un o feibion anwylaf ac enwocaf Rhymni'* (One of Rhymney's most cherished and most famous sons). There is also a memorial plaque in the Public Library.

RUTHIN (W. Rhuthun), Denbighshire; town in the Vale of Clwyd on the junction of the A494, A525 and A526.

It is believed that **Gabriel Goodman** (1528-1601), one of the translators of the English Bible of 1568 (The Bishop's Bible), was born at Axmewe House (now Barclays Bank) or perhaps at Nantclwyd, a much older building on the same side of the street but nearer the castle. He was a benefactor of the town and the founder of Christ's Hospital and the Grammar School. There is a bust of Goodman, who also helped **William Morgan** (1545-1604) with his translation of the Welsh Bible, in the church.

The English writer **Stanley J. Weyman** (1855-1928) lived at Plas Llanrhydd from 1895 until his death. He practised as a barrister in Ruthin and for several years was chairman of the bench of magistrates. He is remembered as the author of romantic novels such as *A Gentleman of France* (1893), *The Red Cockade* (1895), *Under the Red Robe* (1896), *Count Hannibal* (1901) and *Chippinge* (1906). He and his wife are buried in the churchyard of St Meugan's at Llanrhydd under an oak tree in a grave marked by a grey granite cross; he is commemorated by a marble tablet on the S side of the church's nave.

There is a bookshop known as *Siop Elfair* at 16-18 Clwyd Street.

ST ASAPH (W. Llanelwy), Denbighshire; cathedral town on the A55 and A525, 6 m N of Denbigh.

In 1601 **William Morgan** (1545-1604), first translator of the Bible into Welsh, came from the see of Llandaf to that of St Asaph; he is buried in the cathedral, beneath the throne in the presbytery. There is a memorial to him and other translators on the N side of the cathedral.

Felicia Hemans (1793-1835), a poet of great popularity in her day who is now remembered only for her poem 'Casabianca', lived as a girl and again after her marriage at Bronwylfa, a large house on the hillside NE of the town. It was replaced by a later building, which can be seen from Mrs Hemans' Bridge, where she used to sit and write. The bridge can be reached by leaving St Asaph by Chester Street, crossing the dual carriageway and turning left along a narrow lane. She is commemorated in the cathedral by a tablet in the S aisle and a window in the N wall of the chancel. A lock of her hair and a book of her poems are on view in the Cathedral Museum. Her *Collected Works*, in seven volumes, were published with a memoir by her sister in 1839.

H.M. Stanley (1841-1904) was brought up in the workhouse in the town; the local hospital is named after him.

Although most of the tombstones in the parish church have been removed, the grave of the multilingual Dic Aberdaron (Richard Robert Jones;1780-1843) can still be seen here; the *englyn* on his tombstone ends with the line (trans.), 'He is up there now with no language at all.'

ST DAVID'S (W. Tŷ Ddewi), Pembrokeshire; the smallest cathedral city in Britain, on the westernmost bend of the A487 nearly 1 m from the sea.

Giraldus Cambrensis (Gerald de Barri; *c.*1146-1223) was twice elected bishop (in 1176 and 1198) but failed to obtain consecration, probably because the English feared that he would make the Welsh Church independent of Canterbury. He was buried in the cathedral and an effigy in the S choir aisle may be of him.

The bookshop known as *Siop y Dyfrwr* is at 43 Non Street.

ST FAGANS see under **CARDIFF**

SEVERN BRIDGE, Monmouthshire; two bridges which carry the M4 over the Severn Estuary between Gloucestershire and Monmouthshire (although the W ends are not quite in Wales).

For the opening of the first bridge in 1966 **Harri Webb** (1920-94) wrote the well-known squib:

> Two lands at last connected
> Across the waters wide,
> And all the tolls collected
> On the English side.

The second bridge was opened in 1996 but has not yet inspired any verse, as far as is generally known.

STRATA FLORIDA, see under **PONTRHYDFENDIGAID**

SWANSEA (W. Abertawe), Swansea; large seaport and city off the M4 and on the NW shore of Swansea Bay, at the mouth of the Tawe.

The town (it became a city only in 1969) was the most important in Wales at the beginning of the 19th century but had no indigenous literary life until the beginning of the 20th.

Ann Julia Hatton (1764-1838), known to her contemporaries as Ann of Swansea, the sister of the actress Sarah Siddons, settled here in 1799 after taking a lease of Swansea Bathing House. Besides a dozen novels and two volumes of verse, she wrote a play, *Zaffine or the Knight of the Burning Cross*, in which Edmund Keane acted in Swansea in 1810.

The author **Joseph Harris (Gomer**; 1773-1825), a native of Pembrokeshire, became a Baptist minister in the town in 1801; his chapel still stands in Heol Gefn in the middle of Swansea. He also kept a day school, bookshop and printing works. It was he who, in 1814, launched the first weekly newspaper in Welsh, *Seren Gomer*. He made a lasting contribution to the literary life of Wales and it was out of admiration for him that J.D. Lewis (1859-1914) named his press at Llandysul the Gomerian Press (now Gwasg Gomer).

Amy Elizabeth Dillwyn (1845-1935) was born in Swansea and lived most of her life here. After her father's death in 1892 she managed the Dillwyn Spelter Works, her unorthodox views and way of life bringing her a reputation for eccentricity. The first of her six novels, *The Rebecca Rioter* (1880), is set in the Swansea area. From 1906 she lived at Tŷ Gwyn (now the Ocean Heights Nursing Home) in West Cross; her ashes were buried in St Paul's churchyard, Sketty. A plaque and tree commemorate her near the West Cross Hotel on Mumbles Road.

The poet **Gwyrosydd (Daniel Jones**; 1847-1920), who wrote the words of the popular hymn *'Calon Lân'*, is commemorated by a tablet in the public hall at Treboeth on the N side of the city and in the name of a street, Heol Gwyrosydd, on the mountain top near Pen-lan School.

The most famous writer born in Swansea was undoubtedly **Dylan Thomas** (1914-53), who described it as 'this ugly, lovely town'. He was born at 5 Cwmdonkin Drive, which now has a plaque, on the W side of the city in the middle-class district known as the Uplands, and this was his home until he left for London in 1934; he once referred to himself as 'the Rimbaud of Cwmdonkin Drive' and to the house where he lived as 'my nasty provincial address'. His parents sold the house in 1937 and moved to Bishopston; it is now open to the public.

The Grammar School he attended in Mount Pleasant, and where his father was English master, was severely damaged by fire-bombs in 1941, rebuilt in De La Beche Road in Sketty and renamed Bishop Gore School; what remains of the old school is now part of the Swansea Institute of Higher Education and has been renamed the Dylan Thomas Building. Much of the writer's early life forms the background to the stories in *Portrait of the Artist as a Young Dog* (1940) and to the famous *A Child's Christmas in Wales* (1968). Thomas left school in 1931 and found a job with the *South Wales Daily Post* (now the *South Wales Evening Post*).

The simple carved stone monument which stands near the entrance to Cwmdonkin Park, where he played as a child, is inscribed with a quotation from his poem 'Fern Hill':

Oh as I was young and easy in the mercy of his

means,

Time held me green and dying
Though I sang in my chains like the sea.

The shelter near the old bandstand is also a memorial to the poet. The Park is the setting for his poem 'The Hunchback in the Park' and the story 'Patricia, Edith and Arnold'.

The home of Daniel Jones (1912-93), who later became a distinguished composer, was at 8 Eversley Road; the house is still called 'Warmley'. The beginning of the friendship between the two is depicted in Thomas's story 'The Fight'.

At 69 Glanbrydan Avenue, the home of the Communist grocer Bert Trick, the young poet used to meet his friends for discussion of politics and literature.

The bookshop kept by Ralph Wishart (Ralph the Books) was at 60 Alexander Road; after Thomas's death it moved to Dillwyn Street.

The Kardomah Café, also destroyed during the heavy bombing of Swansea, was where Thomas used to meet his artistic friends, who came to be known as 'the Kardomah Boys'.

The Swansea Museum, described by the poet as 'the Museum that should have been in a museum', is in Victoria Road.

The city takes full advantage of its connection with the writer and is a centre of the Dylan Thomas industry; there is even a beer named after him. An annual Dylan Thomas Festival is held in the city and the Dylan Thomas Society of Great Britain, founded in 1977, is located here. One of the poet's favourite haunts was the Uplands Hotel.

A statue to the poet on Dylan Thomas Square is situated in the maritime quarter and in nearby Abernethy Square there is a sculpture by Robert Thomas depicting Captain Cat, one of the characters in *Under Milk Wood* (1954); of the first it has been said that the chair in which the poet sits is a good likeness.

The Dylan Thomas Centre, opened by former US President Jimmy Carter, has a bookshop and permanent exhibition about the poet's life and work. The Dylan Thomas Theatre is situated in the Maritime Quarter at the rear of the Museum.

The Dylan Thomas Centre, Swansea

Dylan's Bookstore is in Salubrious Passage, which links Wind Street with Princess Way.

The poet **Vernon Watkins** (1906-67) lived from 1913 to 1923 in Eaton Grove (now part of Eaton Crescent) and was educated at Swansea Grammar School for a year in 1915/16; his father was manager of the Wind Street Branch of Lloyds Bank. From 1931 to 1941 he lived with his parents at Heatherslade (now The Heatherslade Café) on Pennard Cliffs, some 8 m SW of Swansea, where he wrote *Ballad of the Mari Lwyd* (1941) and some of the poems in *The Lamp and the Veil* (1945) and *The Death Bell* (1954). After serving in the RAF he married in

1946 and settled at The Garth on Pennard Cliffs for the rest of his life. There he wrote the poems in *The Lady with the Unicorn* (1948) and all his subsequent work. For most of his life he worked at Lloyds Bank in St Helen's Road in Swansea; he once described himself as 'the oldest cashier' in the Bank. He died in Seattle, USA, while a visiting lecturer on modern poetry, and his ashes were scattered over the sea at Pennard. A tablet in his memory on the N wall of the church reads:

> Death cannot steal the light
> Which love has kindled
> Nor the years change it.

The *Collected Poems* of Vernon Watkins were published in 1986.

The prose-writer **Alwyn D. Rees** (1911-74) was born at Coalbrook, a house in Grovesend, the son of a winderman in a local pit. When he was a teenager his family moved to 168 Frampton Road in Gorseinon and he attended Penrheol School in that part of Swansea.

The poet **Harri Webb** (1920-94) was born at 45 Tŷ Coch Road in Sketty on the S side of the city and brought up at 58 Catherine Street in St Helen's (a district also known as Sandfields), off Oxford Street and not far from the seafront. He attended the nearby National School (gone) and Glanmor Secondary Boys' School (also gone) before entering Magdalen College, Oxford, to read Medieval and Modern Languages. He never lived in Swansea again but, always considering himself 'a Swansea Jack', he wrote extensively about his native place, notably in *The Green Desert* (1969), *A Crown for Branwen* (1974), *Rampage and Revel* (1977) and *Poems and Points* (1983); his *Collected Poems* appeared in 1995. His view of Swansea was not always rose-tinted, as in 'Redevelopment':

> Twice I have seen my native town
> By wrath and greed to ruin brought down,
> Once from the sky by those called Huns,
> And once again by her own sons.

A good deal of biographical information about Harri Webb is to be found in his books *No Half-Way House* (1997) and *A Militant Muse* (1998), both of which collect his journalistic writings. The poet died at St David's Nursing Home in St Helen's Road, Swansea, and was buried in the churchyard at Pennard, in Gower, where his family had its roots; the headstone on his grave, which is on the right of the main path and near the wall, spells his name Harry.

The poet **John Ormond** (1923-90) was born at 261 Bridge Row near the centre of Dunvant, a village on the B4296 on the W side of the city, and was educated at the University College. He joined the staff of *Picture Post* in London in 1945 but returned to Swansea four years later and became a director and producer of documentary films for BBC Wales.

The writer **Aneirin Talfan Davies (Aneirin ap Talfan**; 1909-80) lived at 78 Sketty Road and kept a chemist's shop in Heathfield Street until it was destroyed by a bomb in 1941, after which he moved to London and joined the BBC. He later returned to Wales and became Head of Programmes with BBC Wales in Cardiff.

The village of Newton, near Mumbles and on the B4593, is the scene of the controversial novel by **Saunders Lewis** (1893-1985), *Monica* (1930; trans. Meic Stephens, 1997). Before he was sacked for his part in the arson at Penyberth in 1936, Lewis was a lecturer in the Welsh Department at University

College, Swansea, and lived at 9 St Peter's Road. The novel is a searing condemnation of suburban values, a portrait of a woman dominated by lust and self-pity, and an indictment of the notion that sexual passion alone is an adequate foundation for marriage.

The village of Bishopston on the B4436 about 4 m W of Swansea was the home of **Edward 'Celtic' Davies** (1756-1831), who held the living from 1805 until his death; he is buried in the churchyard and there is a handsome tablet to his memory in the chancel of the church. Davies was one of 'the old literary clerics' who maintained an interest in the history of things Welsh at a time when such research was frowned upon by the Anglican Church.

The English novelist **Kingsley Amis** (1922-95) was a lecturer in the English Department at the University College from 1949 to 1959, when he left to teach in Cambridge. He and his wife first lived in a flat in Mumbles, then in The Grove in the Uplands and lastly at 53 Glanmor Road in the same district. Both *Lucky Jim* (1954) and *That Uncertain Feeling* (1955) drew on his experiences as a lecturer at Swansea, but whereas the former takes place in a provincial English university, the latter is set against the Welsh background of Swansea, thinly disguised as 'Aberdarcy'. John Lewis, the librarian, works at the town library in Alexandra Road and is taken by the predatory Mrs Gruffydd-Williams on amorous car-trips into the Gower. He secures the post of librarian but throws it away when he realizes that he has been appointed only through the influence of Mrs Gruffydd-Williams on her husband, who is chairman of the Library Committee. The novel is genuinely comic, with many insights into the more pretentious aspects of Welsh middle-class culture, which Amis clearly saw as distracting from the authentic virtues of the Welsh. The novel was made into a film in 1962 under the title *Only Two Can Play* in which Peter Sellers played the hapless librarian John Lewis, Kenneth Griffith his obsequious colleague Ieuan Jenkins and Richard Attenborough the ghastly local playwright, Gareth Probert. Amis dealt with the same milieu in his pamphlet of six poems entitled *The Evans Country* (1962) which is dedicated 'To the Patrons and Staff of the Newton Inn, Mumbles' and ends with the verse:

> There's more to local life today,
> I know, than what I've found to say:
> But when you start recording it
> You've got to tone it down a bit.

Despite his image as an ebullient Englishman, Amis evidently found the town and people of Swansea congenial and also set his late novel *The Old Devils* (1986) there. Alun Weaver, a professional media-Welshman, returns to Wales to write a novel about the country but he has been so long under the shadow of the dead poet Brydan (the resemblance to Dylan Thomas is striking) that he will never create anything of his own. Around him gather a set of ageing friends who are as amusing as they are pathetic, and whose depiction in the novel caused a good deal of speculation as to the real-life people on whom they may have been modelled.

J.R. Jones (1911-70), Professor of Philosophy at the University College from 1952, lived at 64 Eaton Crescent.

The prose-writer and scholar **Thomas John Morgan** (1907-86) lived at Cwrt Herbert in the village of Bishopston. He was Professor of Welsh at the University College from 1961 until his retirement.

A selection of poetry and prose by writers associated with Swansea will be found in James A. Davies (ed.), *A Swansea Anthology* (1996).

SYCHARTH, Denbighshire; house on a minor road very close to the border with England, about 3 m S of Llansilin and reached from the B4396 or B4580.

Here Owain Glyndŵr (*c*.1354-*c*.1416), the national hero of the Welsh, had a home until he rose in revolt against the English Crown in 1400. The poet **Iolo Goch** (*c*.1325-*c*.1398), writing in the 1380s, drew an idyllic picture of life at Sycharth. The site of the house, which is on private land, can be visited by prior arrangement.

TALGARREG, Cardiganshire; village 6 m SE of New Quay at the junction of the B4338 and the B4459.

The cottage known – not surprisingly – as Y Bwthyn where **Dewi Emrys (David Emrys James; 1881-1952)** spent his last years stands opposite the Glanyrafon Arms and just before the school on the road into the village from Synod Inn; the house has a commemorative plaque. The poet is buried in the graveyard of Pisgah chapel where his grave bears the inscription, composed by the poet: '*Melys hedd wedi aml siom / Distawrwydd wedi storom*'. (Sweet peace after many a disappointment / Silence after storm). After serving as a minister with the Independents, he took up journalism in London in 1918, and led a bohemian life in London before returning to Talgarreg in 1940. He won the Crown at the National Eisteddfod in 1926 and the Chair four times between 1929 and 1948. Two volumes of his Welsh verse appeared during his lifetime, namely *Y Cwm Unig* (1929) and *Cerddi'r Bwthyn* (1950); a commemorative collection, *Wedi Storom*, was published in 1965. As **David Emrys** he also published a volume of poems in English, *Rhymes of the Road* (1928).

The poet **Thomas Jacob Thomas** (1873-1945) was born at Sarnicol, a house about 2 m to the W at the junction of two minor roads in the direction of Capel Cynon; he took the name by which he was generally known from this house. A slate plaque is set into a stone wall which forms a gatepost belonging to the farm Allt Maen; it bears the inscription (trans.): 'And I shall come back to this quiet spot / From the four corners of the earth.' Sarnicol, now a ruin, stands in a field about 500 yards away on the other side of the crossroads. He won the Chair at the National Eisteddfod in 1913 and between 1898 and 1944 published ten volumes of verse and prose which were popular because of their local appeal and biting wit. Although he spent many years as a teacher at schools in England and south-east Wales, latterly at Quakers' Yard, near Merthyr Tydfil, where he was headmaster, Sarnicol's milieu as a writer was Banc Siôn Cwilt, the high moorland between Post Bach and Cross Hands, Cardiganshire. He is buried at Bwlch-y-groes.

About 2 m S of Talgarreg, off the B4459, stands Castellhywel, the home of **David Davis** (1745-1827), who was known as **Dafis Castellhywel**. His famous school was opened here in 1782. He is buried in the churchyard at Llanwenog, on the A475 to the E of Rhydowen.

TALLEY, see under **LLANDEILO**

TALSARNAU, Gwynedd; village on the A496 between Harlech and Maentwrog; also the name of the surrounding area.

The writer **Gwyneth Vaughan (Annie Harriet Hughes**; 1852-1910) was born at Talsarnau, a miller's daughter, and is buried near the gate of the churchyard.

The novelist **Richard Hughes** (1900-76) was staying at Harlech for his school holidays when, in 1916, he discovered a one-roomed cottage which he rented out of his pocket-money. The cottage, known as Ysgol Fach, on the estate of Maesyneuadd, can be seen from the mountain road, about 3 m above the village. Hughes returned to Talsarnau with his wife and children in 1947, and settled at Môr Edrin, a house on the shores of the Dwyryd estuary opposite Portmeirion. Here he began to write his long novel *The Human Predicament*, of which the first part, *The Fox in the Attic*, was published in 1961 and the second, *The Wooden Shepherdess*, in 1973. His other major novel is *A High Wind in Jamaica* (1929). He died at his home and is buried in the graveyard of the church at Llanfihangel-y-traethau about 1 m S on the Ynys, where he had been churchwarden.

TALWRN, Anglesey; village less than 2 m NE of Llangefni on the B5109.

The poet **Gruffudd ab yr Ynad Coch** was born in the parish of Llanddyfnan in the 13th century. He is famous for having composed an elegy for Llywelyn ap Gruffudd, the last prince of independent Wales, killed by the forces of Edward I at Cilmeri, near Builth, on 11 December 1282. The poem is the most powerful expression of utter dismay ever written in the Welsh language and conveys the sense of loss and foreboding felt among the Welsh at the death of Llywelyn and the fall of the House of Gwynedd. A memorial to the poet, erected in 1991, stands on the village square.

TAL-Y-BONT-ON-USK, see under **BRECON**

TAL-Y-SARN, Gwynedd; village on the B4418 about 6 m S of Caernarfon.

The poet **Robert Williams Parry** (1884-1956) was born at Rhiwafon, 37 Station Road (now Ffordd yr Orsaf), which has a commemorative plaque. His birth was registered twice within a fortnight; on the first certificate the name of the house was given as Madoc View and on the second, Rhiwafon; the poet always used the latter name. There is a simple but impressive memorial to him in the village which bears his name, dates and the word '*Bardd*' (Poet). He first won a reputation as a poet when he won the Chair at the National Eisteddfod in 1911 with his poem '*Yr Haf*', and thereafter he was known as '*Bardd yr Haf*' (The Poet of Summer).

The writer and journalist **Gwilym R. Jones** (1903-93) lived as a boy at Cloth Hall in the High Street and **Idwal Jones** (1910-85) at 7 Cavour Terrace. The latter is remembered as the author of a series of radio-scripts about the adventures of a private detective named Gari Tryfan, a Welsh equivalent of Dick Barton, special agent, which were broadcast on the Welsh Home Service of the BBC during the 1940s.

TINTERN (W. Tindyrn), Monmouthshire; village on the A466 about 5 m N of Chepstow.

The Cistercian abbey on the bank of the Wye,

founded in 1131, has attracted the attention of many English writers, among the earliest of whom were **Thomas Gray** (1716-71) and **William Gilpin** (1702-1804). The latter's *Observations on the River Wye* (1782) was carried by Dorothy and **William Wordsworth** during their visit to Tintern in 1798 and the poet drew on Gilpin's work when writing his 'Lines composed a few miles above Tintern Abbey', the most famous poem of all those inspired by the countryside hereabouts. It contains the lines:

> How oft, in spirit, have I turned to thee,
> O sylvan Wye! thou wanderer through the woods,
> How often has my spirit turned to thee!

There were more modest responses to the abbey in 'The Banks of Wye' (1811) by **Robert Bloomfield** (1766-1823) and in 'Chepstow' by **Edward Davies** (1718-89). **Francis Kilvert** (1840-79), who visited Tintern in 1875, thought it 'almost too perfect to be entirely picturesque'.

TIR IARLL, see under **LLANGYNWYD**

TRAWSFYNYDD, Gwynedd; village on the W side of the A470 near its junction with the A4212.

A bronze statue in the village commemorates the poet **Ellis Humphrey Evans** (**Hedd Wyn**; 1887-1917), portrayed as a shepherd, who was born at his mother's home, Pen-lan, and brought up at the nearby farm known as Yr Ysgwrn, now a small museum, which stands in a copse on the slopes of Moel Oernant facing Cwm Prysor, less than 1 m along a narrow road from the bridge in the village. One of his most famous poems, '*Atgo*', contains the verse (trans.):

>Only the purple moon
>>On the bare mountain's rim,
>And the sound of the old river Prysor
>>Singing in the cwm.

Evans worked for his father before enlisting with the Royal Welch Fusiliers during the first world war and was killed in action at Pilkem Ridge in July 1917. He was posthumously awarded the Chair at the National Eisteddfod held in Birkenhead in the following September. The announcement of his death was received with great emotion by the audience and during the chairing ceremony the empty chair was draped in black. A collection of his poems was published under the title *Cerddi'r Bugail* in 1918. The story of Hedd Wyn was made into a powerful film in 1992. The inscription on Hedd Wyn's memorial is an *englyn* of his own composition:

>Ei Aberth nid â heibio – ei wyneb
>>Annwyl nid â'n ango,
>Er i'r Almaen ystaenio
>Ei dwrn dur yn ei waed o.

(Trans. His sacrifice will not be in vain, his dear face will not be forgotten, although Germany has stained her iron fist with his blood.) This verse was originally written in memory of Deio Evans of Blaenau Ffestiniog, who was killed at the front in 1916.

TREALAW, Rhondda Cynon Taff; former mining village in the Rhondda Valley on the A4085 about 3 m NW of Porth.

The poet and dramatist **James Kitchener Davies** (1902-52) lived from 1940 until his death at Aeron in Brithweunydd; from 1926 he had lived at 136 Kenry Street in Tonypandy. A militant on behalf of Plaid Cymru, he was a teacher of Welsh at Pentre

Secondary School. His long poem '*Sŵn y Gwynt sy'n Chwythu*', broadcast by the BBC while the poet was on his death-bed, is one of the finest long poems in the Welsh language. It includes the lines (trans.):

> I wanted to save the Rhondda Valley for the nation
> and the nation itself as a fertile garden.

He also wrote a play, *Cwm Glo* (1935) which dealt in plain language with the dire effects of the economic depression on the mining valleys of south Wales. The writer was buried at Llethr Ddu, the cemetery near his home.

TREDEGAR (W. Tredegyr), Caerphilly; industrial town off the B4422 and on the A4048 in the Sirhywi Valley.

The Scottish writer **A.J. Cronin** (1896-1981) lived during the 1930s at The Glen in Poplar Road. A doctor, he worked as a general practitioner and later as an inspector of mines in south Wales. While living in Tredegar he wrote *The Citadel* (1937) and collected material for *The Stars Look Down* (1941), both of which are set in the industrial valleys.

TREFDRAETH, Anglesey; village on a minor road between Llangadwaladr and Cerrigceinwen.

Trefeilyr, the home of the 12th-century court-poets **Meilyr Brydydd**, chief poet to Gruffudd ap Cynan, and his son, **Gwalchmai ap Meilyr**, stands off the B4422. They belonged to an illustrious line of poets who held land in return for their eulogies, a tradition commemorated by the place-names Tremeilyr and Trewalchmai in Anglesey.

The poet **Hwfa Môn (Rowland Williams**; 1823-1905) was born at Pen-y-graig, near the village, but moved with his family when five years old to live at Rhostrehwfa, near Llangefni, and from that place he took his bardic name. Although he published two collections of his verse, both under the title *Gwaith Barddonol* (1883, 1903), he is remembered only as Archdruid, in which office he served from 1895 until his death.

TRE-FIN, Pembrokeshire; village on a minor road off the A487 about 2m NE of Llanrhian.

The poet **Edgar Phillips (Trefin**; 1889-1962) was born at Rose Cottage. A tailor by trade, he was seriously wounded during the first world war and later became a Welsh teacher at Pontllan-fraith in Monmouthshire. He served as Archdruid from 1960 to 1962 and won the Chair at the National Eisteddfod in 1933. He published four collections of verse for children and *Caniadau Trefin* (1950). The famous poem *'Melin Trefin'*, which celebrates the old mill in the village, is not by Phillips but by **William Crwys Williams** (1875-1968).

TREFRIW, Gwynedd; village in the Vale of Conwy on the B5106 about 7 m N of Betws-y-coed.

The poet and printer **Dafydd Jones** (1703-85) lived for many years at Tan-yr-Yw, a small cottage which still bears a plaque proclaiming in Welsh that he was 'the owner of the first printing press in north Wales'. He delighted in collecting and transcribing ancient Welsh manuscripts – he described himself as 'a student of old things'. His press, founded in 1776, when he was 73, turned out some shoddily printed books but they sold well among the common people because they were cheap and in Welsh. Some scholars referred to him derisively, but his contribution to the literacy of the Welsh people was not inconsiderable.

The poet **Ieuan Glan Geirionydd (Evan Evans;** 1795-1855) was born at Tan-y-celyn and educated in the school held in the church and then at the Free School in Llanrwst. He was the most versatile Welsh poet of the 19th century and wrote brilliantly in both the traditional and free metres. Among his most famous poems are *'Ysgoldy Rhad Llanrwst'*, *'Glan Geirionydd'* and *'Caniad y Gog i Arfon'*, and his hymn, *'Ar lan Iorddonen ddofn'* is still sung by Welsh congregations. He is buried in the graveyard of St Mary's Church. The English inscription on his tombstone reads as follows: 'Sacred to the memory of Rev. Evan Evans (Ieuan Glan Geirionydd), incumbent of Rhyl, who brought a life of bardic distinction and ministerial usefulness to a happy close on the 21st day of January, 1855, in the 60th year of his age.'

Gwilym Cowlyd (William John Roberts; 1827-1904) was born at Tyddyn Gwilym in Cwm Cowlyd; he was a nephew of Ieuan Glan Geirionydd and earned a living as a printer and bookseller. As a poet he wrote little of lasting significance but is noteworthy because he tried to establish a Gorsedd of Bards to rival that created by **Iolo Morganwg (Edward Williams;** 1747-1826). He called his assembly *Arwest Glan Geirionydd* and it met annually on the shores of Llyn Geirionydd in Caernarfonshire with himself as Chief Poet. The venture ended in tears, with Gwilym Cowlyd declared bankrupt and generally regarded as a rank eccentric.

The poet **T. Arfon Williams** (1935-98) lived at Y Derlwyn, Rhiw-las, near the village.

TREGARON, Cardiganshire; village on the junction of the A485 and B4343, 14 m S of Aberystwyth and 9 m NE of Lampeter.

The prose-writer and historian **W. Ambrose Bebb** (1894-1955) was brought up at a farm known as Camer Fawr after his family moved here from Goginan, near Aberystwyth, and was educated at the Grammar School in Tregaron. The house is the first farm after leaving Tregaron on the B4343 in the direction of Pontrhydfendigaid.

The poet and dramatist **James Kitchener Davies** (1902-52) was born at Llain near Llwynpiod, to the W of the village. The croft is now a ruin and can be reached only by crossing agricultural land with permission from the owner. His verse-play, *Meini Gwagedd* (1945), is set in Cors Caron, the nearby bog. The writer is commemorated by a plaque on the wall of Llwynpiod chapel, just off the B4578.

TREGARTH, see under **BETHESDA**

TREGROES, Cardiganshire; village on a minor road off the A475 between Rhydlewis and Ffostrasol.

The preacher and hymn-writer **Christmas Evans** (1776-1838), born here on Christmas Day, is commemorated by a plaque on the wall of the school in the centre of the village.

The poet and story-writer **D. Jacob Davies** (1916-74) was born at Penlon, which can be found by turning right at the crossroads in the centre of the village and then proceeding up the hill. A Unitarian minister, he was well-known as a humourist and popular broadcaster. He was the author of more than two thousand radio scripts and his book

Dyddiau Main (1967) is a collection of lively short stories. His finest work is *Y Mynydd Teimladwy* (1970), a collection of poems about the death of his young son Amlyn.

TREGYNON, Powys; village on the B4389 about 5 m N of Newtown.

The hymn-writer and pamphleteer **Thomas Olivers** (1725-99) was born here. He had little formal education and was converted to the Wesleyan cause while working as a shoemaker. Among his tracts were *A Scourge to Calumny* (1774) and *A Rod for the Reviler* (1777) in which he attacked the Calvinistic view of predestination. But he is remembered for two of his hymns: 'Come, Immortal King of Glory' and 'The God of Abram Praise'. Although he was dismissed as an itinerant preacher by John Wesley, their friendship continued and when Olivers died he was buried in the same grave as Wesley.

At Gregynog Hall, now a University of Wales residential centre, a private press was founded in 1923 by the sisters Gwendoline (1882-1951) and Margaret Davies (1884-1963), the grand-daughters of the industrialist David Davies of Llandinam. The press was revived as Gwasg Gregynog by the University in 1974. The workshops are open to the public by prior arrangement.

Among the wardens of Gregynog was the writer **R. Gerallt Jones** (1934-99). The English novelist **B.S. Johnson** (1933-71) was a writer in residence and the house is recognizable in his *House Mother Normal* (1971).

TREHERBERT, Rhondda Cynon Taff; industrial town on the A4058 at the top end of the Rhondda Fawr.

The poet **T. Arfon Williams** (1935-98) was born at Hillside, 5 St Alban's Street in Tŷ Newydd. Discovering an interest in *cynghanedd* in 1974, he quickly mastered it and began writing *englynion* which were notable because they consisted of a single, uninterrupted sentence. He published three collections in his favourite form: *Englynion Arfon* (11978), *Annus Mirabilis* (1984) and *Cerddi Arfon* (1996).

The prose-writer **Ron Berry** (1920-97) lived the latter part of his life at 1 Ael-y-bryn, Treherbert.

TREMADOG, see under **PORTHMADOG**

TREMEIRCHION, Denbighshire; village overlooking the Vale of Clwyd, about 5 m SE of St Asaph, off the A55.

A tablet on the N side of the chancel of the little church of Corpus Christi commemorates **Hester Lynch Piozzi** (1741-1821), who was buried in a vault outside the church but now covered by the N transept, which was built later. The only child of John Salusbury, she grew up at Bach-y-graig (gone), which nestled at the foot of a nearby hill. After her second marriage, to an Italian music-teacher named Gabriel Piozzi, in 1784, she built a new house in the Italian style to which she gave the name Brynbella (an amalgam of the Welsh word *bryn*, a hill, and the Italian, *bella*, beautiful), and there she lived for the rest of her life. She is remembered mainly on account of her friendship and correspondence with Dr Samuel Johnson.

Less than 1 m N of the village, on the E slopes of the Vale of Clwyd, is St Beuno's College, a Jesuit seminary where the English poet **Gerard Manley Hopkins** (1844-89) was a student from 1874 to 1877. An entry in his diary for 6 September 1874 reads: 'Looking all around me but most in looking far up the valley, I felt an instress and charm of Wales.' It was here, too, he wrote his famous poems 'The Wreck of the Deutschland', 'The Windhover' and 'Pied Beauty'. In his poem 'In the Valley of the Elwy' he wrote:

Lovely the woods, waters, meadows, combes, vales,
All the air things wear that build this world of Wales;
Only the inmate does not correspond.

The last line (which is not often quoted in Wales) is thought to refer to the Protestantism of the Welsh people. After three years at St Beuno's Hopkins was ordained priest and left for Derbyshire. But his sojourn in Wales left a permanent mark on his poetry, not least in its use of *cynghanedd*, the traditional prosody of Welsh verse.

TREORCHY (W. Treorci), Rhondda Cynon Taff; former mining village on the A4061 in the valley of the Rhondda Fawr.

The poet **Ben Bowen** (1878-1903) was born at 126 High Street, which has a commemorative plaque bearing the words: *'Un o'r tannau a dorrwyd yn gynnar'* (One of the harpstrings that were broken early). At the age of 12 he became a collier at the Ty'n-y-bedw colliery and later trained for the Baptist ministry in Cardiff. In poor health, he showed great promise as a poet but was excommunicated for heresy by Moriah, the chapel to which he belonged at Ton Pentre. In his diary for 2 December 1901 he wrote (trans.): 'It is easy enough to follow Christ; the difficulty is in following His followers.' After visiting South Africa, where he hoped to regain his health, he died at the age of 24 and was buried in the cemetery at Treorchy, where his gravestone bears the epitaph (in Welsh): 'He talked too much about Wales and Eternity' – the complaint of an adjudicator at the National Eisteddfod. The plaque which commemorates him at 6 Victoria Street, Ton Pentre, which was his sister's home, is inscribed with his *englyn, 'Cystudd'* (Affliction).

Euros Bowen (1904-88), one of the most accomplished Welsh poets of the 20th century, belonged to the same family. He was born at 112 High Street, Treorchy.

TRE-TALIESIN, Cardiganshire; village on the A487, about 9 m NE of Aberystwyth.

A footpath leads 1 m to the E to an ancient stone tomb traditionally regarded as the grave of **Taliesin,** reputedly a poet of the 6th century. Much poetry, probably of a later date, has been ascribed to him. *The Book of Taliesin* (14th century) is a collection of poems by various hands and of different periods.

WAUNFAWR, Gwynedd; village on the A4085 about 4 m SE of Caernarfon.

The cartographer John Evans (1770-99) is commemorated by a monument, the work of Mike Watts, which was unveiled in 1999 at Tŷ Capel (Chapel House) under the auspices of Antur Waunfawr. Evans was recruited by **Iolo Morganwg (Edward Williams;** 1747-1826) to accompany him on an expedition to North America in search of the

'Welsh Indians' said to be the descendants of Madog ab Owain Gwynedd who was reputed to have set sail across the Atlantic about 1170. In the event, Iolo did not make the journey and Evans set out alone in 1792. Four years later he contacted the Mandans, the tribe believed to be the descendants of the Welsh prince and his crew, and remained with them through the harsh Dakota winter. He was the first to map the Missouri some two thousand miles above its confluence with the Mississippi, but eventually reported that the Mandans were not, after all, the 'Welsh Indians' of legend.

WHITFORD, see under **MOSTYN**

WHITLAND (W. Yr Hendy-gwyn ar Daf), Carmarthenshire; village off the A40 about 6 m W of St Clears.

Hywel Dda – the only Welsh king to be called 'the Good' – is commemorated here by a garden and small museum which contain designs and artefacts in enamel, glass, slate and wood by Peter Lord. Hywel, who died in 950, ruled over most of Wales and is associated with the native laws, preserved in about eighty Welsh and Latin manuscripts. According to tradition, they were codified at a convention held at Whitland under the authority of the king. They are a rich source of information about the society and language of medieval Wales and throw a good deal of light on such literary works as **The Mabinogion.**

WREXHAM (W. Wrecsam), Wrexham; large industrial town on the junction of several roads, including the A525, the A483 and the A534.

The Puritan author **Morgan Llwyd** (1619-59) was educated at the Grammar School in Lampit Street and in 1635 was converted by the preaching of Walter Cradock (1610?-59), who was a curate in the town. In his book *Gwaedd yng Nghymru* (1653) he wrote (trans.), 'Enter your secret chamber, which is the light of God within you.' He was buried in the Rhos-ddu Dissenting burial-ground, where a memorial was unveiled in 1912.

A little to the S of the town stands Erddig, a mansion built in 1683, which became the home of **Philip Yorke** (1743-1804) in 1769. He is remembered as the author of *Royal Tribes of Wales* (1799), which was based on printed sources and his correspondence with Welsh scholars of the day. Its erudition contrasts oddly with Yorke's extraordinary gifts as a writer of doggerel, to be found in his book *Crude Ditties* (1914). The history of the house, which is now administered by the National Trust, has been written by Albinia Crust, *Chronicles of Erthig on the Dyke* (1914) and Merlin Watson, *The Servants' Hall* (1980).

The sporting writer **Charles James Apperley (Nimrod; 1779-1843)** was born at Plas Gronow, just outside the town. He contributed regularly to *The Sporting Magazine* and later joined the staff of *The Sporting Review*. Among his ten books the best are *Nimrod's Hunting Tours* (1835), *Memoirs of the Life of John Mytton* (1837), *The Life of a Sportsman* (1842) and *Hunting Reminiscences* (1843).

The critic **Bedwyr Lewis Jones** (1933-92) was born at 4 Rutland Road and later lived at 18 Beechley Road in the town, but grew up in Anglesey.

The poet **Euros Bowen** (1904-88), who had once been a curate in the town, spent the last fifteen years of his life at 5 Ffordd Cynan. He was one of the founders of *Cymdeithas Owain Cyfeiliog*, a literary society named after Owain ap Gruffudd ap Maredudd (*c*.1128-97), Prince of southern Powys, which still flourishes.

The English writer **Alexander Cordell (George Alexander Graber**; 1914-97) lived in Railway Road towards the end of his life. He died near a stream on the Horseshoe Pass above Llangollen in circumstances which at first suggested suicide but his death was later found to be of natural causes.

At Gresford, a village off the A483 to the NE, there occurred one of the worst disasters in the annals of British mining when, on 22 September 1934, 265 men were killed in an explosion and fire at the local colliery. An anonymous ballad, one of the few written in English about coalmining in Wales, commemorates those who lost their lives:

> You've heard of the Gresford Disaster,
>   The terrible price that was paid,
> Two hundred and sixty-two colliers were lost
>   And three of the rescue brigade . . .
>
> The fireman's reports are all missing,
>   The records of forty-two days,
> The colliery manager had them destroyed
>   To cover his criminal ways.
>
> Down there in the dark they are lying,
>   They died for nine shillings a day,
> They've worked out their shift and now they must lie
>   In the darkness until Judgement Day.
>
> The Lord Mayor of London's collecting
>   To help our poor children and wives,
> The owners have sent some white lilies
>   To pay for the poor colliers' lives.

Farewell, our dear wives and our children.
Farewell to our comrades as well,
Don't send your sons down the dark dreary mine,
They'll be damned like the sinners in hell.

YNYS-DDU, see under **CWMFELINFACH**

YNYS-DERW, see under **PONTARDAWE**

YNYS-Y-BWL, Rhondda Cynon Taff; village on the B4273 about 4 m NW of Pontypridd.

The local historian **Glanffrwd (William Thomas**; 1843-90) was born in the village, the son of a wood-cutter. After four years as a schoolmaster, he took charge of a Calvinistic Methodist chapel in Pontypridd, but was then ordained in the Anglican Church and held livings in the dioces of St Asaph. He is remembered chiefly for his *Plwyf Llanwyno* (1888), a history of the parish which lies between the valleys of the Taff and Rhondda Fach. He wrote charmingly about the people of his native parish and the old way of life at a time when this part of upland Glamorgan was mostly Welsh-speaking. An English translation by Thomas Evans was published in 1950.

The village is the setting for the short stories of **J.J. Williams** (1869-1954), a native of Tal-y-bont, Cardiganshire, who worked as a collier here; his book is entitled *Straeon y Gilfach Ddu* (1931).

YSBYTY IFAN, Gwynedd; village on the B4407 off the A5 about 4 m from Pentrefoelas.

The poet **Wiliam Cynwal** (d.1587/88) lived either in a house known as Tyn-y-berth or at Dôl Cynwal, but an autographed manuscript shows that

Cerrigellgwm was his home in 1567; he is buried in an unmarked spot in the churchyard at Ysbyty Ifan. He was an itinerant poet who visited the homes of gentry families throughout north Wales but he also wrote poems of great religious intensity.

YSGEIFIOG, Flintshire; hamlet on a minor road to the N of the A541 between Caerwys and Nannerch.

The poet **Gwilym Callestr (William Edwards**; 1790-1855), also known as **Wil Ysgeifiog**, is buried in the churchyard; he was born at Plas Iolyn near Caerwys. A volume of his poems, *Cell Callestr*, was published in 1815. A millwright by trade, he was a poet of great promise but excessive drinking ruined his health and he died in the Denbigh asylum. His tombstone has the distinction of having six *englynion* and a verse written in his honour by local poets.

YSTALYFERA, Swansea; industrial village on the A4067 in the upper Swansea Valley.

The poet and prose-writer **John Dyfnallt Owen** (1873-1956) was born at Rhiw-fawr, on the slope of the mountain behind the village.

The novelist **Kate Roberts** (1891-1985) taught Welsh at the secondary school from 1915 to 1917, and among her pupils was **David James Jones (Gwenallt**; 1899-1968).

The short-story writer **Islwyn Williams** (1903-57) was born in the village and lived at 49 Allt-y-grug Street. Most of his work is written in the Swansea Valley dialect of Welsh and set in chapel, colliery, trades union, choir, eisteddfod, fair and rugby match. His stories are included in his books *Cap Wil Thomas* (1946), *Storïau a Phortreadau* (1954) and *Côr Mawr Ystalyfera* (1954).

YSTRADGYNLAIS, Powys; industrial town on the A4067 and B4599 at the top end of the Swansea Valley.

Thomas Levi (1825-1916) was born at Penrhos, on the B4599, on the E side of the town. He was set to work in the ironworks at Ynyscedwyn at the age of eight but later became a minister with the Calvinistic Methodists; his last pastorate was at Tabernacl in Aberystwyth. A prolific author, he wrote some thirty books on religious and historical subjects and translated another 60 into Welsh. His most important contribution to the cultural life of Wales was his editorship for nearly 50 years of *Trysorfa y Plant,* a magazine for children which had a monthly circulation of 44,000.

The novelist **Menna Gallie** (1920-90) was born at a house known as Cilhendre in Station Road in the town. Her first novel, *Strike for a Kingdom* (1959) is set during the General Strike of 1926; her second, *Man's Desiring* (1960), draws on her knowledge of university life in Wales and England, and her third, *The Small Mine* (1962), deals with life in a mining valley in south Wales.

Further reading

Raymond Garlick & Roland Mathias (ed.), *Anglo-Welsh Poetry 1480-1990* (Seren, 1990)

Dannie Abse (ed.), *Twentieth Century Anglo-Welsh Poetry* (Seren, 1997)

Tony Conran (trans.), *Welsh Verse* (Seren, 1992)

Alun Richards (ed.), *The New Penguin Book of Welsh Short Stories* (Penguin, 1993)

Meic Stephens (trans.), *Illuminations: an Anthology of Welsh Short Prose* (Welsh Academic Press, 1998)

Roland Mathias, *Anglo-Welsh Literature: an Illustrated History* (Seren, 1984)

Dafydd Johnston, *The Literature of Wales: a Pocket Guide* (University of Wales Press, 1994)

Dafydd Johnston (ed.), *A Guide to Welsh Literature 1900-1996* (University of Wales Press, 1998)

Meic Stephens (ed.), *The New Companion to the Literature of Wales* (University of Wales Press, 1998)

Meic Stephens & R. Brinley Jones (ed.), *Writers of Wales* (90 vols., University of Wales Press, 1970-   )

Meic Stephens, *Literature in Twentieth-century Wales: a Select Bibliography* (The British Council, 1994)

John Davies, *A History of Wales* (Penguin, 1993)

Janet Davies, *The Welsh Language: a Pocket Guide* (University of Wales Press, 1999)

Anthony Conran, *The Cost of Strangeness: Essays on the English Poets of Wales* (Gomer, 1982)

Anthony Conran, *Frontiers in Anglo-Welsh Poetry* (University of Wales Press, 1997)

M. Wynn Thomas, *Internal Difference: Literature in 20th-century Wales* (University of Wales Press, 1992)

M. Wynn Thomas, *Corresponding Cultures: the Two Literatures of Wales* (University of Wales Press, 1999)

Some regional anthologies:

Meic Stephens (ed.), *A Cardiff Anthology* (Seren, 1987)

James Davies (ed.), *A Swansea Anthology* (Seren, 1996)

Dewi Roberts (ed.), *An Anglesey Anthology* (Carreg Gwalch, 1999)

David Rees (ed.), *A Gower Anthology* (Christopher Davies, 1977)

Lynn Hughes (ed.), *A Carmarthenshire Anthology* (Christopher Davies, 1984)

Alan Roderick (ed.), *A Gwent Anthology* (Christopher Davies, 1988)

Meic Stephens (ed.), *A Rhondda Anthology* (Seren, 1993)

Tony Curtis (ed.), *The Poetry of Pembrokeshire* (Seren, 1989)

Tony Curtis (ed.), *The Poetry of Snowdonia* (Seren, 1989)

Dewi Roberts (ed.), *Both Sides of the Border*, An Anthology of writing on the Welsh Border Region (Carreg Gwalch, 1998)

David Kirk (ed.), *Snowdonia, a historical anthology* (Carreg Gwalch, 1994)

INDEX

Bowen, Ben (1878-1903), see under Treorchy
Bowen, Edward Ernest (1836-1901), see under Chepstow
Bowen, Euros (1904-88), see under Llanuwchllyn, Treorchy
    and Wrexham
Bradford, Siôn (1706-85), see under Llangynwyd
Brutus, see Owen, David (1795-1866)
Brynfab, see Williams, Thomas (1848-1927)
Bulkeley, William (1691-1760), see under Llanfechell

Cadrawd, see Evans, T.C. (1846-1918)
Cadwaladr, Dilys (1902-79), see under Bardsey
Caledfryn, see Williams, William (1801-69)
Carneddog, see Griffith, Richard (1861-1947)
Carnhuanawc, see Price, Thomas (1787-1848)
Carroll, Lewis, see Dodgson, C.L. (1832-98)
Carter, Isaac (d.1741), see under Newcastle Emlyn
Cave, Jane (c. 1754-1813), see under Brecon
Ceiriog, see Hughes, John Ceiriog (1832-87)
Celtic Davies, see Davies, Edward (1756-1831)
Chamberlain, Brenda (1912-71), see under Bangor, Bardsey
    and Bethesda
Charles, David (1762-1834), see under Llanfihangel
    Abercywyn
Charles, Thomas (1755-1814), see under Bala, Llanfihangel
    Abercywyn and Llanfihangel-y-pennant
Churchey, Walter (1747-1805), see under Brecon
Coombes, B.L. (1894-1974), see under Resolven
Cordell, Alexander, see Graber, George Alexander (1914-97)
Countess Barcynska, see Sandys, Oliver (1886-1964)
Coward, Noel (1899-1973), see under Portmeirion
Cradock, John, see under Aberglaslyn
Cranogwen, see Rees, Sarah Jane (1839-1916)
Cronin, A.J. (1896-1981), see under Tredegar
Crwys, see Williams, William (1875-1968)
Cybi, see Evans, Robert (1871-1956)
Cynan, see Evans-Jones, Albert (1895-1970)
Cynddelw, see Ellis, Robert (1812-75)

Dafydd ab Edmwnd (fl. 1450-99), see under Carmarthen and
    Hanmer

Dafydd ap Gwilym (*fl.* 1315/20-1350/70), see under Aberystwyth, Bangor, Bodedern, Bro Gynin, Cardiff, Carmel, Flemingston, Llandeilo, Llanfihangel-y-pennant, Newport and Pontrhydfendigaid

Dafydd Ddu Eryri, see Thomas, David (1759-1822)

Dafydd Nanmor (*fl.* 1450-90), see under Nanmor

Dahl, Roald (1916-90), see under Cardiff

Daniel, J.E. (1902-62), see under Bangor

Davies, Aneirin Talfan (Aneirin ap Talfan; 1909-80), see under Cardiff, Newcastle Emlyn and Swansea

Davies, David (1849-1926), see under Rhydargaeau

Davies, David Ivor (Ivor Novello; 1893-1951), see under Cardiff

Davies, D. Jacob (1916-74), see under Tregroes

Davies, Edward (1718-89), see under Tintern

Davies, Edward (Celtic Davies; 1756-1831), see under Builth and Swansea

Davies, E. Tegla (1880-1967), see under Bethesda and Llandegla-yn-Iâl

Davies, George M.Ll. (1880-1949), see under Dolwyddelan

Davies, Idris (1905-53), see under Rhymney

Davies, J. Eirian (1918-98), see under Nantgaredig

Davies, Jennie Eirian (1925-82), see under Nantgaredig

Davies, J. Kitchener (1902-52), see under Trealaw and Tregaron

Davies, John (*c.*1557-1644), see under Llanferres and Mallwyd

Davies, John (Ossian Dyfed; 1852-1916), see under Cardigan

Davies, John Humphreys (1871-1926), see under Llangeitho

Davies, Pennar (1911-96), see under Mountain Ash and Pentre

Davies, Rhys (1901-78), see under Blaenclydach and Llantrisant

Davies, Richard (Mynyddog; 1833-77), see under Llanbryn-mair

Davies, T. Glynne (1926-88), see under Llanrwst

Davies, Walter (Gwallter Mechain; 11761-1849), see under Llanfechain and Llanrhaeadr-ym-mochnant

Davies, William (Gwilym Teilo; 1831-92), see under Bethlehem

Davies, W.H. (1871-1940), see under Newport

Davis, David (1745-1827), see under Llangybi (Carms.) and Talgarreg

Deio ab Ieuan Du (*fl.* 1450-80), see under Aberystwyth

Derfel, R.J. (1824-1905), see under Llandderfel

Dewi Emrys, see James, David Emrys (1881-1952)

Dewi Havesp, see Roberts, David (1831-84)

Dewi Wyn o Eifion, see Owen, David (1784-1841)

Dic Dywyll, see Williams, Richard (*c.*1805-*c.*1865)

Dic Tryfan, see Williams, Richard Hughes (1878?-1919)

Dillwyn, Amy Elizabeth (1845-1935), see under Swansea

Dodgson, C.L. (Carroll, Lewis, 1832-98), see under Llandudno

Doyle, Arthur Conan (1859-1930), see under Clyro

Dwnn, James (*c.*1570-*c.*1660), see under Betws Cedewain

Dwnn, Lewys (*fl.* 1568-1616), see under Betws Cedewain

Dyer, John (1699-1757), see under Llanfynydd and Llangathen

Dyment, Clifford (1914-70), see under Caerleon

Earley, Tom (1911-98), see under Mountain Ash

Eben Fardd. see Thomas, Ebenezer (1802-63)

Edelman, Maurice (1911-75), see under Cardiff

Edwards, Charles (1628-91?), see under Llansilin

Edwards, Dorothy (1903-34), see under Cardiff

Edwards, Huw Lloyd (1916-75), see under Penisa'r-waun

Edwards, J.M. (1903-78), see under Llanrhystud and Mynydd Bach

Edwards, John (Eos Glan Twrch; 1806-87), see under Llanuwchllyn

Edwards, Lewis (1809-87), see under Bala and Capel Bangor

Edwards, O.M. (1858-1920), see under Aberystwyth, Glynllifon and Llanuwchllyn

Edwards, Roger (1811-86), see under Bala

Edwards, Thomas (Twm o'r Nant; 1738-1810), see under Denbigh

Edwards, William (Gwilym Callestr; Wil Ysceifiog; 1790-1855), see under Ysceifiog

Eifion Wyn, see Williams, Eliseus (1867-1926)

Elfed, see Lewis, Howell Elvet (1860-1953)

Elis o'r Nant, see Pierce, Ellis (1841-1912)

Elis Wyn o Wyrfai, see Roberts, Ellis (1827-95)

Ellis, David (1893-1918), see under Llangwm
Ellis, Robert (Cynddelw; 1812-75), see under
  Pen-y-bont-fawr
Ellis, T.I. (1899-1970), see under Aberystwyth
Emrys, see Ambrose, William (1813-73)
Emrys ap Iwan, see Jones, Robert Ambrose (1848-1906)
Eos Glan Twrch, see Edwards, John (1806-87)
Evans, Anne Adaliza (Allen Raine; 1836-1908), see under
  Newcastle Emlyn
Evans, Caradoc (1878-1945), see under Aberystwyth,
  Llanfihangel ar Arth, New Cross and Rhydlewis
Evans, Christmas (1776-1838), see under Tregroes
Evans, D. Silvan (1818-1903), see under Dinas Mawddwy
  and Llanarth
Evans, Ellis Humphrey (Hedd Wyn; 1887-1917), see under
  Trawsfynydd
Evans, Evan (Ieuan Fardd; Ieuan Brydydd Hir; 1731-88), see
  under Lledrod, Llansilin and Newport
Evans, Evan (Ieuan Glan Geirionydd; 1795-1855), see under
  Trefriw
Evans, Eynon (1904-89), see under Caerphilly and Nelson
Evans, George Ewart (1909-88), see under Abercynon
Evans, Hugh (1854-1934), see under Llangwm
Evans, Frederic (Michael Gareth Llewelyn; 1881-1958), see
  under Llangynwyd
Evans, John (Y Bardd Cocos; 1826-88), see under
  Menai Bridge
Evans, John Gwenogvryn (1852-1930), see under
  Llanybydder
Evans, Robert (Cybi; 1871-1956), see under Llangybi
  (Gwynedd) Evans, Theophilus (1693-1767), see under
  Newcastle Emlyn
Evans, Thomas (Tomos Glyn Cothi; 1764-1833), see under
  Gwernogle
Evans, Thomas (Telynog; 1840-65), see under Cardigan and
  Mountain Ash
Evans, T.C. (Cadrawd; 1846-1918), see under Llangynwyd
Evans, William (Wil Ifan; 1888-1968), see under Bridgend
  and Llanwinio

Evans-Jones, Albert (Cynan; 1895-1970), see under Aberdaron, Bangor, Bodedern, Llangybi (Gwynedd), Menai Bridge and Pwllheli

Firbank, Ronald (1886-1926), see under Newport
Foster, Idris Ll. (1911-84), see under Bethesda
Francis, J.O. (1882-1956), see under Merthyr Tydfil

Gallie, Menna (1920-90), see under Ystradgynlais
Gee, Thomas (1815-98), see under Denbigh
Geoffrey of Monmouth (c.1090-1155), see under Abermule, Brecon, Caerleon, Cardiff, Carmarthen and Old Radnor
Gerald de Barri, see Giraldus Cambrensis (c.1146-1223)
Gilpin, William (1702-1804), see under Tintern
Giraldus Cambrensis (Gerald de Barri; c. 1146-1223), see under Cardiff, Manorbier, Pencader and St David's
Glanffrwd, see Thomas, William (1843-90)
Glasynys, see Jones, Owen Wynne (1828-70)
Gomer, see Harris, Joseph (1773-1825)
Goodman, Gabriel (1528-1601), see under Ruthin
Goodwin, Geraint (1903-41), see under Corris, Montgomery and Newtown
Graber, George Alexander (Alexander Cordell; 1914-97), see under Bangor, Merthyr Tydfil, Wrexham and Pontypool
Graves, Robert (1895-1985), see under Barmouth and Harlech
Gray, Thomas (1716-71), see under Tintern
Griffith, Richard (Carneddog; 1861-1947), see under Nanmor
Griffith, W.J. (1875-1931), see under Aberffraw
Griffiths, Ann (1776-1805), see under Llanfihangel-yng-ngwynfa
Griffiths, David Rees (Amanwy; 1882-1953), see under Ammanford
Gruffudd ab yr Ynad Coch (fl. 1277-82), see under Abbey Cwm-hir and Talwrn
Gruffudd Gryg (fl. 1357-70), see under Bodedern and Llandeilo
Gruffydd Bodwrda (c.1578-1649), see under Aberdaron
Gruffydd, Ifan (1896-1971), see under Llangristiolus
Gruffydd, W.J. (1881-1954), see under Bangor, Bethel, Cardiff and Llanllyfni
Guest, Lady Charlotte (11812-95), see under Hergest,

Llandovery and Merthyr Tydfil
Gwalchmai, see Parry, Richard (1803-97)
Gwalchmai ap Meilyr (*fl.* 1130-80), see under Trefdraeth
Gwallter Mechain, see Davies, Walter (1761-1849)
Gweirydd ap Rhys, see Pryse, Robert John (1807-89)
Gwenallt, see Jones, David Gwenallt (1899-1968)
Gwili, see Jenkins, John (1872-1936)
Gwilym Callestr, see Edwards, William (1790-1855)
Gwilym Cowlyd, see Roberts, William John (1827-1904)
Gwilym Hiraethog, see Rees, William (1802-83)
Gwilym Marles, see Thomas, William (1834-79)
Gwilym Teilo, see Davies, William (1831-92)
Gwynn, Cyril (1897-1988), see under Oystermouth
Gwyrosydd, see Jones, Daniel (1847-1920)

Hanley, James (1901-85), see under Llanfechain
Harris, Joseph (Gomer; 1773-1825), see under Swansea
Hatton, Ann Julia (1764-1838), see under Swansea
Haycock, Myfanwy (1913-63), see under Pontnewynydd
Hedd Wyn, see Evans, Ellis Humphrey (1887-1917)
Hemans, Felicia (1793-1835), see under Abergele,
    Cadair Idris and St Asaph
Hooson, I.D. (1880-1948), see under Llangollen
Hopcyn, Wil (1704-41), see under Llangynwyd
Hopkins, B.T. (1897-1981), see under Mynydd Bach
Hopkins, Gerard Manley (1844-89), see under Holywell,
    Penmaenpool and Tremeirchion
Howell, James (1593-1666), see under Aber-nant
Howell, John (Ioan ap Hywel; 1774-1830), see under
    Abergwili
Hughes, Annie Harriet (Gwyneth Vaughan; 1852-1910), see
    under Talsarnau
Hughes, Cledwyn (1920-78), see under Arthog
Hughes, Isaac Craigfryn (1852-1928), see under Llangynwyd
Hughes, John Ceiriog (1832-87), see under Aberdovey, Glyn
    Ceiriog, Llanarmon Dyffryn Ceiriog and Llangollen
Hughes, Mathonwy (1901-99), see under Llanllyfni
Hughes, Richard (1900-76), see under Laugharne and
    Talsarnau
Hughes, T. Rowland (1903-49), see under Aberdare,
    Aberdovey, Bangor, Bethesda, Brynrefail, Cardiff,

Harlech and Llanberis

Humphreys, E. Morgan (1882-1953), see under Dyffryn Ardudwy

Huw Menai, see Williams, Huw Owen (1888-1961)

Hwfa Môn, see Williams, Rowland (1823-1905)

Hywel ab Owain Gwynedd (*fl.* 1140-70), see under Bangor and Benllech

Hywel ap Rheinallt (*fl.* 1461-1506), see under Bardsey

Ieuan ap Iago, see James, Evan (1809-78)

Ieuan Brydydd Hir, see Evans, Evan (1731-88)

Ieuan Fardd, see Evans, Evan (1731-88)

Ieuan Glan Geirionydd, see Evans, Evan (1795-1855)

Ieuan Gwynedd, see Jones, Evan (1820-52)

Inglis-Jones, Elizabeth (1900-94), see under Betws Cedewain

Ioan ap Hywel, see Howell, John (1774-1830)

Ioan Tegid, see Jones, John (1792-1852)

Iolo Goch (*c.*1325-*c.*1398), see under Sycharth

Iolo Morganwg, see Williams, Edward (1747-1826)

Iorwerth Fynglwyd (*fl.* 1485-1527), see under Aberpergwm

Islwyn, see Thomas, William (1832-78)

Jac Glan-y-gors, see Jones, John (1766-1821)

James, David Emrys (Dewi Emrys; 1881-1952), see under Fishguard, New Quay and Talgarreg

James, Evan (Ieuan ap Iago; 1809-78), see under Pontypridd

Jarman, A.O.H. (1911-99), see under Bangor and Cardiff

Jenkins, John (Gwili; 1872-1936), see under Pontarddulais

Jenkins, R.T. (1881-1969), see under Bala

Jôb, J.T. (1867-1938), see under Bethesda

Johnson, B.S. (1933-73), see under Tregynon

Jones, Arthur Llewellyn, see Machen, Arthur (1863-1947)

Jones, Bedwyr Lewis (1933-92), see under Bangor, Penysarn and Wrexham

Jones, Dafydd (1703-85), see under Trefriw

Jones, Dafydd (1711-77), see under Caeo

Jones, Daniel (Gwyrosydd; 1847-1920), see under Swansea

Jones, David (1895-1974), see under Capel-y-ffin and Cardiff

Jones, David Gwenallt (1899-1968), see under Aberystwyth, Llandeilo, Llansawel, Penmachno, Pontardawe and Ystalyfera

Jones, Edmund (1702-93), see under Pontypool

Jones, Edward (Bardd y Brenin; 1752-1824), see under
Llandderfel

Jones, Edward (1761-1836), see under Llanrhaeadr
Dyffryn Clwyd

Jones, Elizabeth Mary (Moelona; 1878-1953), see under
Rhydlewis

Jones, Ernest (1879-1958), see under Oystermouth

Jones, Evan (Ieuan Gwynedd; 1820-52), see under Caerphilly
and Dolgellau

Jones, Glyn (1905-95), see under Cardiff, Llanstephan and
Merthyr Tydfil

Jones, Griffith (1683-1761), see under Llanddowror

Jones, Gwilym R. (1903-93), see under Tal-y-sarn

Jones, Gwyn (1907-99), see under Aberystwyth and Cardiff

Jones, Henry (1852-1922), see under Llangernyw

Jones, Hugh (1749-1825), see under Dinas Mawddwy

Jones, Idwal (1895-1937), see under Lampeter

Jones, Idwal (1910-85), see under Tal-y-sarn

Jones, Jack (1884-1970), see under Cardiff and
Merthyr Tydfil

Jones, Jeremiah (1855-1902), see under Llangrannog

Jones, John (Jac Glan-y-gors; 1766-1821), see under
Cerrigydrudion

Jones, John (Ioan Tegid; 1792-1852), see under Bala

Jones, John (1796-1857), see under Dolwyddelan

Jones, John (Talhaiarn; 1810-69), see under
Llanfair Talhaiarn

Jones, John Gwilym (1904-88), see under Bangor, Glynllifon,
Groeslon and Llandwrog

Jones, John Puleston (1862-1925), see under Bala

Jones, John Robert (1911-70), see under Pwllheli and
Swansea

Jones, Lewis (1897-1939), see under Blaenclydach and
Cardiff

Jones, Moses Glyn (1913-94), see under Mynytho

Jones, Owen Wynne (Glasynys; 1828-70), see under
Llandwrog and Rhostryfan

Jones, Percy Mansell (1889-1968), see under Carmarthen

Jones, Rhys (1713-1801), see under Llanfachreth

Jones, Robert Ambrose (Emrys ap Iwan; 1848-1906), see
under Abergele and Rhewl

Jones, Robert Gerallt (1934-99), see under Aberystwyth,
  Bardsey, Morfa Nefyn, Penysarn and Tregynon
Jones, Robert Lloyd (1878-1962), see under Bethesda
Jones, R. Tudur (1921-98), see under Llanystumdwy
Jones, Thomas (1870-1955), see under Harlech and Rhymney
Jones, Thomas Gwynn (1871-1949), see under Aberystwyth,
  Betws-yn-rhos and Llangollen
Jones, T.H. (1921-65), see under Builth
Jones, Tom Parri (1905-95), see under Bodorgan
Jones, William (1755-1821), see under Abergavenny
Jones, William (1896-1961), see under Porthmadog
Jones, William Ronald Rees, see Rhys, Keidrych (1915-87)

Keating, Joseph (1871-1934), see under Mountain Ash
Kilvert, Francis (1840-79), see under Aberedw, Capel-y-ffin,
  Clyro, Hay-on-Wye and Tintern

Landor, Walter Savage (1775-1864), see under Llanthony
  and Oystermouth
Lawrence, T.E. (1888-1935), see under Porthmadog
Levi, Thomas (1825-1916), see under Aberystwyth and
  Ystradgynlais
Lewis Glyn Cothi (c.1420-89), see under Bardsey and
  Llanybydder
Lewis, Alun (1915-44), see under Aberdare, Aberystwyth,
  Bethesda and Cowbridge
Lewis, Alun T. (1905-86), see under Llanrwst
Lewis, George Cornewall (1806-63), see under Old Radnor
Lewis, Howell Elvet (Elfed; 1860-1953), see under
  Cynwyl Elfed
Lewis, John (1548?-1616?), see under Old Radnor
Lewis, Saunders (1893-1985), see under Abergwyngregyn,
  Aberystwyth, Cardiff, Glynllifon, Merthyr Tydfil,
  Penarth, Pwllheli and Swansea
Lewis, Thomas (1759-1842), see under Llandeilo
Lewis, William Lewis (Llew Llwyfo; 1831-1901), see under
  Penysarn
Linklater, Eric (1899-1974), see under Cardiff
Llew Llwyfo, see Lewis, William Lewis (1831-1901)
Llewellyn, Richard, see Lloyd, Vivian (1906-83)
Llewelyn, Michael Gareth, see Evans, Frederic (1881-1958)

Llinos, see Williams, Maria Jane (1795-1873)

Lloyd, D. Tecwyn (1914-92), see under Carmarthen, Corwen and Penysarn

Lloyd, John (1797-1875), see under Brecon

Lloyd, John (1833-1915), see under Brecon

Lloyd, Robert (Llwyd o'r Bryn; 1888-1961), see under Cefnddwysarn

Lloyd, Vivian (Richard Llewellyn; 1906-83), see under Gilfach Goch

Llwyd o'r Bryn, see Lloyd, Robert (1888-1961)

Llwyd, Angharad (1780-1866), see under Caerwys

Llwyd, Huw (1568?-1630?), see under Blaenau Ffestiniog

Llwyd, Morgan (1619-59), see under Bala, Blaenau Ffestiniog and Wrexham

Llwyd, Richard (Bard of Snowdon; 1752-1835), see under Beaumaris

Llywelyn Goch ap Meurig Hen (fl. 1350-90), see under Llangynhafal and Pennal

Llywelyn-Williams, Alun (1913-88), see under Bangor and Cardiff

Lord Tennyson, see Alfred, Lord Tennyson (1809-92)

Mabinogion, The, see under Abercuch, Aberffraw, Aberystwyth, Bethesda, Blaenau Ffestiniog, Harlech, Llanddeusant (Anglesey), Llandovery and Whitland

Machen, Arthur (Arthur Llewellyn Jones; 1863-1947), see under Caerleon

Malory, Thomas (d.1471), see under Caerleon

Meilyr Brydydd (fl. 1100-37), see under Trefdraeth

Milton, John (1608-74), see under Abermule

Moelona, see Jones, Elizabeth Mary (1878-1953)

Monsarrat, Nicholas (1910- 79), see under Llanarmon Dyffryn Ceiriog

Morgan, Dyfnallt (1917-94), see under Bangor and Merthyr Tydfil

Morgan, Elena Puw (1900-73), see under Corwen

Morgan, Robert (1921-94), see under Mountain Ash

Morgan, T.J. (1907-86), see under Glais and Swansea

Morgan, William (1545-1604), see under Cardiff, Glyn Ceiriog, Llanrhaeadr-ym-mochnant, Penmachno and St Asaph

Morris Brothers (18th cent.), see under
    Llanfihangel-tre'r-beirdd
Morris, Edward (1607-89), see under Cerrigydrudion
Morris, Lewis (1701-65), see under Aberystwyth and
    Lledrod
Morris, Sir Lewis (1833-1907), see under Carmarthen and
    Llangunnor
Morris, William (1889-1979), see under Blaenau Ffestiniog
Morris-Jones, John (1864-1929), see under Bangor and
    Llanfair Pwllgwyngyll
Mynyddog, see Davies, Richard (1833-77)

Nantlais, see Williams, William (1874-1959)
Nicander, see Williams, Morris (1809-74)
Nicholas, T.E. (Niclas y Glais;1878-1971), see under
    Aberystwyth and Glais
Niclas y Glais, see Nicholas, T. E. (1878-1971)
Nicolas, Dafydd (1705?-74), see under Aberpergwm
Nimrod, see Apperley, C.J. (1779-1843)
Novello, Ivor, see Davies, David Ivor (1893-1951)

Olivers, Thomas (1725-99), see under Tregynon
Onions, Oliver (1873-1961), see under Aberdovey
Ormond, John (1923-90), see under Cardiff and Swansea
Owen, Bob (1885-1962), see under Croesor
Owen, Daniel (1836-95), see under Mold
Owen, David (Dewi Wyn o Eifion; 1784-1841), see under
    Llangybi (Gwynedd) and Llanystumdwy
Owen, David (Brutus; 1795-1866), see under Llanpumpsaint
Owen, Goronwy (1723-69), see under Bangor, Benllech,
    Llangeitho and Llanystumdwy
Owen, John (1564?-1628?), see under Llanarmon
Owen, John Dyfnallt (1873-1956), see under Carmarthen and
    Ystalyfera
Owen, Robert (1771-1858), see under Newtown
Owen, W.D. (1874-1925), see under Bodedern

Pantycelyn, see Williams, William (1717-91)
Parry, Gwenlyn (1932-91), see under Cardiff, Deiniolen and
    Pencader
Parry, Richard (Gwalchmai; 1803-97), see Llanerch-y-medd
Parry, Robert Williams (1884-1956), see under Aberystwyth,

Afon-wen, Bangor, Bethesda, Cardiff, Cefnddwysarn,
   Llanrhystud, Mynytho, Penysarn, Pwllheli and
   Tal-y-sarn
Parry, Thomas (1904-85), see under Bangor, Bro Gynin and
   Carmel
Parry-Williams, T.H. (1887-1975), see under Aberdaron,
   Aberystwyth, Beddgelert and Rhyd-ddu
Payne, Ffransis G. (1900-92), see under Hergest
Peacock, Thomas Love (1785-1866), see under Aberdovey,
   Cadair Idris and Caerleon
Peate, Iorwerth C. (1901-82), see under Cardiff and
   Llanbryn-mair
Pennant, Thomas (1726-98), see under Caerwys,
   Dinas Mawddwy, Llanberis and Mostyn
Penry, John (1563-93), see under Llanwrtyd
Phillips, Edgar (Trefin; 1889-1962), see under Tre-fin
Phylip, Siôn (c.1543-1620), see under Harlech
Phylip, Wiliam (1579-1669), see under Dyffryn Ardudwy
Physicians of Myddfai, see under Myddfai
Pierce, Ellis, (Elis o'r Nant; 1841-1912), see under
   Dolwyddelan
Piozzi, Hester Lynch (1741-1821), see under Tremeirchion
Poet of Mount Pleasant, see Williams, William (1850-1917)
Powell, Vavasor (1617-70), see under Knucklas
Powys, John Cowper (1872-1963), see under
   Blaenau Ffestiniog, Corwen and Llangollen
Price, John (1502-55), see under Brecon
Price, Richard (1723-91), see under Bridgend and Llangeinor
Price, Thomas (Carnhuanawc; 1787-1848), see under Builth
Prichard, Caradog (1904-80), see under Bethesda
Prichard, Rhys (1579-1644), see under Llandovery
Prichard, T.J.Ll. (1790-1862), see under Builth
Prys, Edmund (1543/4-1623), see under Bangor,
   Blaenau Ffestiniog and Llanrwst
Prys-Jones, A.G. (1888-1987), see under Denbigh
Pryse, Robert John (Gweirydd ap Rhys; 1807-89), see under
   Llanbadrig
Pugh, Ellis (1656-1718), see under Dolgellau
Pughe, William Owen (1759-1835), see under Barmouth and
   Llanfihangel-y-pennant

Raine, Allen, see Evans, Anne Adaliza (1836-1908)

Rees, Alwyn D. (1911-74), see under Aberystwyth and Swansea

Rees, Goronwy (1909-70), see under Aberystwyth

Rees, Ioan Bowen (1929-99), see under Bethesda

Rees, Sarah Jane (Cranogwen; 1839-1916), see under Llangrannog

Rees, T. Ifor (1890-1977), see under Llandre

Rees, William (Gwilym Hiraethog; 1802-83), see under Llansannan

Rees, William (1808-73), see under Llandovery

Rees, W.J. (1772-1855), see under Cascob

Rhys Goch Eryri (*fl.* 11385-1448), see under Beddgelert

Rhys, Ernest (1859-1946), see under Carmarthen

Rhys, E. Prosser (1901-45), see under Aberystwyth and Mynydd Bach

Rhys, John (1840-1915), see under Ponterwyd

Rhys, Keidrych (William Ronald Rees Jones;1915-87), see under Bethlehem and Carmarthen

Rhys, Morgan (1716-79), see under Cil-y-cwm and Llanfynydd

Rhys, Siôn Dafydd (1534-*c.*1619), see under Brecon and Llanfaethlu

Richards, Brinley (1904-81), see Llangynwyd

Richards, W. Leslie (1916-89), see under Llandeilo

Robert ap Gwilym Ddu, see Williams, Robert (1766-1850)

Roberts, Barbara Dew (1885?-1963), see under Llanfechell

Roberts, David (Dewi Havesp; 1831-84), see under Llandderfel

Roberts, Elis (Elis Wyn o Wyrfai; 1827-95), see under Llandwrog

Roberts, Gomer M. (1904-93), see under Llanybydder

Roberts, Kate (1891-1985), see under Bangor, Denbigh, Rhosgadfan and Ystalyfera

Roberts, Lynette (1909-95), see under Bethlehem

Roberts, Robert (Y Sgolor Mawr; 1834-85), see under Llangernyw

Roberts, R. Silyn (1871-1930), see under Bangor and Llanllyfni

Roberts, Samuel (1800-85), see under Llanbryn-mair

Roberts, William John (Gwilym Cowlyd), see under Trefriw
Rolfe, Frederick (1860-1913), see under Holywell
Rowland, R.D. (Anthropos; 1853?-1944), see under
    Caernarfon and Corwen
Rowlands, Ifan (1879-1977), see under Llandderfel
Rowlands, John, see Stanley, H.M. (1841-1904)
Ruck, Berta (1878-1978), see under Aberdovey
Ruck, Richard (1887-1973), see under Aberdovey and
    Llanberis
Ruddock, Gilbert (1938-98), see under Cardiff

Salesbury, William (*c.* 1520-1584?), see under Llanrwst and
    Llansannan
Sandys, Oliver (Marguerite, Countess Barcynska
    (1886-1964), see under Aberystwyth
Sarnicol, see Thomas, Thomas Jacob (1873-1945)
Sassoon, Siegfried (1886-1967), see under Llansanffraid
Scott, Clement (1841-1904), see under Mumbles
Sgolor Mawr, see Roberts, Robert (1834-85)
Shelley, Percy Bysshe (1792-1822), see under Elan Valley and
    Porthmadog
Silyn, see Roberts, Robert (1871-1930)
Spencer, W.R. (1769-1834), see under Beddgelert
Spring, Howard (1889-1965), see under Cardiff
Stanley, H.M. (1841-1904), see under Denbigh and St Asaph
Steele, Richard (1672-1729), see under Carmarthen and
    Llangunnor
Stephens, Thomas (1821-75), see under Abergavenny and
    Merthyr Tydfil
Stowe, Harriet Beecher (1811-96), see under Llanddewibrefi

Talhaiarn, see Jones, John (1810-69)
Taliesin (*fl.* late 6th cent.), see under Bethesda and
    Tre-taliesin
Taliesin ab Iolo, see Williams, Taliesin (1787-1847)
Taylor, Jeremy (1613-67), see under Golden Grove
Telynog, see Evans, Thomas (1840-65)
Tennyson, see Alfred, Lord Tennyson
Thomas, David (Dafydd Ddu Eryri; 1759-1822), see under
    Llanrug
Thomas, Dylan (1914-53), see under Bethesda, Cardiff,
    Carmarthen, Laugharne, Llandysul, Llangain, Mumbles,

New Quay and Swansea

Thomas, Ebenezer (Eben Fardd; 1802-63), see under
  Clynnog Fawr and Llangybi (Gwynedd)

Thomas, Edward (1878-1917), see under Ammanford and
  Pontarddulais

Thomas, Ernest Lewis (Richard Vaughan; 1904-83), see
  under Llanddeusant (Carms.)

Thomas, Gwyn (1913-81), see under Cardiff, Merthyr Tydfil
  and Porth

Thomas, Jennie (1898-1979), see under Bethesda

Thomas, Robert (Ap Vychan; 1809-80), see under
  Llanuwchllyn

Thomas, Thomas Jacob (Sarnicol; 1873-1945), see under
  Merthyr Tydfil and Talgarreg

Thomas, William (Islwyn; 1832-78), see under Cwmfelinfach

Thomas, William (Gwilym Marles; 1834-79), see under
  Llandysul

Thomas, William (Glanffrwd; 1843-90), see under
  Ynys-y-bwl

Thompson, Francis (1859-1907), see under Holywell

Thrale, Mrs, see Piozzi, Hester Lynch (1741-1821)

Tilsley, Gwilym R. (1911-97), see under Aberdare,
  Llanidloes, Llanrwst and Prestatyn

Tomos Glyn Cothi, see Evans, Thomas (1764-1833)

Trebor Mai, see Williams, Robert (1830-77)

Trefin, see Phillips, Edgar (1889-1962)

Tripp, John (1927-86), see under Cardiff

Tudur Aled (c.1465-c.1525), see under Carmarthen

Tudur Penllyn (c.1420-c.1485), see under Llanuwchllyn

Twm o'r Nant, see Edwards, Thomas (1738-1810)

Valentine, Lewis (1893-1986), see under Pwllheli

Vaughan, Gwyneth, see Hughes, Annie Harriet (1852-1910)

Vaughan, Henry (1621-95), see under Llansanffraid

Vaughan, Hilda (1892-1985), see under Builth

Vaughan, Richard, see Thomas, Ernest Lewis (1904-83)

Vaughan, Rowland (c.1587-1667), see under Llanuwchllyn

Vaughan-Thomas, Wynford (1908-87), see under Dylife

Watcyn Wyn, see Williams, Watkin Hezekiah (1844-1905)

Watkins, Vernon (1906-97), see under Cardiff, Carmarthen, Maesteg and Swansea
Watts, Isaac (1674-1748), see under Caeo
Waugh, Evelyn (1903-66), see under Llanddulas
Webb, Harri (1920-94), see under Abbey Cwm-hir, Afon-wen, Cardiff, Carmarthen, Merthyr Tydfil, Mountain Ash, Oystermouth. Pontrhydfendigaid, Porthmadog, Severn Bridge and Swansea
Weyman, Stanley J. (1855-1928), see under Ruthin
Wil Ifan, see Evans, William (1888-1968)
Wil Ysceifiog, see Edwards, William (1790-1855)
Wiliam Cynwal (d. 1587/8), see under Penmynydd and Ysbyty Ifan
Wiliam, Thomas (1761-1844), see under Llantwit Major
William, Dafydd (1720/21-94), see under Llanedi
Williams, Alice Mallt (1867-1950), see under Brecon
Williams, David (1738-1816), see under Caerphilly
Williams, D.J. (1885-1970), see under Aberystwyth, Fishguard, Llansawel and Pwllheli
Williams, D. Matthew (1900-70), see under Cellan
Williams, Edward (Iolo Morganwg; 1747-1826), see under Carmarthen, Cellan, Cowbridge, Flemingston, Gwaelod-y-garth, Llancarfan, Llandderfel, Llandeilo, Llanfihangel-y-pennant, Llangynwyd, Llanover, Newport, Porthmadog, Trefriw and Waunfawr
Williams, Eliseus (Eifion Wyn; 1867-1926), see under Cwm Pennant and Porthmadog
Williams, Emlyn (1905-87), see under Mostyn
Williams, G.J. (1892-1963), see under Cellan and Gwaelod-y-garth
Williams, Gwyn (1904-90), see under Aberystwyth and Mynydd Bach
Williams, Gwyn A. (1925-95), see under Merthyr Tydfil and Newcastle Emlyn
Williams, Huw Owen (Huw Menai; 1888-1961), see under Caernarfon
Williams, Ifor (1881-1965), see under Bethesda, Clynnog Fawr and Menai Bridge
Williams, Isaac (1802-65), see under Aberystwyth
Williams, Islwyn (1903-57), see under Ystalyfera
Williams, John (Ab Ithel; 1811-62), see under Dinas

Mawddwy, Dyffryn Ardudwy and Llangynhafal

Williams, J.E. Caerwyn (1912-99), see under Aberystwyth

Williams, J.G. (1915-87), see under Cricieth

Williams, J.J. (1869-1954), see under Ynys-y-bwl

Williams, J.O. (1892-1973), see under Bethesda

Williams, Maria Jane (Llinos; 1795-1873), see under Aberpergwm

Williams, Morris (Nicander; 1809-74), see under Bangor and Llangybi (Gwynedd)

Williams, Raymond (1921-88), see under Pandy

Williams, Rhydwen (1916-97), see under Aberdare, Merthyr Tydfil, Mountain Ash, Pentre and Porth

Williams, Richard (Dic Dywyll; c.1805-c.1865), see under Llanerch-y-medd

Williams, R. Bryn (1902-81), see under Blaenau Ffestiniog

Williams, Richard Hughes (Dic Tryfan; 1878?-1919), see under Aberystwyth and Rhosgadfan

Williams, Robert (Robert ap Gwilym Ddu; 1766-1850), see under Aber-erch and Llanystumdwy

Williams, Robert (Trebor Mai; 1830-77), see under Llanrwst

Williams, Rowland (Hwfa Môn; 1823-1905), see under Trefdraeth

Williams, Taliesin (Taliesin ab Iolo; 1787-1847), see under Flemingston and Llanover

Williams, Thomas (Brynfab; 1848-1927), see under Pontypridd

Williams, T. Arfon (1935-95), see under Caeathro, Cardiff, Trefriw and Treherbert

Williams, Waldo (1904-71), see under Aberystwyth, Fishguard, Haverfordwest, Llandysilio and Mynachlog-ddu

Williams, Watkin Hezekiah (Watcyn Wyn; 1844-1905), see under Ammanford

Williams, William (Pantycelyn; 1717-91), see under Cardiff, Llandovery, Llanfihangel-yng-ngwynfa and Llangybi (Gwynedd)

Williams, William (Caledfryn; 1801-69), see under Caerphilly

Williams, William (Poet of Mount Pleasant; 1850-1917, see under Abergavenny and Pontnewynydd

Williams, William (Crwys; 1875-1968), see under Craig-cefn-parc and Tre-fin

Williams, W.D. (1900-85), see under Barmouth and Corwen
Williams, William Nantlais (1874-1959), see under
    Ammanford and Pencader
Williams-Ellis, Amabel (1894-1984), see under Portmeirion
Williams-Ellis, Clough (1883-1978), see under Portmeirion
Wordsworth, William (1770-1850), see under Llangynhafal
Wynn, Sir John (1553-1627), see under Caerwys and
    Llanrwst
Wynne, Ellis (1671-1734), see under Harlech and
    Llanfair Ardudwy

Yorke, Phillip (1743-1804), see under Wrexham

Zangwill, Israel (1864-1926), see under Beddgelert